A Simple Mistake

Chris Oswald

NEWMORE PUBLISHING

First edition published in 2019 by Newmore Publishing.

ISBN 978-1-9160719-3-3

Cover design by Book Beaver.

Book design and layout by Heddon Publishing.

Chris Oswald has lived in America, Scotland and England and is now living in Dorset with his wife, Suzanne, and six children. For many years he was in international business but now has a little more time to follow his love of writing. His books have been described as dystopian but they are more about individual choice, human frailty and how our history influences the decisions we make, also about how quickly things can go so wrong.

For my brother and sisters, Tim, Lis, Goggy and Sam.

Still a family after all these years!

Cast of Characters

Mainly Dorset

Thomas Davenport, second son and third child of Luke and Rebecca Davenport, builder.

Elizabeth Taylor, née Davenport, elder daughter and second child of Luke and Rebecca Davenport, married to Simon, known by friends as Lizzie.

Matthew Davenport, oldest child of the Davenport family, recently married Lady Eliza Merriman.

Eliza Davenport, née Merriman, owner of Bagber Manor.

Lord Merriman, father of Eliza.

Amelia Taylor, daughter of Simon Taylor, lives at Bagber Manor, known to her friends as Mealie.

Grace Sherborne, Countess of Sherborne, wife to Henry, daughter of Luke Davenport.

Henry Sherborne, Earl of Sherborne and illegitimate son of Eliza Davenport.

Lady (Alice) Roakes, previously Mrs Beatrice before she married Sir Beatrice Roakes. Sir Beatrice was murdered in *It Takes a Rogue* but leaves her and her unborn child ownership of the Great Little Estate.

Penelope Wiltshire, Dowager Duchess of Wiltshire.

Sally Black, Penelope's maid and lover.

Amy Barratt, serving girl at the Red Lion in Dorchester.

Mr Amiss, owner of the Red Lion in Dorchester.

Paul Tabard, government contractor at Sanderson and Sanderson who flees London when his mentor, Mr Sanderson, is murdered and the company taken over.

Mr Milligan, builder who trained Thomas before turning over the firm to him.

Sarah and Kitty, sisters, maids to Eliza Davenport at Bagber Manor.

Grimes, henchman to Simon Taylor and Parchman.

Big Jim, friend to Thomas and Grace, owns a successful hauliers firm in Dorset.

Plain Jane, friend to Thomas and Grace, married to Big Jim.

John Parsons, godfather to Milly.

Duke of Wiltshire, inherited following the death of Penelope's husband in the fire at Great Little (*It Takes a Rogue*).

Tomkins, factor at the Great Little estate.

Adam Jollice, bailiff for North Dorset.

Sir Philip Lacey, leading lawyer, based in Dorchester.

Colonel James Hansen, friend of Thomas and Grace, Colonel in the Dorset militia.

Milly, maid to Eliza Davenport in London, moves to Dorset.

Eric Turner, footman in the London household of Matthew and Eliza Davenport.

Mainly Ireland

James Stuart, previously King of England, Scotland and Ireland. Parliament declared his abdication from the throne after he fled London in December 1688 in *It Takes a Rogue*.

Tristan Browne, Irishman born in Barbados.

Bridget Browne, young historian, living in Londonderry during the siege, cousin to Tristan Browne.

Tobias Browne, father of Bridget and uncle to Tristan, farmer near Londonderry.

Cartwright, right-hand man to Parchman.

Fanshawe, Cartwright's deputy.

Duke of Schomberg, becomes Commander-in-Chief of William's Irish army.

Miles Denby, butcher and part-time solider in Londonderry.

Sean Murphy, leading citizen in Ballydalgagan, a village in the middle of Ireland.

Fr O'Toole, parish priest for Ballydalgagan.

Mrs O'Keefe, housekeeper and neighbour to Fr O'Toole.

Matthew Davies/Matthew Derwent, aliases for Matthew Davenport while spying in Ireland.

Paul Jensen, manager of the new Londonderry branch of Sanderson and Sanderson.

Mr Caverns, Chief Clerk to Paul Jensen.

Mainly London

William III, Prince of Orange, becomes King of England, Scotland and Ireland when Parliament offers the throne following their declaration of James Stuart's abdication. He is married to Mary and is the nephew and son-in-law of James Stuart.

Mary II, Mary Stuart, becomes Queen and co-reigns with her husband, William III. She is the daughter of James Stuart by his first marriage to Anne Hyde.

Jacob Avercamps, Dutch civil servant and key aide to William III.

Parchman, government agent with responsibility under Robert Candles for espionage in Ireland, key person in the prior imprisonment of Lady Merriman, has a deep-rooted grudge against several Dorset families, particularly the Davenports, the Merrimans and the Roakes.

Robert Candles/Robert Ferguson, agent managing Irish espionage for the new government. He employs Parchman. In a previous life, Ferguson was a Presbyterian minister and a jealous rival of Luke Davenport.

George Allingham, Chief Clerk to Matthew Davenport while Matthew helps draft the Bill of Rights for Parliament.

Mr Prendegast, a successful publisher in London nearing the end of his life.

Michael Frampton, personal assistant to Mr Paterson

Mrs Frampton, wife of Michael Frampton.

Mr Sanderson, owner of Sanderson and Sanderson, government contractors, before his murder.

A Simple Mistake

Chapter 1

It was a simple mistake to make. He had thought it Wednesday when it was only Tuesday.

But it had enormous consequences.

Thomas went to Bagber Manor, as he did every Wednesday and Sunday, for church. He went the normal way; across the bridge he had helped to build and which had been his introduction to the building profession. He always crossed it with a mixture of pleasure and pride. Then along the southern bank for a few hundred yards, right at the mill, and up the track that followed the Stour to the Divelish. He crossed this tributary where the road dipped under the water and went across the fields to the trees, following the Divelish all the way. He had seen that stream in every mode from raging torrent to sleepy trickle but that day it was somewhere in between, with lazy loops of water in slow but constant motion, as if searching for their essence or their character; for how they would be that year.

He knew every inch of the route for he was a frequent visitor, especially now that he was walking out with Amelia Taylor.

He thought of her long and often, wondering what she was doing that moment and how she would react to a particular topic running through his mind. He saw things through her eyes, knew she did the same. It was as if they were an elderly couple celebrating a life spent in each other's company.

Sometimes, like today, he held conversations with her as he walked. Mostly, these were confined to his head but that evening he spoke out loud, as befitted the glorious April day with new growth everywhere; plants stacking up to blossom in a few short weeks.

He stopped abruptly when she answered his chatter. It was her voice, for certain, although the words were muffled. It came from the trees ahead, just where the stream bent to the south and a large flat stone made a natural point to sit and dangle feet

1

in the water below. Her voice was as well-known to him as his own breathing patterns. He made to talk, then stopped again; she was not answering him but another and her voice was light and playful. Then he heard her words, as if delayed by lingering a while in the new leaves on the oak and ash and blackthorn above and around:

Let me scratch your back if it itches so, my dear.

The words sent a shaft into his heart.

He edged forwards to the rock ledge, obscured from view by a bank of early nettles and brambles. It prevented sight of her but also hid his proximity. He listened again to her beautiful laughter. She was teasing someone, giggling quietly as if acting in a private play. Incensed, he strode forwards, remembering afterwards the young nettles attacking his skin with their vicious stings.

"Mealy, what brings you…" He never finished his sentence, instead backed away, for she was almost naked; just a loose and soaking-wet undergarment from bosom to knees but riding up at the side so that her left thigh was half visible. His eyes rested on that thigh and, for a moment that went on and on, he could not look away. Yet his brain was working on the outrage, the deceit. And it worked on its own schedule, to its own tempo.

Amelia looked up, blushed deep red and grasped for an item of clothing, anything within reach. She held a dress upside down so that the skirt covered her breasts and shoulders and the top made partial cover only for her legs. He could still see her thigh although his vision was watery, as if he had dipped his eyes in the same Divelish she had patently been in. But his wetness sprung from tears and those tears were of anger, with a dash of wonder at what he had seen.

"Thomas!" she cried, standing up and backing away. "Cover your eyes." He covered his eyes, backed away, not wanting to see what he had next seen.

For lying next to Amelia, similar in attire, was his sister, Elizabeth.

Amelia had offered to scratch Elizabeth's half-bare back.

And, presumably, would be scratched in turn herself.

With both hands to his eyes, as if one were not enough, he

turned and stumbled, coming down heavily in the bramble and nettle patch that cropped the edge of the rock. Amelia, dressing quicker than Elizabeth, was by his side; no stays, no corset, no petticoats, just her dress clinging to her body like a sheet on a ghost.

"Thomas, are you alright? Have you hurt yourself?" She reached out for his face but he shook her off.

"Leave me alone, you… devil." He scrambled back, oblivious to the stings and thorns feasting on his limbs. After five yards of scrabbling on the ground, he hit upon a tree stump, used it to raise his shocked body up the shortened trunk so that he was standing, looking down at the girl he had hoped to marry. His backbone would not carry him so he leaned upon the stump like a discarded puppet after the show was over.

"It's not what you think, Thomas," came from left and right, slightly out of time so that the one seemed an echo of the other.

"It's not what you think… what you think…" mocked at him from both sides; faces he knew so well, could draw on blank paper from memory, now bobbed at his tear-struck vision like a badly written scene in a badly written play.

Two female voices that moments before had been lying together against nature and the law of God. For some reason, his head was filled with Penelope Wiltshire and her little black servant girl. But it was different to take a servant girl. It was not the same thing at all as this that he had stumbled upon on that beautiful, fresh and light evening that only April could offer to the world.

And they both were claiming innocence in defiance of what he had seen with his own eyes.

"Thomas, please listen. It's not…" But Thomas was moving away, picking up a peculiar pace somewhere between a trot and a canter as the trees thinned out.

And shock entered in.

He ran towards Bagber Manor, for that was the way he had intended, thinking it was Wednesday when it was only Tuesday. But half way across the lawn, he stopped still as a wave of horror swept over him. He had imagined settling down with Amelia, had rehearsed proposing to her. And all this time she was lying with his sister. He turned to go back to the stream, then turned again and again, like a weathercock in changeable conditions. His mind was a turmoil of indecision; he desperately wanted an explanation from Amelia but had walked away, refusing the very thing he longed for.

Finally, he set off at a right angle to his previous course from stream to manor; a round-about route home, he supposed, that would avoid contact with anyone, still less Amelia or Elizabeth. His walk was speedy and seemingly full of resolution, not something to be broken into.

Yet that resolution was as feigned as Amelia's ridiculous explanations he had blocked from his mind. Many times, he stopped. Many times, he wished if only he could turn back the clock, miss church that Wednesday, be called away on sudden business.

Anything, any course of events, so that he did not have to know.

Sometime later he arrived home, righteous anger and misery worked into his face. He went straight to his attic bedroom and slammed the door, ignoring the staff who did not know whether to serve his meal or take him a glass of wine, and so did nothing until the food went cold and they retired to bed.

And much later that night, when the tears and rage were worn out, he started to make plans. He pulled out his diary and saw that it was only Tuesday, not Wednesday.

He had not needed to walk by the Divelish that April evening at all.

Thomas was a man of business and could not act immediately. He had arrangements to make. Mr Milligan was happy to come back to work for a while. William Baker could step up to take extra responsibility but would need to be briefed on each building project underway.

"If you have to go away," Mr Milligan said, "I believe it best if I handle estimates for new business and also the Great Little contract, because I have familiarity with it. Mr Baker, can you manage the other projects? Good, then we have a working plan.

When will you go, Thomas?"

Thomas did not know as to when or where, just that he had to go. It was Mr Milligan who gave him ideas.

"Go to London. They have new houses springing up everywhere. New squares appear over night!"

But was London far enough? Would it punish Amelia enough; hold sufficient mystery and adventure to ensure maximum concern?

"They have need of builders in Ireland, I hear," Thomas replied.

Ireland was dangerous, filled with war. James, the old King, had arrived five weeks earlier, on March 12th; just about the whole country had fallen in behind him. "Perhaps I could get work on the fortifications at Londonderry."

"Londonderry is under siege, Thomas. At least go to London first, seek out the odds of getting employment in Ireland for it is London where the decisions are made. Then, if it proves impossible, you are already in the capital and can get work easily enough there." It was an old man talking from experience and it made sense. And it was argued with fervour, for Mr Milligan prayed Thomas would not fill his head with the Americas; they were too far away and held little chance of returning.

It was the obvious destination for a jilted lover.

It was agreed that he would go at the end of the week, allowing a few more days to hand over his various responsibilities.

He had missed the real Wednesday church service and now planned to avoid the Sunday meeting as well. But he was torn right down the middle. A half of him did not want to go; wanted to put his arms around Amelia and draw her to him; to hear an acceptable explanation, however shaky it might be.

And the biggest part wanted to see that naked thigh again; the way the wet undergarment clung to her body, sending rivulets across her pale pink skin.

But that was not the part of him that addressed Amelia when she came to see him on Friday evening, the eve of his departure.

She seemed sorrowful and serious as the housekeeper let her

in. Thomas was upstairs packing but came automatically, as if driven, to the landing when he heard the doorbell.

He knew it would be her and had rehearsed a thousand times how it would go.

Now, from his vantage of height, he could see her head, hat and shoulders and the swish of her elegant skirts as she proceeded through the hall with its faded wooden floor. He counted seventeen clacks of her footfall before she disappeared into the parlour.

"Sir, Miss Taylor has come to see you," the housekeeper called up the stairs, sensing that he was there and that this was no ordinary event.

"Thank you, Mrs Bush. I'll be down directly."

He desperately wanted to be in the room with her but, for some reason, delayed. He returned to his attic room, up the steep stairs that he and Grace, his sister and closest in age and friendship, had often trod to get away from the others. He brushed his hair, straightened his clothes, as if preparing for a prize ceremony rather than an interview with the girl he had planned to wed.

He noted the use of the past tense and grimaced to himself. Could he go through with this?

"Thomas, I want to explain…"

"Miss Taylor, what brings you here?"

She should have shot straight through his wall of formality, smashing his resistance. But she was as human as he and she treated him nervously, knowing that she was on the brink of losing him. She had waited for Thomas to establish himself in his profession, turning away others, or at least cooling their declarations. Now she risked losing what she had played the long game for.

"Thomas, please just listen to me."

He reacted with choice pomposity, pulling out his father's pocket watch and stating that she had three minutes, implying that his time was precious and could be divided and divided again into small particles that still had value.

"I love you, Thomas, but if you cannot give me more than three minutes for a serious explanation, then I bid you safe travels and wish you well. Good day, sir."

Thomas felt anger as she left the room. But all too soon there was nothing to put that anger up against. Except a closed door and the echo of her shoes on the wood as Amelia hurried down the hall and outside.

In the morning, Thomas rode out alone, seen off by just his housekeeper, maid and groom. He rode into fine rain that soaked cleverly, surreptitiously, leaving him uncomfortable and irritable in no time at all. But it was nothing next to the disorder in his mind.

That fine rain hid those watching from the corner of the street, even when Thomas looked around in hope of some hook that would pull him back, wind him in again. Elizabeth and Amelia stood by the intricate cornerstones that marked the edge of the Luke Davenport Home for the Homeless, the one-time place of worship where Luke Davenport had reigned in his splendid glory.

And they watched Luke's son ride away, for want of knowing what else to do.

Chapter 2

Matthew had a choice to make. He laid the big leather-bound bible on the table and looked at his wife of three weeks; Lady Merriman, or, more correctly, Mrs Davenport.

"What shall I do, dearest?"

"Whatever's in your heart, my love," came the soft reply.

But he had known her answer even before he had put the question. She was a heart-follower but with a head perched somewhere. She was busy making up for lost time; the time taken from her. Life was short enough without the theft of two decades.

"My heart says...says to do it." Besides, they might see Thomas, Matthew's younger brother, who had left Sturminster Newton so abruptly two weeks earlier. Matthew had no idea why he had left but suspected it was connected to Amelia Taylor, who lived with them at Bagber Manor and had been morose since Thomas' sudden departure.

And so they went to London, leaving the next day.

"We can stay at the George Inn while we find a house to rent," Eliza said in the carriage, playing with his hand as she spoke, tracing her finger up and down his. She slowed down as she reached each tip, as if undecided, then raced down the slope to the valley below.

He responded by pushing her finger to arch it backwards, then raising her delicate hand to his lips.

"My love," he said between his kisses.

"Sir," she said, with respect close to reverence. "I am so pleased to be with you, Matthew," she added, as if it was her mission to boost his confidence. "And by the fact that you have been chosen above all others."

"It's a rare privilege," he said modestly.

"It's a rare achievement," she replied, still in boost mode.

Eliza Davenport, nee Merriman, had decided two things from the beginning of her marriage and she had written them in the little notebook that had belonged to her mother.

1. *My husband is a remarkable man.*
2. *I shall do everything I can to support and bolster him.*

Unknowing to Eliza, Matthew had written something similar in his copy of *Fox's Book of Martyrs*.

1. *I love my wife with every fibre in my body.*
2. *She is a wonderful lady.*
3. *She is my reason, next only to God Almighty.*
4. *I will do everything in my power to make her happy and fulfilled.*

The invitation had come in the name of the King but actually was written out by a senior clerk, who met Matthew with a grave nod and, "Welcome to Parliament's employ, Mr Davenport."

"Are we to work together, sir?" Matthew asked, taking in the worn furniture and stacks of papers everywhere. The early morning sun drew patterns of pale yellow across the room, flickering like a dying lantern, yet the day was new. Every surface seemed covered in thick dust, which Matthew imagined to be laid years earlier when the world was first begun.

Was this to be his place of work for the foreseeable future? Had he given up the pleasing views and gentle air of Bagber Manor, his wife's ancestral home, for this tired and shabby room?

"Of course, sir." The clerk's watery eyes dwelled on Matthew a moment, seemed to understand everything. "But this is just the records office, Mr Davenport. You've come in the back way, is all. Allow me to show you to your study, sir. You have two junior clerks and myself to aid you in your work." The elderly clerk looked at Matthew a moment longer, trying to decide whether to go a step further. Matthew, in response, studied the plaster cracks in the painted walls, following each twist and turn from source to delta. "Sir, I knew your father when we were both young. We fought together in the civil war," the clerk continued.

"Did you now, Mr...?"

"Allingham, sir. George Allingham. And in later years I always enjoyed a sermon of an evening and your father's were particularly fine. My late wife used to read one each night while we sat by the fire. We often did the Tower of Babel; I believe that was our favourite."

"That's very kind of you, Mr Allingham," Matthew replied, thinking back to penning the sermon on the Tower of Babel. Much of it had been his work, his ideas. But it had gone out in Luke Davenport's name, for his father had added the flair that took dry and dusty words and made them dance and storm in front of the congregation.

Matthew had often wanted to have that extra spice in his words but had never managed it. And now he was facing the huge job of helping to draft a new law to guarantee the liberty of the English people for all time.

"Leave the practical matters to me, my dear," Eliza had said. "You should concentrate on your work." And a week after coming to London, they moved from the George to a pretty house on the east side of Southampton Square. She hired servants and purchased elegant furniture to complement what was provided. The front door opened onto the street, down five broad steps. In the back, there was a quiet garden with a young oak tree leaning against the carriage house at the bottom, as if it was too gangly to hold itself upright.

"Can we afford this, Eliza?"

"Not on your salary, Matthew. But with the profits from our property in Dorset we could afford a palace if we so desired," she laughed back.

"I do not want a palace, just somewhere warm and dry with a modicum of comfort," he replied seriously, making Eliza Davenport gaze at the man she had married.

"I love you, Mr Davenport," she said as it welled up inside her.

But in the other task she had set herself, of finding Thomas, she had completely failed. She had no friends in London, having spent most of her adult years in cruel seclusion, first in Yorkshire, then chained to a laundry sink in Bristol. She pressed Mr Allingham, her husband's chief clerk, for who to ask in the government and who in the main building firms.

"He would have come looking for building work, probably here but possibly in Ireland," she had said, first to George Allingham and then to a series of officials she was sent to. But all looked through their books and shrugged their shoulders. There was no note of a Thomas Davenport, builder from Dorset, in any of their records.

"Thomas seems to have totally disappeared," she concluded to her husband one Sunday morning in May. It was a day of rainbows, many slight and washed-out-looking but a few painted in vibrant colours. The frequent light showers that caused the rainbows seemed to glance off the coats and jackets and hats of those out in the strong sunlight; as if the human race had developed immunity to the weather in this great capital city.

After church, set in a tiny building along a narrow lane that joined the square next to theirs, they had walked in Hyde Park, along with dozens of others. Mr Allingham had recommended the backstreet church as having a rattling good preacher and Mr Allingham was there in the congregation of twenty or thirty. It had been that bit too rattling for Eliza, who liked her religion to be steady; almost mundane and ordinary. But her husband had clearly enjoyed it.

They discussed Thomas throughout their time in the park but got no closer to solving the mystery.

"I shall write to Amelia, of course. But I had so hoped to have positive news to send her."

"Do you miss the lively household at Bagber, my dear?" Matthew asked. Bagber Manor was their home but also housed the Taylor family. Simon Taylor, once a lawyer until he had suffered a stroke in '85, was now her land agent, despite his continuing disablements, with speech in particular. His wife was Elizabeth, Matthew's sister. Amelia was the daughter of Simon's first marriage and was the same age as Elizabeth, now her best friend.

"Of course I miss it, Matthew," Eliza replied thoughtfully. "It is my childhood home and it is ingrained in me. It is a part of who I am. But now I am yours, sir. I am your chattel and go where you will take me, with a glad and grateful heart."

"Nicely said, my dearest, but I would have you be happy. My work here will only last a short while and then we shall return to Bagber and go on as before."

"That would certainly please me, dearest Matthew, but only when you are ready."

Late spring of 1689 at Bagber Manor was like any other spring for over three hundred years. The house had been started before the Black Death raged across England, causing one in three to die and taking a clutch of Merrimans along with it. The manor had stood for several years as a shell, echoing with the cries of children as they played amongst the half-built walls, making adventures of stone and mortar.

"There was no one to do the building work." Her father, Lord Merriman, had often told the story when she was a girl. "So eventually, an enterprising forefather of ours found some workers by going to the towns and ports and offering a cottage and some land for each one who would work every day except Sundays for a year. Our ancestor ensured that they worked first to build their own cottages and only then turned their efforts to the manor. Thus, it was built with consideration for others, so as to be a happy place."

"Is that why there are so many freeholders in Bagber?" Eliza would ask and her father would nod and tell a tale or two about their independent thinking, followed by a gentle lecture on the demise of the feudal system and the rise of small landholders without any obligation to give service or payment to their lords.

"It started with the Black Death," he would say and she could still hear his clear voice thirty years later.

At other times, they would go back further with their history lesson, all the way to the previous house. He would talk of a time long ago, before the Conquest, when the Merrimans had been major landowners with holdings stretching across three counties.

"Much was taken from us when the Normans came."

But Eliza Merriman was busy buying land back, aided by the considerable skills of Simon Taylor in locating land and negotiating the best price, doing so despite his slurred speech and inability to always find the right word. He just seemed to have a knack for buying it. The Bagber Manor she had inherited was just over a thousand acres. She had almost doubled the initial holding and was investing in the land as well; this was where her expertise came in. She experimented with new crops and new methods of harvesting and drainage. She had rebuilt a third of the buildings, giving Thomas' firm a constant supply of work.

She did it because the Merrimans had done such things stretching back into history.

But now there was a new chapter to her life. Not just because of marriage to Matthew but because she had come to London with him.

Matthew found the work both tedious and fascinating. The actual detail was everyday stuff; examining drafts and changing nuances here and there before resubmitting the evolving text to the scribes. He worked as one of a dozen. Several, like Matthew, had been suggested to Parliament by Jacob Avercamps, a key behind-the-scenes adviser to William and Mary and a major driving force in the invasion the previous year. Matthew and his colleagues had thus become known as the Dutch Gang, although all were Englishmen, displaying Avercamps' wisdom in selecting home-grown talent.

The fascination came late in the day, when all twelve drafters gathered to discuss concepts and progress towards their goal.

And, amidst collective groans across the group, they heard feedback from the parliamentary committee responsible for drafting the new bill. Matthew loved this part of the day; for the first time ever, he felt he belonged to a brotherhood, a common cause.

Chapter 3

Paul Tabard was down to his last two shillings. He ordered a tankard of the cheapest ale, along with some bread and cheese, asking if the inn had any stale bread from yesterday at a discount, explaining self-consciously that it would be a modest boost to the landlord's profit if old bread could be resurrected rather than discarded. The landlord at the Red Lion did not care for profit any longer. He had just sold his whole business to his rival at the White Lion for a reasonable sum. As soon as the legal work was done, he would be out, his pockets bulging with cash.

He took a penny for food and drink combined, pocketed it and told the serving maid to surprise the young man, who looked as thin as a beggar.

Ten minutes later, she served a bowl of rich soup, followed by a plate laden with roast beef and a glass of good whisky to wash it down.

"To what and who do I owe this kind gesture?" Paul asked.

"Mr Amiss, the landlord, is retiring, sir. He has sold out to Mr Weston. He just told me to surprise you, sir. I hope I've done so."

"You have surprised me supremely. Thank you, Miss...?" He looked again at her; she had a beauty that cut through him.

"It's Amy, sir, Amy Barratt."

"And will you stay with the new owner, Amy?"

"No, sir. I won't work for him, not even if I was starving! He's as mean as anything, sir."

Paul wanted to invite her to starve with him. Going hungry was his norm these days but it would be so much more bearable to share that poverty with someone. But her in particular; he had never met anyone before who could enter his soul.

She was quite a beauty; something to work with, as his old employer would have said in jest, rubbing his hands together, then making a pyramid of fingers under his chin. For a moment he thought back to happy days, learning the trade under a man who knew it inside out and treated him like a son.

But his employer, Mr Sanderson, was dead, his capital confiscated and his contacts terrified into silence.

And Paul Tabard was completely on his own in this world.

Leaving London had been the obvious thing to do. If they had found him, they would have killed him too. He was sure about that. After nine years in the trade, he knew the business as well as his employer, making him every bit as dangerous to them, whoever they were.

They had made it appear a common case of theft gone wrong, resulting in the death of a leading city merchant. But Paul suspected otherwise, not believing it a muddled robbery and accidental death.

"Your bed is ready, sir." Amy came back into the main bar, where a few souls drifted around seeking free beer and Paul had fallen asleep at the table where he had eaten, his empty whisky glass threatening to topple out of his hand to the floor.

"I'm sorry, I cannot afford a bed."

"What nonsense is that? You've already paid, sir." Amy was taking this surprise to the extreme, aware that Mr Amiss did not care and she was in her last week of employment before Mr Weston took over. She spoke in a loud voice, stressing the next few words, one at a time so that they settled on the mildly drunk patrons. "And, sir, you also paid for several rounds of drinks for all tonight. It was very generous of you, sir, was that not so?" She turned to watch the six or eight in the bar wake to the prospect of free drinks.

It was a giggling Amy Barratt who helped a slightly tipsy Paul Tabard to his private room an hour and a half later. In that time, she had managed to get him to eat half a rabbit pie, a plate of fresh clams, and several more slices of cold roast beef.

"Sleep well, sir," she said as she closed the door after placing a glass and a big jug of water by his bed.

"Stay with me, Amy, stay with me."

"I can't do that, sir, I'm a good Christian girl," she chuckled and was still chuckling when she reached the attic bedroom she shared with two other serving maids, both of whom were staying on to try their chances with the new owner.

Paul did not come down for breakfast in the morning. There was no sound from his room through the door. Amy returned several times, wondering if she had given him too much to drink the previous night. On the fourth trip back, still silence from inside, she determined to enter. Just as she placed her hand on the doorknob, it turned, making her jump back in surprise. The door opened and Paul Tabard stood there, his thinning red hair standing on end from sleep.

"Good morning, Amy."

Seeing again the cheeky grin he wore, surrounded by freckles from tiny to vast, she knew exactly why she had treated him so specially the night before.

"Good morning, sir. I was just about to come and wake you, to see what you desired for breakfast."

"And that is included in the penny I paid yesterday as well?"

"For sure, sir. A penny goes a long way in Dorset."

"Then I am wealthy, Amy, but not for my possessions or any hoards of silver but because of who I met yesterday."

He risked a kiss then, first one on her right cheek, the second on her lips. She remembered afterwards the way his red hair tickled her face as they kissed. He remembered how warm she was to hold in his arms.

"I have the afternoon off, sir," she breathed through his hair.

"You must call me Paul."

"Yes, sir, Paul, sir." She broke contact and danced away. "Now I have work to be getting on with… Paul. But, will I see you later?"

They made love in her attic bedroom, a chair propped against the door handle in case the other occupants returned for an article of clothing or some such thing. But they were undisturbed all afternoon, lying together on the bed long into the May evening. They talked endlessly, slipping naturally from "What will you do?" to "What shall we do?" And a plan emerged as May 14th turned, as days do, into May 15th. Her room mates had bedded down in other rooms, gossiping as to

16

what was going on behind the fastened door.

Outside, the clouds scuttled as the light wind blew in Heaven knew not. For the country of England was changing before their eyes, leaping forward yet anchored so solidly in the past; it took its old ways with it in a way no other country has ever done.

All change at Great Little, too. The new house was rising from the ashes of the old; bigger, bolder, better.

"I declare, the only substantial thing remaining from the old house is the painted glass on the main staircase," Sally said that evening, as Alice Roakes and Penelope Wiltshire sat with her in the long, narrow library with wallpaper tinged by flames, aging it in faded yellow patches running up the walls.

"Did the flames really get that far up the wall?" Penelope said, pointing between the two French windows that looked over the terrace. "And this was the least damaged room."

"Except the stained glass on the staircase." Sally stuck to her point. The depiction, done long ago, was of the Little family at feast. It wound up the main staircase like a story told by another generation. Wimples on the women and horned cups, no doubt containing mead, for the lower tables. Those at the upper table all had chalices of silver or gold, in imitation of the Last Supper. Sally had often counted the people at the high table. There were thirteen places and only twelve occupants.

Had Judas left already to collect his thirty pieces of silver?

In a way, it was the Last Supper, for it seemed whatever happened to the house, the Littles would always be feasting on the staircase, frozen in their state of joy.

Every time Sally used the new staircase, built of oak from distant Kent, she saw something else in the picture; something she had not seen before.

And Penelope, her lover, the Dowager Duchess of Wiltshire, had told her that it was exactly the same for her.

Mr Milligan had been visiting that day, explaining the absence of Thomas Davenport and stating that he would be running the project for a while. He was pleased with progress, although they lacked sufficient stone and it was becoming ever scarcer.

"The quarry at Melbury Abbas has a long waiting list for deliveries," he had told them, adding that he had sent riders out to various other quarries in the area. Each one carried a sample of the Dorset limestone that went into Great Little. "No one has yet reported back on spare stone but I am confident we will find some and Melbury Abbas has promised deliveries to recommence in a few weeks at a steady pace. Last year, nobody was building and this year, everybody is."

"Optimism sprouts like weeds in the hedgerow," Alice Roakes laughed. "But do not fret too much, I am not going to rebuild Great Little in one year. Besides, I have the baby due next month. Now, I've done some sketches of the kitchen garden leading down to the stables. You must let me know what you think."

"Would you consider one wing in brick?" Mr Milligan asked, thinking around the problem. "It might look striking to have the clay offset the limestone. I was thinking of the new library we are building so this one can be combined with the great hall. Brick can look particularly gracious when it is laid well."

"That would be lovely," Penelope said, then added that it was not for her to say.

"But it is for you to have a say, my dear," Alice replied. "For you are in this together with me. This is to be your home every bit as much as it is to be mine." As she said this, she looked at Sally, standing quietly by the door since Mr Milligan had arrived; keeping up the pretence of mistress and servant. Penelope saw this look and knew that Alice meant Sally to be included in this largesse.

"That is kind of you, Alice. We certainly feel like it is our home here, even if it is just a building site!" And because Penelope threw the words at Alice but looked at Sally, Mr Milligan knew who Penelope meant when she used the plural pronoun.

Chapter 4

Thomas came to his senses to the rocking of the ship on the swell. His drink-fuddled brain recalled with horror the cries of, "Next stop Charlestown!" that had bounced down the passenger berths the night before.

Why had he done the exact opposite of what he had agreed with Mr Milligan? "Go to London, son, it is far enough yet near enough." He had understood exactly what the old man meant. Yet at the crossroads in Shaftesbury he had stubbornly turned his horse west for Bristol and a ship for the new world. He should have turned east for London. In the capital he would have found work or, at the very least, secured government employment in Ireland, then hopped across the Irish Sea, a comfortable distance from Dorset rather than a yawning gap.

In making that decision at the Shaftesbury crossroads, he had only thought of the effect on Amelia when she heard he had gone far away.

In striking back at Amelia, he was scourging himself on the back, salt on the wounds.

He lay in his cot. Too small to take his body stretched out, the cot took most of the tiny cabin he had spent a quarter of his capital on.

He could have sailed as a deck passenger for a much smaller sum but the same irrational mood that had dominated for three weeks now made him part with five pounds for a ticket in this stuffy, windowless box that they called a 'gentleman's berth'.

And then last night, the night before sailing, he had gone ashore with two fellows from the ship. They had drunk far too much and mixed their drinks, starting on beer, then rough wine with the pretence of a meal, followed by stronger liquids in different shades of brown. Every time he had looked, there seemed to be another glass on the table before him.

His two colleagues seemed to manage their drink easily. Occasionally, Thomas had caught them looking smugly at each other. Then, one or the other would call out and more glasses would appear. A memory came to him of large and heaving bosoms brushing against him as the drinks were placed on the table. The serving girl was actually a matron with sagging skin and a hoarse voice like iron moving against iron. She had made repeated coarse jokes. They had laughed at each one long and hard, yet it was the drink laughing, not Thomas; not one of the jokes could he remember now.

He closed his eyes; it hurt to keep them open. His brain felt like the server's voice; metal grating on metal, grinding into consciousness.

It did not have to be this way. He had been foolish but could unwind the petulant decisions he had taken. Five pounds had been wasted but he could leave the ship and still have sufficient to keep him in London while he looked for work.

He rose suddenly from his cot as if resolved. He just avoided striking his head on a beam that would have knocked him out. He put his fingers to his head, wondering at the near miss, then feeling a large lump in the middle of the back of his head. There was dried blood making a sticky mat of his hair. He must have fallen on the way back to his cabin.

It was overpowering to stand so he lowered himself carefully back down on his cot, closed his eyes once again, this time concentrating on getting better. He examined first the peripheries. There was nothing wrong with his feet and legs, other than a little cramp that he solved by placing his foot on the deck and putting pressure on it. His right hand was stinging. Opening one eye like the shutter on a lantern, he examined it. It was grazed, as if run against a rough wall. A vague memory came to him of being hit on the head and falling against something, putting out his hand to break his fall.

What had happened last night?

Next in line for attention was his stomach. For several minutes, he lay motionless, trying to quell the storm within. The head posed a greater problem. He concentrated first on the throb in the temples, willing it away. A pint of water from a flask he had by the cot helped a little. But the bigger problem remained; somehow, he had cut his head badly. The blood had dried but the pain and cloudiness endured.

Slowly now, he stood again and made his way out of the cabin, up the ladder and to the main deck. Was it his hangover or the bang to his head that caused him to sway so much? No, it was none of these. The ship was moving, chopping and slicing through the waves that hit from the right, just ahead of the centre of the vessel.

"Captain, we are underway!"

"Yes, Mr Davenport, we are underway. I applaud your powers of observation, sir." The captain had sold berths to a hundred young men going to America, knew the types well enough.

"But, I have changed my mind, Captain. I was coming to say I would not be sailing after all."

'It's too late now, Mr Davenport. We cannot turn around on this tide."

Thomas argued until it was obvious the captain was losing patience.

"I'll tell you what I'll do, Mr Davenport. For five pounds more, I'll drop you in Ireland, somewhere on the south coast. It's a beautiful land and you will be able to get passage back to England from there. Is that a prospect you can live with, sir?"

"It is, Captain. I'll just get the money." It was another drain on his capital but it was all part of correcting his silly pride.

But, down below in his cramped cabin, his capital was much depleted. He searched his purse, his bag, his overcoat, everything, in case he had put some of it elsewhere for safe-keeping. There was not a farthing anywhere, except for five pounds in silver in his purse.

He was left with the exact amount he needed to pay the captain to drop him at an Irish port.

He would ask his colleagues from last night what they knew of his money. But nobody had seen two men answering that description on board. The purser went through the entire passenger list while the captain jangled new coins in his pocket, contemplating how there were a dozen ways to make a living out of the passenger trade to and from America.

Thomas retired to his cabin in a state of outrage and self-pity. When the steward knocked and opened the door several hours later, he saw a young man on his knees, offering his despair to his Lord.

"I thought you were suffering from seasickness, sir," he said, his jollity cutting through Thomas' prayers. "I brought a little bread and cheese and a tot of brandy to settle your stomach. The name's Browne, sir, and I'm here to help you gents in any way I can."

Thomas looked up at him, marvelling that the Lord had acted so swiftly in answer to his prayers. For an idea had seeped into his befuddled head that moment, prompted by the sight of the cheery steward with the largest grin stretched across his kindly face.

"Mr Browne, you can do something for me. Run and fetch the bottle the brandy came from and another glass. Then, if you have the time, I need to know how this ship works."

"I'm no sailor, sir."

"I'm not thinking of the sails and the wind and the ropes that run everywhere waiting to trip me; rather, how the ship is organised, both legitimately and otherwise, if you get my meaning."

"I do, sir, and will be back directly."

The steward poured another glass of brandy then sat next to Thomas on the child-size cot. He was tall, with long legs that buckled up to almost reach his nose.

"You're hardly built for this work, Mr Browne," Thomas commented.

"Well, I'll be giving it up in a day or two." His soft Irish accent was washed out, as if he had spent years in foreign places, yet he looked the same age as Thomas.

"What will you do next?"

"I'm going home, Mr Davenport. At last, I'm going home." He went on to explain that he had been born in Barbados. His father had been an overseer on a plantation. "He was fired several times and consequently often without work for he would not whip the slaves. He and Ma were friends with the slaves, helping them where they could." He stopped then, his otherwise perpetual grin falling to nothing, to blankness pierced through with sad memories.

"What happened to your parents?" Thomas heard the voice but was not conscious of asking the question.

"They died," he said quietly, took a mouthful of brandy, refilled both glasses. "They were killed by the slaves in a mad uprising six years ago, when I was sixteen."

"You mean the same slaves who were his friends?"

"Yes, I mean the same. But it was not their fault. They were fighting the plantation owners with stolen firearms. Ma and Pa were trying to stop the fighting and they got caught in the crossfire."

"I'm sorry to hear this tragedy." He was doubly sorry, for Browne was obviously a good man.

"Since then I have been working at anything I could, trying to get back to Ireland, to cousins and grandparents I have never met."

"Well, I am going to Ireland, too. I paid the captain to stop."

"Why pay him, sir? We were stopping anyway. I agreed to work my passage over to Ireland. We were always going to stop there."

Thomas' outrage, recently quelled through talking to the Lord, with a little help from the steward's brandy, was back again in full force. "Of all the lying, thieving tricksters!" he shouted through the wooden ceiling to the deck above.

Chapter 5

It was a habit long ingrained; always take the roundabout route, use the back streets and avoid the main thoroughfares.

He could never be an aristocrat, travelling in pomp down the Strand or up the Mall. But, then, he did not want to be an aristocrat, and was perfectly happy as a ruthless agent working with stealth and secrecy to undermine whatever his target was.

And build up his wealth and independence steadily.

It was, so they declared, the hottest day of the year so far. The late May sun beat down on London with a fierce determination to burn whatever it landed upon. On the main routes, there would be ladies waving fans with hopeless vigour, men perspiring in darkened woollen coats and hats to match. But Parchman, travelling by the back streets, could avoid the conventions of fashion and keep to the shady places in the narrow, high-sided lanes that wound around the place. He kept his coat over his arm or flung over one shoulder, hooked with a thumb. He would put it on only when he reached Whitehall, arriving cool and undisturbed by the heat outside.

It was a critical day. He had done his preparatory work carefully, going three times undercover to Ireland to check practices and procedures. The last time had been particularly thrilling, slipping in and out under the nose of James Stuart and his growing army. These trips had been at his own cost but he saw it as an investment.

An investment in a gold mine. And not just for him but also for his associates, his hangers-on. Cartwright and Franshaw would be chuckling when they heard of the scheme. But first he had to get it past Candles.

"It's easy, remarkably easy," he said in private conference with Robert Candles, the Scotsman with a most unlikely surname for a Scot. "We bid for the supply of the army in Ireland."

"What army? Oh, you mean the one we are recommending

to send? But we can't do that, I mean…"

"It's simple, Robert. You and I have responsibility for security in Ireland." This was pushing the truth a little for, strictly, Parchman worked for Candles rather than sharing responsibility. Also, they were responsible for espionage, not security in all its aspects. "Our agents reported back consistently that James was planning to land there."

Candles nodded. The old King had landed on March 12th, just as they had predicted would happen. "Hence, we recommended that King William sends an army to counter the forces of James that now control most of the country. That army is being prepared as we speak. We have recommended Schomberg to lead it but no appointment is yet made."

"Exactly," Parchman continued. "Might I remind you, Robert, who suggested Schomberg in the first place."

"It was you."

"I was insistent, was I not?"

"You were insistent, sir. Please tell me the significance of this choice rather than play games with me."

"Yes, of course." Had he gone a little too far in his familiarity? It would pay to seem an ounce more respectful. "I had an inkling of the idea even then, sir." He reflected while he talked that 'sir' could be a mark of respect, as he had intended it just then, or one of impatience, as Candles had employed in addressing him. It went up the chain with deference and slid down again as an affront of arrogance. "I thought that if we could secure an elderly foreigner to lead the army, we might have a freer rein with the supply and accounting for that supply."

"But you forget one thing, Parchman, and in doing so expose the futility of your grand exercise. We are agents of espionage and as such are not responsible for running an army. There you have the weakness in your plan. Others will choose who supplies the army, not us."

"Who will, sir? Make that decision, I mean."

"Why sir, the King or perhaps one of his ministers, I suppose." Deference up and impatience back down.

"There is no one currently. I propose that we put ourselves

forward for this thankless task of unceasing toil and organisation."

"And then award the contract to ourselves? Can we do that?" Candles was still not wholly convinced but Parchman noticed he was now listening.

"Only at arm's length, Robert." Parchman edged back to the more familiar as the argument settled on his employer. "Just think, with a contract to supply the army with everything from powder to rations, we will be in the unique position of being both customer and supplier."

"I like it, Parchman, but will it really work? I don't want to end up with my head in a noose."

Parchman shuddered, as he always did when mention was made of the hangman.

"We keep the two sides completely apart, of course. I have a man who will run the trading operation and we, as government employees, place the demand on the apparently separate business."

Parchman had gone a step further than this but did not see the need to bother his employer with it at present. He had located the firm of Sanderson and Sanderson, brought about the sudden and violent death of the principal, and taken control of the operation. Sanderson and Sanderson had experience in supplying armies stretching back to before Cromwell's time. It was the perfect cover.

For a perfect operation.

And Parchman knew exactly what he would do with his new wealth.

Sanderson and Sanderson reopened their doors on May 25th. Cartwright walked into the office on the ground floor of the Sanderson home, with a cluster of draft contracts in hand. It just needed the royal seal and they were fabulously rich men.

Parchman was confident that seal would come soon; confident enough that he put the next leg of his plan in operation. This was the private part that nobody in London need know about.

"Everything is in place, Robert, and the first of many

contracts should come our way within the month. I'm going to be away for ten days, with your permission of course, as I have some pressing personal matters to deal with."

"Of course, but don't be longer than ten days," Candles replied, anxious that Parchman, as the mastermind behind this plan, should not be away when the contract came through but rather relishing the thought of ten days without his company.

With Candles' share of the proceeds, he could retire from government service, return to being a Presbyterian preacher, and publish a brilliant set of sermons to rival those of Luke Davenport. He would be remembered partly for his sterling government work but mainly for the superiority of his sermons. He could see the volume in his mind now; heavy pages, laden with insight. Why, he would dedicate the first book to King William. In return, William would keep one by his bedside and read a new sermon to himself before going to sleep each night.

Parchman had a long ride to Dorset and a clandestine meeting with a certain Mr Simon Taylor, who he knew of old. Taylor had suffered a stroke a few years earlier but had achieved a remarkable recovery. He had, for some reason, decided to keep that recovery from his family. This gave Parchman the perfect cover for his planned activities.

Taylor was the vehicle of revenge for Parchman and would benefit enormously from the demise of his enemies.

"I'm targeting two people who have done me great injustices," he said in a corner of a remote and almost deserted inn a quarter way from Shaftesbury to Sturminster Newton. Simon's manservant, who had driven him there, had been told he could visit his mother in Shaftesbury and to be back in three hours.

To all intents and purposes, they were alone.

"I know one but not the other," Simon replied, warming to the furtive looks his companion gave out. Parchman was his type of man, dependable in his underhand ways, consistent in his plotting and able and willing to back it up with unrestrained force when required.

"One is your employer; Lady Merriman as was, Mrs Davenport now."

"She is not my employer," Simon replied hotly, reality stinging.

"Your business partner, then." This was said with carelessness, as if it mattered not whether Simon Taylor was his own man; Parchman only wanted certain skills.

And when he explained what skills he wanted and how they would be applied, Simon Taylor was rubbing his hands with glee.

For there is a neatness when two resolute people's revenge coincides, causing a near unstoppable force to bring others down.

Chapter 6

Amy Barratt decided she would not slip away, preferring the bold approach.

"I'm leaving early, sir. Would you be able to pay me for the work I've done? I'm going with Mr Tabard, the guest you were very kind to."

"I thought you would," he replied. "There's something about you two together."

"Oh, did you notice? Was it that obvious?" Amy seemed flattered to have had her feelings confirmed.

"No, not that obvious, Amy. But I have not entirely been taken up by my sudden good fortune in selling this flea-infested pit for a tidy sum. I've always prided myself on character judgement. You two are suited to each other." He pulled out a handful of coins and counted out two pounds in shillings, florins and sixpences. Then added four more half-crowns taken from another pocket.

"Fifty shillings, sir? That is far too much. I'm only owed about…"

"Take it, girl, and go with my blessing. You stood by me during the hard times so it is only fair you should benefit a little from my good fortune."

"Thank you, Mr Amiss."

"Do the same for someone else when you can one day."

"I will, Mr Amiss."

"What will you do now that you are free of this place?"

"We will get married first, sir, as soon as we can. Paul asked me yesterday and I said…"

"Well, what did you say?"

"I said," she was suddenly shy, "that I wanted very much to but that he should ask your permission as the closest thing I have to a father."

"Oh Amy, you've made an old man very happy. Of course, you have my blessing but I am concerned beyond giving a

29

blessing. Unfortunately, people cannot live on love alone."

"I know, sir. We have a plan. Paul is very skilled at government contracting, having served an apprenticeship and become almost a junior partner in the firm he worked for in London. He lacks the capital to start in his own name so when we are married he will take employment hereabouts with a view to raising capital to start his own firm as he finds backers."

"Amy, have you asked why he left London?"

"Yes, Mr Amiss. His employer was killed by thugs. Paul thinks they were acting for a rival firm and are after him also. It is a dangerous business because it can be so profitable. It attracts all sorts on the fringes, sir."

The landlord was tempted to invest but, on enquiring how much was needed, it was clear that it was most of the proceeds from selling the inn. It was too big a risk to take. But perhaps he could help in a smaller way.

"Oh, sir. I didn't mean to ask you for this sum. I am mortified to think…"

"Well, less thinking and certainly less mortification please, Amy, my dear. Go with events for a little while. I expect the Lord will show you a clear path."

They parted with happy tears but not before Mr Amiss cheekily suggested that Paul formally seek permission from him to marry her and they would enjoy a little harmless fun out of the situation. He was reluctant to see the back of Amy and her new husband-to-be.

Only, it got a lot more serious than Mr Amiss had imagined.

Their little diversion worked well. Amy pushed Paul to ask the innkeeper for permission to marry. He came to see Mr Amiss, turning his hat in his hand, as if presenting plans to a minister of the Crown. Amy had slipped into the next room to listen at the doorway.

"Wait a minute, Mr Tabard, let me understand you correctly. You waltz in here, take a view on the situation and next thing we know you are proposing to my charge, Amy Barratt." This stretched the truth a little. Amy was twenty-three years old and of sound mind; she was nobody's charge.

"That's correct, sir."

"This is the most preposterous thing I've ever heard." Mr Amiss had spent decades as a showman running the Red Lion; his acting skills were well honed. "Tell me why on God's earth I should give my blessing to such a union?"

"I love her, sir. She is like a soulmate to me." Amy's heart jumped and hovered a yard above her head as she heard his words through the door cracked slightly open.

"Tell me, Mr Tabard, how do you intend to support Amy? Keep her in hats and all?"

"I have much commercial experience, sir, particularly in the management of government contracts for a healthy profit."

"So, you have no immediate income, just the promise of some in the future? How many times have I seen promises made in the heat of the moment? It won't do, Mr Tabard. It certainly will not do."

"Sir, I love Amy and will do anything to keep her secure and well. I will take employment immediately in whatever position I can secure in Dorchester in order to put a roof over her head. There are sufficient trading houses here for me to get a position as clerk, perhaps even a senior clerk. It is likely I will earn thirty pounds a year."

"You will do no such thing."

"I will, sir, if it will provide security for Amy. I will work my way up from the bottom again."

"I'll tell you what I'll do." He scowled for effect, such that Amy, through the crack in the door, saw him and let out a quickly muffled giggle. Paul turned to see what the noise was but saw nothing but the door slightly ajar. "Mr Tabard, do you intend to listen to me or stare into open space like a half-wit?" He could see it would be hard to hold the pretence much longer.

"Yes, sir, of course I intend to listen to you." But the head kept turning towards the door.

Mr Amiss, having saved carefully all his life and with a windfall on top from the sale of his inn, made an irrational decision; something he had done less than a handful of times over his sixty years.

"For Amy's sake, I'll put up one quarter of the capital you require, provided you can source the other three quarters within the next six months. In addition, I will give you an allowance of thirty shillings a month and free board at the house in Dorchester I am moving to. It is a fine house and I will complete on the purchase next week. It is narrow and tall, but you may have a whole floor to yourselves."

"Does that mean...?" Paul was scrabbling to take this generosity in but wanted, above all, to ensure his understanding with regard to marrying Amy.

But Mr Amiss could not resist another chance to tease him.

"Yes, Mr Tabard, it means you will have three whole rooms at my house."

"But, sir, can we wed with your blessing?"

"Mr Tabard, it also means you two have my blessing."

Paul heard the door open and turned to see Amy, smiling broadly.

"You were listening all along?" he gasped, then broke into laughter with them.

Paul Tabard took employment three days a week at a local importer of silk, giving him three days to look for backing for his planned enterprise. He moved temporarily into a lodging house until they were married in the middle of June. Meanwhile, Amy prepared the three rooms on the fourth floor for their wedding night.

Mr Amiss was content to spread his good fortune a bit. He had never married and was happy to have two people share his home, ignoring the rumours that Amy was his love child.

"Why else would he shower her with such benefice?" the gossips asked each other. "And what do we ever hear of her parentage? Surely there is something behind the devotion he shows her?"

It could not be random kindness, in their eyes, for they were unaware of this quality that appears in men and women from time to time.

But one thing Mr Amiss could not do was help Paul Tabard find backers. He introduced him to many potential investors, desperately hoping they would prove to be the one. Only the silk importer, seeing Tabard's qualities at work and anxious not to lose him, offered a shilling for every pound he needed.

And even then, there were strings attached; Paul was to continue working at the firm for at least two days a week.

"I don't see how I can do this, Mr Amiss," he reported on the evening of the offer. "When I raise the capital, I will need to dedicate my time wholly to my new enterprise."

"Take it as a mark of respect for your capabilities, son," Mr Amiss replied, wishing he had sufficient to back him fully, wishing he had the nerve to take the risk.

As the clocks moved through the days and the days moved into high summer, Paul and Amy, blissful newly-weds, began to wonder whether they would ever raise the capital they needed.

"Do you think we should leave Dorchester?" Amy asked her husband one light and breezy evening, with the airiness belying their concerns.

"In London, I could get work easily but we cannot go there. Besides, there is Mr Amiss to think about."

It was remarkable how quickly the older man had become a father figure to Paul, matching what he had always been to Amy.

Chapter 7

Bridget Browne asked a boy to cup his hands together to make a platform for her feet. The ragged boy obliged, delighting in the view it gave him of her ankles. Once, when she squirmed to get a better view, her plain cotton dress, the only one she had left to wear, caught on a knob of stone and rode up a little, giving the boy a perfect view of both lightly stockinged calves, glorious in their shapeliness. He wavered slightly in his stance as he forgot the perpetual hunger, replaced briefly with another hunger.

"Careful, boy, don't let me fall." Which address was a cheek for Bridget, at nineteen, was maybe a year or two older than the boy.

"What can you see?" the boy asked, hoping he had the strength to continue holding her forever, shifting his body to lean against the parapet.

"I see ships, lots of ships. Well, not exactly the ships themselves but masts and sails. The sails are coming down, I think."

"They are anchoring below Culmore Point," a nearby soldier told the pair. "They must be the relief fleet."

Suddenly, all around were cries of, "It's the relief fleet!" and then, as the news passed along the wall and down into Londonderry, the implications were voiced. "Food is coming. We are saved. We are saved."

"Don't believe it," the soldier said.

"Why, sir?" Bridget replied, her own euphoria dampened by his words.

"It is certainly the relief fleet bearing food a plenty but a miss is as good as a mile, as they say. It has sailed to within sight of our city but can go no further. Like Tantalus and the grapes, it is forever out of reach of its goal."

"How, sir?"

"The boom, young miss. The Jacobites have put giant chains

across the river that will prevent any ship coming up to us."

"Oh!" And at that moment the boy gave up the struggle against hunger and the weariness it sent with it. He broke his cupped hands, stumbling backwards and falling onto the stone ledge. Bridget Browne fell a foot, grabbed the parapet above her with both hands and was left dangling there until the soldier carefully lowered her, assisted by the embarrassed boy, who was now back on his feet.

"Are you hurt?" the soldier asked.

"No, sir." But when she looked her dress was torn badly. "I need to repair my dress is all," she laughed from relief and because laughter was all you could fall back on in times of despair. Laughter as the glue that binds humans into humanity.

The soldier whisked off the light cloak he wore and wrapped it around her shoulders to cover the tear.

"There we are, quite the soldier now!" he laughed too. "All you need is a sword and musket."

"I'll use them happily if the Jacobites scale our walls," she replied.

"They're trying to starve us out and doing a good job of it, too. My name is Miles Denby and I live above the first shop on Butcher Street on the right from the gate; just so you know where to return the cloak when you have gone home to change is why I tell you, miss."

"You are a butcher? I'm Bridget Browne of Halebrook Farm. We quite likely supply your shop in normal…"

"Times! Yes, I know Tobias Browne. Is he your father?"

"Yes, sir."

"A good and honest farmer. But there has been no meat these four weeks, as you well know. When I close my eyes at night, all I see is chops and choice cuts in abundance! So, instead of plying my trade, I must guard these walls with my fellow citizens. But what of you, miss? What brings you to starve behind these walls with us town folk? Halebrook is at Ballymagorry, is it not, some dozen or more miles south of here?"

Bridget, suddenly fighting back childish tears, explained that she had been caught in the city when James Stuart had arrived at Bishop's Gate, one of the four entrances to Londonderry, two months earlier.

"Last October, I came to stay with some friends in order to study a while under Dr Fielding, the historian. I brought a trunk of clothes, for I intended to stay several months. I became so engrossed in my studies and ended up staying longer than anticipated. I had written to my parents, saying I would return home in the second part of April and then, as you well know, James Stuart arrived with his army on the eighteenth and I was trapped. When the refugees started coming in from the countryside, I gave most of my clothes away and spent my spare money on food for them." Mention of food made her stomach ache; a dull gnawing pain that grew and grew inside.

"And now there is no food left, not even a rat to be caught in the sewers."

"Too true, Mr Denby. I will return your cloak this evening, sir. And thank you for your kind assistance." She had eaten rat and would happily do so again. Leather from shoes, too, added to the watery soup that had become their sustenance.

She had no trouble locating the butcher's shop, in fact had frequently queued there in the early days of the siege, watching the display of meat gradually diminish. The butcher-turned-soldier and his young wife welcomed her and gave her a glass of watered-down beer.

"It's mostly water with just a touch of beer now, it has been diluted so many times."

"Well, it is delicious and the first drink I have had for two weeks that has not been water." Bridget could sense the few particles of energy that remained in the beer coursing through her veins, spreading a morsel of goodness to her tired and weakened bones.

They talked for a few minutes of the siege. It was the only conversation that made sense, other than prayer. And usually people's prayers turned back to the siege and the terrible hunger imposed on them for their defiance.

"Do you think we should have surrendered when James Stuart came in April, sir?" Bridget asked.

"No, I do not, most certainly not. We shouted 'No surrender' then and we should still now, even with empty bellies and feeble heads."

"Well, I must go, Mr Denby. Thank you again for the loan of your cloak."

"Miss Browne, do you have paper and ink?"

"I do, sir, quite a good supply."

"Are you a writer?"

"I would like to be. I was researching our family history, back to Elizabethan times, when we first came to Ireland."

The suggestion that came next threw Bridget completely.

"You should write a history of the siege."

It was a perfect idea. She had arrived several months before the siege began and would, in all likelihood, be in Londonderry the day it ended. Writing was her love and she knew she could do it with grace and style.

She thanked the Denbys for their hospitality and for the idea then left to return to her friend's home. After a supper of vegetable soup, more watered-down than the beer, and only a few mouthfuls for the rest would be stock for the next day's soup with more water added, she retired to her room, pulled out the ink, quill and paper she had purchased on her arrival in Londonderry and sat down to write.

The Siege of Londonderry by a Woman of Some Education Who Lived through it All.

She had a very pleasant neat hand at writing; her long fingers controlled the quill easily so there were minimal blots. Her mind was also at work, thinking things through carefully, making notes on an extra piece of paper. The result was an easy to read, clear and excellently-flowing recording of events in and around Londonderry that year. And with a developing insight that, on re-reading it, pleased her and, she hoped, would please others.

She was also surprisingly modest, for her education against that of most nineteen-year-olds was vastly superior. She spoke French fluently and understood both Latin and Greek. Her father, Tobias Browne, had introduced her to Herodotus when eight years old and she had never stopped devouring history books ever since. Under Dr Fielding, she had also studied mathematics, geology and a little of the other sciences, as well as philosophy. She brought great purpose to being a student, several times writing to her parents to request an extension to her tutoring.

Afterwards, when the siege was over and Londonderry stood proud in its defiance, she sent the first short chapter to a publisher in London. The manuscript rose to the head of the firm of Prendegast and Son, underlings recognising the sweet, non-fussy style and the topical subject. One afternoon in late summer, Mr Prendegast found the sun through the window and sat back in an armchair in the corner of his office. He would read the opening chapter one more time and then make a decision on publication, although he had really made that decision already and merely sought the joy of another reading.

It can all be said to have commenced with a letter known as the Comber Letter sent to Lord Mount-Alexander in early December of 1688. William of Orange had arrived in England and had progressed to London, although with the distance from Londonderry, we knew only that he was moving through the West Country with the crown of England, Scotland and our beloved Ireland his objective. The letter in question was said to be from an acquaintance and warned his aristocratic friend of dire things plotted against the Protestants of Ireland.

This letter was copied many times over and passed by hand and word of mouth throughout Ireland in quick order. It understandably caused much concern, even panic. Then, a few days after the Comber Letter was made public, Colonel Phillips, once a Governor of Londonderry, sent urgent message to our city to close the gates to the Redshanks who could any day approach and demand entry. The Redshanks are the Earl of Antrim's forces and, indeed, the following day they arrived, causing panic in our streets. I remember this day well. Perhaps the most outstanding observation is the power of rumour, building on panic and causing great distortions and exaggerations to the truth. The Redshanks were said to eat babies and slaughter everyone in their path. There were hordes of them; one person was heard to say one hundred thousand Redshanks; for certain the ranks of soldiers filled the land to the horizon and beyond.

The truth would be known only after the events, when historians set to work. But the damage is done at the time; more so through exaggeration than fact.

Here we have the first true dilemma of the Siege of Londonderry and out of this dilemma came the first historic moment that marks this siege in the history books. The Bishop in his cathedral would have us open the gates and let the Redshanks have the city. However, this was not to be for Henry Campsie and a band of apprentices seized all four gates and took charge of the magazine. They shouted defiance and, out of that defiance, came strength and resolve to all citizens.

It was an uneasy Christmas that year for no one knew what the future held. It could be death and destruction or fame and fortune. Only the Lord, our Father in Heaven, knew and, despite our constant and many prayers, he was not divulging this outcome, as is the way of God with His Kingdom on earth. We knew afterwards of great happenings in England but even good news is sometimes slow to travel and throughout December we had to content ourselves with rumours of William of Orange's progress towards the three crowns of England, Scotland and Ireland.

At the beginning of January, Lieutenant-Colonel Robert Lundy came onto the scene as our new Military Governor. He spent much time that month improving the walls and defences. The walls were still quite sound, originating some seventy years earlier when King James I, the grandfather of James Stuart, granted a Royal Charter to our city and sent us out from England to settle the land. But Colonel Lundy had many improvements in mind and ensured these were carried out in quick order. Many Protestants were fleeing into the city at this time, fearing for their lives if they remained outside the walls. My family came to visit me from my home in Ballymagorry, but not to stay. They explained that if they left the farm, their livelihood would suffer with the animals being uncared for. They also feared they would not be allowed to return to the farm in the event that James Stuart succeeded in taking over the country. This heightened my personal determination to defy the forces of James Stuart and, no doubt, each defender had a personal story to boost their resolve and morale, building into a giant body of defiance from many small contributions.

The influx of people was so great it had another effect on me at this time. I had been given three rooms in my friend's house; a bedroom, a study and a sitting room, all provided for a modest charge arranged with my father and to include meals. I went to my friends as the incomers kept coming and suggested I kept just my bedroom and the other two rooms be rented out to a family seeking sanctuary. This was gratefully received as it would increase their income quite considerably.

I make no bones about skipping over the intervening months. We lived in a state of tension and anxiety which was finally brought to a head on April 18th when James Stuart arrived with a large army and started the blockade that continues to this day.

And so, the Siege of Londonderry commenced. In subsequent chapters, I will detail the events that occurred each day and, in time, the conclusion of our dreadful trials which, we hope and pray, will bring triumph to our cause and peace and harmony again to our lives.

But we do not yet know how events will play out as this is a story in the making.

Mr Prendegast read again the final sentence several times. He had enough imagination to see how it had been for the residents of Londonderry. Of course, he knew how it had all ended for it was several months in the past now, but to face starvation and deprivation without any indication of the end or the outcome?

He closed the manuscript, returned to his desk and rang the little bell for his assistant.

"Ah, Mr Frampton, be so kind as to compose a letter from me to Miss Browne of Halebrook Farm, Ballymagorry. Say that I have read her first chapter with great interest and would very much appreciate seeing the whole book. Ask her to send a copy by return and indicate that if the remainder lives up to the standard of the first chapter, we will be delighted to publish."

"Yes, right away, Mr Prendegast." Frampton had read the manuscript and fully agreed with the principal of the firm.

Chapter 8

It took the ship six days in difficult and changing winds to reach a safe anchorage off Ireland.

Six days in which Thomas Davenport and Tristan Browne worked hard, Tristan doubly so for he also had his work as passengers' steward.

On the evening they dropped anchor in Kinsale Harbour, both went to see the captain; one in search of his agreed minimal wages, both seeking justice from a corrupt man. They had three written statements from crew members that they handed to the captain. In return, Tristan received the wages due and Thomas his five pounds returned.

"Don't ever seek passage or work on my vessel again," the captain growled. Like most bullies and cheats, he was a bad loser. "I hope for your sakes our paths never cross again."

"Oh, they will, dear Captain," Thomas muttered as they left his spacious cabin. "For one day we will give evidence against you in court." As well as their own signed statements, they had four more from crew members, including those of the master and the purser.

The captain had sold himself for only a little part of the story against him. He let the two youngsters go free, thinking he had solved the problem they presented. A wiser and more cautious man would have kept them on board all the way to Charleston. Or silenced them forever somewhere in the vast Atlantic Ocean where he, as captain, was the source of all justice. And was, also, the writer of the ship's log.

Thomas and Tristan took no chances and stayed awake all night, waiting for the first boat of the morning. They stayed in Thomas' tiny cabin, twice hearing the door handle rattle. One of those times a weight was put against it but there was no movement for they had stolen a chair and placed it to jam the door shut.

On landing in Kinsale the next day, there were no magistrates willing to give the pair any time. They asked anyone with a cloak of officialdom but spent several hours getting nowhere, walking from office to office through rain so fine it felt like brushing against silk. They did not know that the captain had sent coffee and tobacco to both local magistrates, warning them of petty troublemakers from his ship and suggesting all officials ignore them.

History was being written by the side that got their story out first. And spread the news with gifts of value.

The place was seething with soldiers, marching with purpose, spreading from this southern tip of Ireland throughout the land.

"You know this is where King James landed back in March? And he has covered much of the country since then," the first talkative innkeeper they could find told them. "I hear that only Londonderry holds out against the true King of Ireland, Scotland and England."

"And to take ship back to…" Thomas started but Tristan cut him short, kicking him in the shins.

"Come, Thomas, we must be on our way or we shall never get back with the cow we are to buy," Tristan insisted, pulling at his new friend's arm, finishing his drink with a single swallow.

"Why the hurry?" Thomas preferred to find out more information then make a plan as to what to do, how best to get back to England.

"The whole country is united against the English. It is not safe for you to be here at all. Not really safe for me, either."

"Why is that? This is your country, is it not?"

"Where do you think my family are based, Thomas? Yes, Londonderry. I am as Protestant as you and somehow have to play the good Catholic for the entire length of this troubled country."

They stuck together, for who does not seek companionship when faced by danger? There was no moment of agreement, no grand arrangement and not even a whispered suggestion. They simply moved off together.

They walked because with the army all around there was no hope of buying horses. Besides, two youngsters riding would invite questions. Better, they reasoned, to be plain folk walking from one parish to another.

And then the next parish and the one after that.

"How far to Londonderry?" Thomas asked at the start of their third day on the road.

"Heaven alone knows, and don't go asking strangers, for it will be taken badly, especially with your accent." Thomas noticed that Tristan's own voice had changed, melting into the environment, taking on the lilt of the area. It was a good, practical disguise. But not one he had any hope of following.

"We will just have to hope that no one requires you to say anything of substance."

Not that they talked much with others; mainly odd grunted greetings and to buy food, which Tristan covered, once explaining to a sharp-eyed woman that his companion was a mute simpleton he was taking to see a celebrated expert in Cork.

"For the love of God, I hope the man can do something for Seamus for he is a trial to watch over as he is."

At night, rather than stop at inns and risk detection, they took off at right angles to the road, going back three or four fields until they found a secluded spot with water.

Tristan insisted, at these stops, that they wash and clean and tidy their clothes, even producing a brush for their hair.

"I want it to seem like we've just set out this morning from the previous village back along the road." Sometimes, as they walked along, Tristan rehearsed in a half-talk and half-whisper, what their next story would be.

"We heard our Aunt Esmerelda, that is our mother's mother, was dying and…"

"We should not be brothers as we are too much the same age and too different in our looks," Thomas replied. And he was right. They had discovered that Tristan was a week older than Thomas. Tristan was taller and thinner but also much darker than his new English friend, with jet-black hair and a rounded face, ever ready to break into a smile.

"What, then?"

"Cousins, maybe?"

They worked on their stories as they trod out the miles, walking with the beautiful July yellow sun on their right in the morning and their left in the afternoon.

That way they knew they were heading north and would eventually get to Londonderry.

Thomas saw two Irelands rolled into one. Normal life went on; markets were held and inns visited by the thirsty with stories to tell. Carts trundled this way and that, like ladybirds crawling on a chequered quilt. Workers were bent over in the fields, their metal-edged tools flashing in the brilliant sunshine. But overlaying this picture of a rural economy in its perpetual cycles, were bands of soldiers and officials who moved with an altogether different gait. It was as if they were planted there by God as an afterthought, then continually dug up and repositioned; their momentum, their purpose, oddly against the solid rhythm of the other Ireland.

After five days of walking, sleeping under trees and melting into their surroundings whenever soldiers came into view, the weather broke. Cracks of thunder preceded a downpour that hit the ground with incredible force, soaking them both within seconds.

"There's a house, quick, run!" Tristan called, slinging the words behind him as he picked up speed. Thomas, coming from behind, started to catch up as he stretched his legs. But then he slipped on the new-made mud and came down heavily. Tristan ran on a few steps, sensed his friend was not behind him, and came to a stop.

"What's up? Oh…" he burst out laughing. "You are covered in mud from head to foot." But it was worse than the cosmetic, for Thomas struggled to get himself up off the ground.

"I can't put any weight on my foot," he said, trying again with both hands taking the strain, leveraging on a tree stump.

But it took Tristan, grinning through the heavy rain, to lift his heavier friend and take his weight; a human crutch. They wobbled along like a duo of drunkards caught by the weather and caring little for the soaking they received.

It was a bedraggled pair that arrived seven minutes later at the door to the house Tristan had spotted. They hesitated before knocking. It was substantial; a long, low building like a farmhouse but without any of the accoutrements that made a farm. There were no barns, no chicken houses, no ploughs rusting in the rain, not even dogs to bark at their arrival. Instead, the house sat in a pleasant garden of several acres with rhododendrons flowering everywhere.

They did not need to knock, for the door opened and a man of about forty stood in the doorway. He was stick-thin and very tall, giving adequate view behind him of a long and low-ceilinged hallway with a fireplace at the far end. The flames flickered their welcome.

"Two weary travellers, I must imagine." He smiled as he talked so that the words would seem warm, whatever message he gave. Thomas felt uneasy; the smile seemed painted on his face.

But for now, the words were warm and welcoming.

"I expect you need some hot soup, time to dry your clothes, maybe to sleep a while?"

"Yes, sir, we would very much appreciate some warmth and a bite to eat if you can manage it."

"Manage it? Dear travellers, you have stumbled upon Sean Murphy of Horseshoe House in fair Ballydalgagan, I trust the happiest household in all of Ireland. It behoves me to welcome the weary traveller, to aid a fellow human being on their never-ceasing journey across our globe. And you might be?" They were still on the doorstep, looking in to warmth and dryness from the wet and cold.

"I'm also a Sean, sir, Sean Kilkenny, and this is my simple cousin, Patrick Kilkenny. He is dumb with regard to speech and a little different in how he sees the world but he has the same needs as you and me, sir."

"Welcome, Kilkennys, both simple and more complex! Please come in and warm yourselves at the hearth." He flung the door open in an extravagant gesture and called to a Mrs Bellew to bring soup, bread, glasses and a decanter of something to add fire to their conversation.

Which it did, at least for Murphy for he talked almost non-stop while they ate and drank and warmed their wet clothing. Every movement, every gesture, was loud, generous, flamboyant. And engaging.

"Dear God in Heaven, is that the time?" he cried suddenly, leaping to his feet. "Listen to me chattering on while you are exhausted. No, I insist that you stay the night. It is late now, thanks to my tireless tongue, and it is cold and wet outdoors. No, I insist." He took Thomas and Tristan up the stairs to another low-ceilinged room. "I trust this will be comfortable."

"You are very kind, sir."

"Please call me Sean, everyone does. In the morning, come with me to Mass and then we can set you on your way again after a full breakfast. Where did you say you were going?"

"Just to Mallow to pick up a cow my uncle, Patrick's father, bought."

"I see, well Mallow is south of here and you said earlier you were going north." Murphy paused a moment to let his words settle in. "You are certainly two lost travellers, that is a fact, but far from the first we've seen in our little outpost. Well, I'll say goodnight now and see you in the morning."

He closed the door, seemed to rest his hand on the door handle a moment.

"He's a bit rich in his use of language," Thomas said. "I'm not at all sure that I like him."

"Quiet," Tristan whispered. "I wonder if he is listening at the door."

They got into the two beds lining the wall, one each side. Both were instantly asleep. But Thomas woke, it seemed an hour later, but he could not be sure. It was dark outside and the storm clattered against the window, trying to find a way in, to vent its rage on the whitewashed plaster walls that made Horseshoe Lodge. He got out of bed and shook Tristan awake.

"We did not say grace before we ate," he whispered but with force of direction so that Tristan could easily hear above the cries of the storm outside.

"So? I did actually, to myself. I always do. Did you wake me the first time forever in a real bed to suggest to me that I did not give thanks for my last meal?"

"No, Tristan. But we did not cross ourselves... like Catholics do."

Tristan sat up in bed, suddenly awake with fear.

"He would have noticed that," Tristan said, getting out of bed and walking to the door.

It was locked. Tristan shook the door handle, frustration mixing with fear.

"What shall we do?" He turned back to Thomas, squinting across the room in the gloom.

"Easy, we go to Mass," Thomas replied.

"But I don't want to... oh, I see."

"But first we get some more sleep."

They got back into their beds. Thomas pulled the covers right up, as if he could shut the threatening world out. He did not think he would sleep but moments after hearing Tristan's gentle snores, he drifted off himself. The two competed with their snoring throughout the night and Sean Murphy, coming down to check on his prizes, chuckled when he heard the rumbles from within the room.

He had caught a couple of good ones for sure. Protestants were worth a pretty penny.

And he had heard of the dumb and simple ruse before. Either the tall quiet one was someone of importance travelling incognito or, even better, an Englishman.

He could see the fat reward, feel the weight of coin in his hands.

He returned to bed, padding almost silently on the bare floorboards, rubbing his hands together like a magician about to produce something out of his hat.

Chapter 9

"Time to get up, my friends." The call came as the door banged open. Thomas and Tristan gave evidence to their sleepiness, both sitting bolt upright in their beds and rubbing their eyes, then stretching arms towards the ceiling.

It was a little contrived but Murphy was seeing a purse full of coins rather than a pair of slightly suspicious men acting poorly.

"You've just got time to eat something before communion," Murphy said. This time he did note the surprise on their faces.

Yes, I've got you! No Catholic would be puzzled by the requirement to fast an hour before receiving the body and blood of Christ.

"Come along, we have eggs, gammon and cheese. After Mass, we will eat properly but you must have something to keep you going." *Going to the gallows, that is.*

And they ate well, for they did not know when they would next eat. Even when Murphy insisted they leave for church, they were cramming food into their mouths, throwing glasses of small beer to chase it down.

The church was very small for Ballydalgagan was just a hamlet lying under the frowning watch of a craggy hill known as the Gagan. Just off the main road from Mallow to Limerick, it was dwarfed by other places around; places that had inns and multiple shops. Ballydalgagan had one shop and several farms that sold eggs, cheese and meat. The church was the centre of the village and was narrow; barely space for four people each side of a central aisle. It was beautifully decorated with fluted half-columns standing out from the walls and a stained-glass window with a depiction of the Last Supper. Thomas noted that the Last Supper table was tilted, as if the originator had wanted to show to all the food on offer. It reminded him of the Littles feasting in the hall at Great Little, never tiring of their perpetual merriment.

Did death mean being painted into a picture somewhere,

forever stationary, frozen in an act and posture decided on a whim by the artist, no account taken of comfort or of amusement to stave off boredom? And, Thomas wondered, was that Heaven or Hell?

The priest looked like he was getting ready to join Our Lord at the never-ending feast, as he made his way slowly around the altar, setting the chalice and plate and smoothing the clean white cloths. His wrinkled face spread up over his bald head. It was the type of head you could detach and turn upside down and it would still look like it belonged.

All this Thomas observed from the back of the church, looking down the nave like into a telescope reversed. He looked around, wondering how and why his eyes were immediately focused on the altar, more so than in any other church he had been in. His professional eye noted an illusion caused by the pillars near the altar standing closer to the centre of the church. He noticed that each set of pillars protruded an inch or two beyond the pair before. Probably less than six inches either side in total but it served to channel the eye onto the altar. From behind the altar, the stained-glass Last Supper sent jets of multi-coloured sunlight to the scene, like spills of red wine and honey dripping down towards the congregation.

"Welcome newcomers to this House of God." The priest had turned from the tabernacle and saw Murphy leading the two strangers in through the main door.

In fact, it seemed the only door. Which made escape difficult. Rather, it would be impossible, for Murphy had whispered something and, looking back, they saw two heavy men taking up station either side of the door, like guardian angels.

But what were they guarding?

In nomine Patris, et Filii, et Spiritus Sancti.
Amen

Everyone settled, Murphy herded Thomas and Tristan into the front row on the right-hand side, then placed himself on the same bench but nearest the aisle. They were doubly locked in; to get out of the pew they had to get past Murphy. Then, to get outside they would have to tackle the angels either side of the doorway at the back of the church.

No doubt they would also face resistance from the rest of the congregation, united in their determination to rid the world of two more Protestants.

Introibo ad altare Dei.

Thomas knew enough Latin to grimace at the irony of these words. They had not so much gone to the altar of God as been funnelled there.

Ad Deum qui laetificat juventutem meam.

The congregation chanted back: "To God the joy of my youth."

Yet was God's church to be used as a vehicle of capture, a trap for two young Protestants going about their own business?

Beside him, Tristan nudged Thomas then whispered urgently.

"Remember the sign of the cross and kneel when the others kneel. Act as if you know what you're doing." But it was too late for that; everyone knew they were not Catholics. They had not even genuflected before taking their seats.

Soon, Thomas was lost to the beautiful Latin words flowing from the celebrant's lips, like the honey that spilled from the Last Supper at the front of the church. He did not understand it all yet had to admit that he loved the intonation, the rhythm of the chant, even the formality of repetition by rote; host rising up, host coming down, chalice up and chalice down, fingers washed and dried so delicately and ineffectually for not much real dirt would be removed from such a modest rinse of the fingertips.

Then, lulled by the chanting, he started to look at the architecture of the church, examining the construction in detail. It was not an elaborate building; simply built of stone, its two main features were already noted by Thomas, the narrowing fluted columns and the beautiful stained-glass window. He felt a conflict, appreciating the beauty yet disapproving of such ornament in a place of worship. But then he stopped himself. Had he not commissioned a carving of Moses receiving the Ten Commandments for the church he had almost completed in Sturminster Newton? But his carving was of simple stone. He had built of brick mainly but with large stone panels between plain brick columns. Into the largest stone panel, he had put the carving of Moses. Rough cut into the stone, it barely compared with the flood of colour and light spilling out of the feast before him in the little church at Ballydalgagan, somewhere in the hinterland of Ireland.

Thinking of home made him think of Amelia and how he had left her so suddenly, refusing to even talk sensibly at the end. Yet she had been in the wrong. It was not him who had acted against God's law.

And now he was talking to that same God in a different country and in a church of an abhorrent religion; the religion of superstition; the religion that spoke kindly but brandished a stick to enforce its words. Yet, it was strangely comforting to give way to the sweet incense and chant that rose and fell like the tide in a gentle backwater.

He should leave before he was corrupted. But how could he manage that? He looked backwards and the same heavy men were standing either side of the door. One caught him looking and smiled, then unfolded his hands and thumped one fist into the palm of the other hand.

Speaking kindly but brandishing a big stick.

Corpus Christi

Amen

Corpus Christi

Amen

Corpus Christi

The congregation was moving forwards for Communion. To maintain the pretence, Thomas and Tristan would have to move up to the altar rail.

Murphy seemed surprised when they stood. A wave of panic crept over his face; perhaps he was mistaken and they were Catholics after all? No, his instinct in such matters was usually right. He checked the guards at the door at the back of the church then stood up to join the queue for communion, thus allowing Thomas and Tristan to do the same.

Corpus Christi

Amen

They shuffled up towards the altar rail. They knelt at it when their turn came. Murphy had been forced by a vacancy to go left while they went right.

The old priest was not so old when Thomas saw him close up; just weathered, presumably from time spent outside. He gave a host to the person on Thomas' right, placing it in his open mouth. The man rose almost immediately, crossing himself and returning to his seat.

Now it was Thomas' turn. Could he go so far as to take the host? His heart beat violently and his mouth was totally dry. The priest reached into his cup and took a host from it.

But his next action was completely different.

Ad cionibus sacristie

Amen

ostium in dextera tua

Amen

The host never entered Thomas' mouth, even though he had opened wide in expectation. Instead the priest did some trickery, seeming to place it but whisking it away, covering it with the sleeve of his vestment until it was safely back in the cup.

Thomas had forgotten to be a mute, replying with what first came into his head but 'Amen' was the perfect answer. If anyone had heard something different to the normal mumbling of Corpus Christi by the priest, they would assume the simpleton had a few words and be reassured by the correct response.

He did not rise immediately from his kneeling position at the railing. Instead, he leaned forward as if in deep prayer. In actual fact, his mind was rattling through his fading Latin vocabulary. *Ostium* was door, *dextera* was right.

They were being told to take the door on the right that led to the sacristy.

The priest moved on to Tristan, spoke even more quietly so that Thomas strained to listen.

mihi crede

That was easy – the priest was asking for them to trust him.

viridi ostium domus mea est

Ostium again so another door. *Domus mea* had to be my house. Was the priest telling them to go to his house? And what on earth did *viridi* mean?

It was the same clever trick with Tristan. Clearly, the priest knew they were not Catholics, and was not going to let a heretic partake of Holy Communion. His deft hands worked their magic. He moved on to the next communicant, probably offering the same host he had presented to Thomas and then to Tristan.

They rose and went back to their seats, squeezing past Murphy, who looked at them quizzically. They, in return, sent blank stares back; the stares of those who plead innocence in the face of overwhelming evidence of guilt.

What did all this mean? Was the priest playing with them while he had a chance? Or was he genuinely trying to help? He seemed to be indicating that they should leave through the sacristy door but how on earth would they get out of the pew with Murphy in the first seat?

The priest carried on with Mass, moving steadily towards the concluding rite. The Latin with an Irish lilt seemed to settle on everyone lightly. Everything was slowed down, as if the priest could dictate the passage of time, bending it to his purpose. Perhaps it was not the priest, Thomas thought, but God acting through the priest. The God of fierce love and wrath he knew so well was transformed by chanted Latin and incense swinging freely through the musty air. Thomas felt lulled into sleepiness.

Then his mind sat up straight. He knew exactly what the priest would do. The priest turned briefly to face the congregation. Their eyes met and Thomas knew what the old-but-young-man-really had been communicating at communion.

"Be ready to move, Tristan," he whispered. "We'll be going

forward and to that door on the right."

Tristan nodded. Without any Latin, he had been miles behind Thomas but saw the look in the priest's eyes and knew the man was going to help them.

Suddenly, just before the final blessing, the priest tripped and fell heavily on the step that the altar sat on. He crashed into a lectern used for the gospel readings, collapsing it so it fell onto the first pew on the right.

It fell on Murphy and just avoided Tristan and Thomas.

"Go," shouted Thomas, vaulting over the kneeler in front of him.

In a moment, they were through the sacristy door, as far as they could tell unnoticed by the congregation, whose attention was first on the priest flailing around on the floor and then on Sean Murphy, neatly knocked out by the heavy book on the lectern.

He had been hit by the Catholic Bible, allowing Thomas and Tristan to make their escape.

The sacristy was a tiny room with two cupboards, a table, a chair and a kneeler sitting underneath a crucifix. But it also had the only other door out of the church, leading directly onto a grassy graveyard with stones leaning at every angle. Beyond was a row of houses, just over the churchyard wall. The village was deserted, everyone being in church.

"Where now?" Tristan asked. "Do we run for it?"

"No, the priest told us where to go, only I did not understand. It is something to do with the Latin word 'viridi' but, for the life of me, I cannot remember what that word means.

"That's easy," Tristan replied. "'Viridi Hibernia' means 'Green Ireland'. It stems from the green flag of Owen O'Neill in the rebellion of '41, the reason my parents had to leave Ireland. There was a big uprising against Protestants and…"

"More later, please Tristan. So, he meant his house has the green door. He was telling us to go to his house to hide. Let's get over the wall and look for a house with a green door."

"Well, that's easy," Tristan replied. "The very first door in that row is green. Besides, the priest's house is always nearest to the church."

The door was open and they let themselves in. All was quiet as they entered. Then from the window they saw people spill out of the church. The first two out were the guardian angels, seeking their lost charges, full of grim purpose as their share of the purse of silver faded.

There was no sign of Murphy. But the priest came out after the main rush had died down. He used the sacristy door and followed the path around the long way to the front of his house.

"Are you there, my sons?" he called as he closed the door behind him. "Good, now you best stay upstairs quietly until nightfall. I'll get my housekeeper to make up some supplies for you later, under the pretence they are for me while I search for the runaway Protestants." So, it was obvious that they were not Catholic; everyone in the church had known. "She cannot be trusted totally. She... well, let's just say that she likes to wag her tongue." His grin was bashful and took years, decades even, off his face. He was probably no more than forty, just had a strongly weathered look and a total absence of any hair. "I was a ship's boy and then a sailor," he explained, seeing the thoughts go through their minds. "I went everywhere, both with the navy and with commercial vessels. Then ten years ago, I decided to become a priest. I don't know why to this day. Something just changed within me. I was up in the crow's nest on watch duty on a huge sixty-four-gun monstrosity and I guess I got a bit too close to God in Heaven for he spoke to me and said I had wandered the world long enough! He was calling me to his work now."

Later that evening, when sharing a meal of stew with them, he told them he had known the situation because Sean Murphy had sent a message to him earlier in the day. "But he misjudged me, my friends, for I would never let my church be used as a net to catch Protestants. More so because I have many Protestant friends and believe firmly that we should be living together rather than fighting each other."

Chapter 10

Simon Taylor liked to add swear words to his everyday speech, slurring them deliberately so that his wife, Elizabeth, and his daughter, Amelia, could never be quite sure whether they were profanities or not.

Life was good, he considered, as he wheeled himself from his study to the library, where he always took a glass of madeira at six o'clock. His circumstances were actually better since his stroke four years earlier. His family cared for him considerably, as did Lady Merriman. Only now she was Mrs Davenport after marrying that pious fool, Matthew. Lady Merriman, as he always thought of her, appreciated his efforts in adding to her property holdings. He had purchased an additional 787 acres since '85 and had another almost 300 in discussion with the sellers.

They always sold to him in the end. Perhaps it was a knack he had. Or perhaps it was the charmless sidekick he employed. Grimes, his old gamekeeper when he had owned the Bagber estate, used tactics Simon did not want or need to know about. All he cared was that the sellers happily sold to him at a discount; the relief on their worried faces proving to him that a good deal brought something to each party.

It worked well. The bonuses accumulated and his bank balance grew. He had already bought a small farm at Durweston, not in his name but in a partnership with Grimes but with Simon owning the vast majority of the firm. To his family, he was recovering from a stroke, a stroke that had given him certain disabilities. But it went further than that for he seemed to them to have a miracle touch with real estate, particularly farm land. Yet, like most stroke victims, he found speaking and walking difficult. The family supposed that whatever had gone on with blood amassing in his head had destroyed much of his mind but had also altered his perception of the world; adding a curious ability to sniff out land deals.

What utter nonsense they believed. He had simply made a faster recovery than expected, hidden it from his family by pretending continued difficulty with movement and speech, and then developed interesting ways to obtain farmland at enormously discounted prices. These included the tactics employed by Grimes and ignored by Simon.

His mistress, Florence Holmes, knew it as a sham, of course. But Simon took care to ensure no one person knew everything. Flo, for instance, knew that he could walk and talk easily but she knew nothing of Grimes and the part he was playing in amassing Simon Taylor's new fortune.

It was like a play with each act interweaving and influencing both prior and later scenes unknowingly, bending all the rules of man and nature to achieve the overall effect. And Simon delighted in playing a different role in each of the acts that made his play.

And now there was this new act, announced by Parchman with hushed words in a clandestine meeting. He disliked Parchman, of course; nobody could actually like the man. But the proposition was so intriguing and so delightful, it would even tempt Jesus on his forty days in the wilderness.

He finished his madeira, held the glass up for refill by Kitty or Sarah; he never could tell the two maids apart. As the amber liquid tumbled deliciously into his glass, he allowed himself to imagine Jesus resisting the devil time and time again while fasting in the red-yellow dusty desert. Then, at close to midnight on the fortieth day, cold descending with the dark rising, along would come Simon Taylor, wobbling over the barren rocks in his wheelchair.

Which he did not need but added to the effect.

I've resisted the devil for almost forty days, my child.

Jesus addressed everybody as children, yet Simon was almost twenty years his senior. He did not remember his childhood, other than the stern words and straight sticks.

Well, I have an interesting proposition for you, my son.

After all, he was a son.

Jesus was famous for being a son above all else.

And Jesus would toss his filthy long hair back from his face, scratch his lousy beard and laugh as Simon went into the preliminaries. Such was the arrogance of God.

But it would be Simon doing the laughing as midnight approached and Jesus lapped up the proposition, falling into line behind Simon; waiting to follow orders.

Orders that would take him down the crooked, rutted but delightful path of sin.

"Is something amusing you, sir?" Sarah asked, wondering if her bodice was undone or her skirts hitched up to reveal what a man should not see.

"Just a flight of the imagination," he slurred back.

"Too much madeira I would say, sir." That was forward of her, insolent too but he would let it pass. He did not want to lose the picture of Jesus kneeling at his feet, begging for his next set of instructions.

The deal proposed by Parchman over the bare-planked table in the inn near Shaftesbury would accelerate all his plans.

Just as well for he was over fifty and wanted to enjoy his remaining years, was fed up of playing the invalid and desperate to be young and lithe again.

And it was so simple to carry out. He had gone through the requirements, marking in his mind why he was ideally suited to this job.

"It involves buying real estate," he reminded himself. "And it does not disturb the current cosy arrangement so there is no need to stop drawing my salary from Lady Merriman each quarter. It is a good outlet also for my inventiveness."

"What was that, sir?"

No matter, Kitty, you can go."

"It's Sarah, sir. Kitty is my sister."

"Go, whatever your name is… and, thank you, Ki… Sarah, for looking after an elderly man restrained by his inability."

"Sir, have you tried walking?" Sarah asked because she had seen him. Weeks ago, she had opened the door to the library and seen Mr Taylor standing at the madeira decanter, then walk with refilled glass back towards his chair by the window. She had closed the door quickly and soundlessly and come back five minutes later when he was settled.

She was also questioning his age for he was far from an elderly man, with jet black hair just tinged with a few grey specks and a silver group above his left ear.

But all Sarah really concerned herself with was the deceit to her mistress, Lady Merriman. Should she tell her when she came back from London? Or perhaps write to her in Southampton Square? Or would it just create a big row between two people who were good business partners? Everywhere there were signs of Bagber Manor's success; buildings going up, refurbishments, new experiments and methods on the land.

And most months at least a field or two were added to the collection.

The next time Simon Taylor spoke to his wife and daughter, he almost forgot to slur his words; it became a tail of a slur, remembering half way through the sentence and degenerating into an exaggerated confusion of sounds and words.

Amelia and Elizabeth looked at each other, then both looked at Simon. Aware that he had made a critical error, he stressed the slurring like a lying child trying to give credence to a fib.

"I have to go away for a few days," he said. But all they could understand was 'I' and 'days'; the rest lost to the human ear.

"Say it again, Father," Amelia said, patiently and tenderly. She and Elizabeth both took responsibility for their charge with complete seriousness. It had become a package made of tenderness and familiarity, like gift paper wrapped in a bow. Love did not enter into it; rather it was duty, compassion and, on occasion, a little dose of fondness.

Simon repeated himself, daring to go a little clearer to get his words across. They wanted to know why, of course, which meant more knife-edge dialogue between the two extremes – crystal clearness and a hopeless slurry of words running into each other.

Because he did not want to give away his secret just yet.

Besides, he rather liked the extra light in their eyes as they studied his mouth movements and concentrated on what he was trying to say. It was a wholesome, virtuous look he loved to see in others.

Particularly those he despised.

It took twenty minutes to get the meaning across. Simon did not consider this a theft of his family's time because they would just be caring for him anyway.

"So, Father, your land searches are taking you further away from home where we can care for you in comfort?"

I need to get out from your stifling care, daughter dear. I need to be a man again.

"Yes, daughter, I do not want to go but duty calls."

"Who will look after you, sir?" Elizabeth asked.

Why, Flo, of course. She shall be my comfort and warmth and take care of my every need. That comes part and parcel with the role of mistress, does it not?

"Grimes has said he will go with me."

"I do not like that man, sir. Please consider that Amelia and I come with you."

That would totally defeat all my purposes, both primary and secondary. It must not happen.

"Dear wife, your role must be to keep house here, particularly as our dear host might be back any day now."

"She has not communicated that to me, sir." Elizabeth pulled out her last letter and raced her eyes across the page.

"I meant, wife, that she could be back at any moment. It is quite like her not to declare her intentions and just to turn up."

"Remarkable!" Elizabeth replied. Then added to his raised eyebrows, that he had said that last sentence with no distortion at all 'as clear as a church bell'.

Simon responded with a grunt, turning his chair around and leaving the room. He was running out of time with his pretence. He needed to be away from here for a while, partly to get away from the suffocating care but also to be able to operate effectively without the masquerade of disability.

The real beauty of the plan Parchman had outlined was that it allowed Taylor to operate on several plains at once, providing a multiplicity of income and gains. He was being funded to attack the Great Little Estate operated by Lady Roakes who, Parchman had explained, was no lady at all but a rogue of the highest order struck exceedingly lucky. The object was to undermine its operations at every level.

"Nothing short of bankruptcy will please me," Parchman had said over the planked table in the darkest corner of the near-deserted inn outside Shaftesbury.

"That should not be a problem but what is in it for me?" Simon had replied.

And what was in it for him was considerable bonus payments on success in this objective plus a monthly stipend he could draw upon immediately. This would allow him to continue buying land for Lady Merriman but, crucially, to acquire the best land in the name of Grimes and Company, Simon being the 'company' which was also the controlling interest. He had lacked the capital before to divert the best land to his own ownership; it had proved to be a slow process to accumulate such funds, even with his lucrative arrangements with Lady Merriman. The additional considerable payments from Parchman allowed for a decades-long process to be consolidated into a year or two.

He rubbed his hands in joy at the anticipation and got down to work.

"Grimes, I have a list for you to get started on."

"Thank you, sir. I will enjoy working on it."

And Simon knew this to be the case for Grimes was paid a tiny monthly salary plus the rent on a half-derelict cottage on the northern extremity of the Bagber lands. He had never asked for more and Simon had not offered it.

There were some people not motivated by money and Simon Taylor had found one of them.

Chapter 11

Eliza Davenport, nee Merriman, loved to serve tea to her husband in the morning.

The problem was that Matthew liked to do the same for his wife. The moment the maid knocked on the door, two figures would scramble up from bed and make for the door, laughing and pulling at the night clothes of the other to hold them back.

Downstairs, in the kitchen, the staff had a running book on who would fling open the door first and grab the tray. Each servant who wanted to play put in a few pennies a week. If Eliza was first at least four times out of seven, the winning pennies went to the female staff. If Matthew beat his wife to the door more often than not, the male servants took the prize.

It went from Sunday to Saturday and today was Saturday. Milly, the youngest maid in the household, knocked tentatively on the door. The master and mistress were tied at three times each that week. Today was the deciding day.

Milly's heart thumped as she heard the scrambling following her knock. It was her birthday and all the female staff had said she would keep the entire winnings should Eliza Davenport make it to the door first. The men, in contrast, had said they would spend it on beer and gin and drink her good health.

The door opened, then closed and opened again. Eliza Davenport's beautiful, sleep-tussled head was out of the door first, her slender hands upon the tray. The mistress had won.

But it was Matthew who took the day.

"Good morning, Milly. I wish you joy on this anniversary day."

"Thank… thank you, sir." She beamed from ear to ear, beating the July sun in its brilliance.

"Why, is it your birthday, Milly?"

"Yes, madam."

"Well, please add my joyous wishes to those of my husband."

"Thank you, madam." Milly took up station outside the door, waiting to be summoned back in to collect the tray, dying to share her good fortune with the rest of the staff.

"How did you know it was Milly's birthday, husband?" Eliza poured some tea and took it over to him in bed, bending to kiss him as he reached out for the tea.

"I keep a book," he replied between the kisses. "It's a diary with each staff's birthdate in it. And at the back, I list each staff member and note where they are from and if married and any other personal information." He reached to the cabinet beside his bed and pulled out a brown, leather-bound book. "You see, today Milly is fourteen. Ah, I see also she is from Wiltshire and is the oldest of a family with four other children. Her father died when she was ten years old." He turned over the page and continued reading. "Apparently, he was put in charge of a new threshing machine driven by two oxen. He stumbled on a loose bail of straw and fell under the oxen."

"How terrible," Eliza said.

"Yes, but he survived that ordeal, maimed terribly but still able to work, and then died four years later of a growth in his stomach."

"Equally awful." She shuddered, just as Parchman did when mention was made of the hangman. She hated a life cut short for she was determined to live every moment of hers following her enforced captivity for half her lifetime.

Later, after breakfast, taken in the small dining room with bright yellow walls, she went to seek Milly, who was making their big bed with her slender arms enveloped in huge white sheets. Eliza pressed two half-crowns into her little white hand.

"Spend it wisely, Milly. I've got some ribbon here for you also, so you don't waste the money on trivial adornments." The ribbon was almost a yard of blue silk and young Milly was speechless.

"Oh, miss, I won't waste it. I am saving up." There was something about the way she said it that made Eliza concentrate.

"What for, Milly? Sit down a minute and tell me about it."

Most servants would have remained standing, waiting for the mistress of the house to insist they sit in her presence. But Milly did immediately as she was told, walking to the deep window seat that looked over the square outside. It was still early but well-dressed servants were up and about, several carrying shopping baskets with fresh bread, one with a bunch of roses in yellow and red, the colours seeming to merge with the distance. A gentleman hurried by, clearly late for an early appointment. Eliza, following Milly to the window seat, wondered whether the flowers and the gentleman were connected and what the story linking the two would be.

Milly's story had nothing to do with flowers and romantic appointments. Instead, it was a simple and heartfelt tale that saw Eliza take her young maid's hands and grip them tightly.

Milly talked quickly and covered much ground, aware that she had a full day's work ahead of her and the housekeeper would forget it was her birthday if she slipped behind in her tasks.

Eliza held her hand throughout the six minutes of Milly's story.

To evidence her purpose, as Milly talked, she held her purse up in her left hand. It was bulging with pennies from her winnings and, at the bottom, the sixpences she had saved each week since coming to London eight weeks ago.

She did not open the purse and count the money; that would have eaten into her busy timeframe. Rather, she felt its weight, jingling it slightly, as if the coins were dear old friends.

"Eleven shillings at least," she said as her sad tale finished its allotted time.

When she had fifty pounds, she knew exactly what she was going to do.

And it had very little to do with being a maid.

Eliza Davenport returned to the dining room where Matthew was finishing his porridge.

"I have to go, my dearest." He stood up as Eliza entered the room. "I have a meeting in Whitehall."

"Oh, I hoped you would stay with me today." She sat back in

64

her chair and put her head in her hands. "You have been working so hard these last few weeks. And…"

"Yes, Eliza? What is it?" He came around the table and knelt by her chair, taking her hand and raising it to his lips. For a delightful moment she thought he was proposing all over again.

"Nothing Matthew, nothing at all. Now, off you go. I will be here when you return. No, you must go. Your work is so important, my dear."

She walked him to the door, placed his hat upon his head and kissed him on the doorstep.

"I love you, Matthew." She closed the door on his affirmation that he also loved her, leaned back against the door and let the tears flow.

Her tears were a river with three distinct sources. As to be expected, joy was one source, so often given to tears for some strange reason; the happier we are the more inclined to stand reason on its head and send streams tumbling down the hillside to the river in the bottom. The second source supported this theory for sorrow is a cousin to joy and loneliness a cousin to sorrow. She was desperately lonely yet sublimely happy; this being because she loved another so intensely that sacrifice on his behalf, in this case enduring loneliness, was a joy in itself.

But the third source was strange to her and did not fit any neat pattern of nature. It had elements of fear, lazily meandering with malintent, but also of a great sadness rushing down steep banks in a terrible hurry. How can one stretch of tributary be lazy and rushing all at once?

The answer was, of course, that jumble of emotions that we call compassion, or rather compassion mixing with nervousness, distaste, duty and honour. Eliza had walked its banks once before, when Simon Taylor, an instrument of the cruel captivity she had been held in for most of her adulthood, had been struck down with the bleeding in his head. But at that time, she had been walking on the banks of the river. Now, she was rowing upstream, desperate to make headway; to help young Milly Smith, who had only an appalling naivety to shield her.

Matthew walked less speedily than normal, as if pulled back by strong elastic or wading through deep sand. He had an important meeting that morning to determine his next position. The drafting of the Bill of Rights was complete; beautifully inscribed words laid down on parchment that would, God willing, be the bedrock of the new country of England and its liberty-loving people. He had met King William a few times in Holland and once in Whitehall a few weeks ago. Matthew warmed to the severity of his expression, his serious countenance and his plain sense of humour. He was a Calvinist rather than a Presbyterian but it was close enough for trust in regards to religion.

And the overriding principle behind the Bill of Rights had been toleration as a cornerstone of English liberty. As a co-author, he could hardly complain that his monarch was one brand of Protestant while he was another.

The idea that the words and clauses of the bill he had worked on so hard for the last three months would soon become an effective, unbreakable shackle upon both King William and all future monarchs, was a sobering thought.

Freedom strangely embraced by shackles. Freedom because of those shackles.

Freedom is a cousin of restraint, just as wilfulness is wed to liberty lost.

As is so often the way.

But his thoughts were dwelling on the past, on the backward pull of that elastic. Now, he needed to rebound into the future and what lay next for him.

"Sir, please take a seat. The King will be available presently."

"The King?" Matthew felt his heart quicken. But the official had moved away, long list in hand and worried expression to check it once again.

Matthew waited on the only free chair in the anteroom. It was an elaborate stool with legs that crossed over each other to form the seat of padded red velvet. The legs were a deep rich wood he did not recognise; probably from some distant place like Africa or the Americas. It was low down so his long legs had to cross over in imitation of the stool's legs or else his knees would be above his chest; hardly a dignified pose.

But, as soon as he was settled and had a look around at his fellows, recognising and nodding at one or two, his name was called by the same official who had told him to take a seat.

"This way, sir," he used his two arms in a sweep to indicate passage through to the next room and then on through two others into the heart of the palace.

Matthew wanted to ask the official why he was seeing the King but he kept a professional two steps ahead, denying the possibility of discussion.

He was left alone in a small room with delicate white plaster lacing standing out from pale blue walls. Both windows looked over a courtyard garden with an abundance of roses, climbing along the walls. An old gardener was showing a young lad how to deadhead the flowers that were past their best, collecting them in a trog that was almost full. A light wind made the leaves sway in communion with the gardeners and their never-tiring rhythm of work. Matthew watched them, marvelling that everyone had their place in God's world. Once that old gardener was a young lad himself, learning the practices from another old gardener, who had learned them himself in his youth. Contentment eased out of the pair at work, timelessness in God's wonderful world.

"Mr Davenport, sir." Matthew turned and bowed low from the waist. "Thank you for coming to see me."

"The pleasure is all mine, Your Majesty."

"Kind in you, sir. And, I recall we have met before now I see your face."

"Yes, Your Majesty. We met three times in the Low Countries when I was in exile and working for Mr Candles. And then once last month as part of a delegation that presented the draft bill to Your Majesties." Queen Mary had been there as well, deferring to her husband but, nevertheless, queen in her own right.

"You are the man, then, who made the recommendation to land our forces in Devon?"

"Well, Your Majesty, I suppose so. I wrote a paper outlining the advantages and then others developed the idea into a real possibility."

"Your modesty does you credit. But also leads me to ask another favour of someone with your evident capabilities." William, still standing, now took a seat in a large chair with wooden sides, carved to show some hunting scene or long forgotten battle; Matthew could not make the details out. He moved away from the window to face directly towards the King, sensing it to be a more respectful pose.

"I need someone in Ireland," the King said. "I need someone to go incognito, someone who is unknown, yet carries my warrant should they need it." William explained the situation. He would prefer to go himself to lead the army that would confront James Stuart but feared both rebellion at home and a French invasion. "I am reluctant to stay in England and reluctant to go to Ireland. It presents a quandary."

"I see, Your Majesty. But I do not understand how someone with my limited experience of the world might help in this matter. I am certainly no politician, sir." Matthew's three months in London had shown him the truth of this statement. He veered time and time again to the honest, straightforward and moral approach, whatever the problem. "Your Majesty, I am more than willing to assist in any way you desire but others run rings around me in terms of sophistry and argument."

"Exactly!" William thumped the arm of the chair with force and the force of kings broke the wood and sent splinters across the floor. "I never liked this chair," he said, giving a rare grin.

The two laughed together for thirty seconds exactly, as if God in Heaven had turned an hourglass over, set for exactly the period that laughter was allowed for.

"Back to business."

"Yes, Your Majesty."

"I do not require a political figure for this mission. I seek instead a straightforward, bluff and honest body. I need someone people will not be suspicious about and, hence, will bring into their confidences."

Matthew had to admit that he fitted this description. He listened intently as William gave succinct details about the mission before passing him on to an aide to brief him more fully.

"I'm relying on you, Mr Davenport."

"I won't let you down, Your Majesty."

The aide turned out to be Jacob Avercamps, the Dutchman who had befriended Matthew when Candles had been determined to put him down at every chance. They were friends in a respectful, professional way; both had time for each other.

"Matthew, whatever you do, only report back to either me, or His Majesty should I be unavailable, the preference is to me. Can we work out a code?"

"I will do that this afternoon, sir. Might I come and visit you tonight perhaps to pass it on by word of mouth?"

"Excellent, Matthew. Remember, only report to me, and to the King should something happen to me."

"I am worried about you, Matthew." After the briefing, he had gone straight to tell Eliza. "Also, we've not been a night apart since we were married. Can I not come with you to Ireland?"

"They were adamant that it is not a place for ladies. Of course, normally it would be fine but James Stuart is there, causing mayhem."

"Which you will be right in the middle of, Matthew dearest."

"I am not a soldier, Eliza, nor will I ever be. I am there to do a survey of the quality of wool they produce as part of a longer-term study the Earl of Sherborne has commissioned into farming improvements."

Eliza winced on hearing this name. Henry Sherborne was her illegitimate son, re-discovered after the years she had spent in isolation. Only a handful of people knew this to be the case, for his illegitimacy barred him from inheriting and the Earldom would die out, there being no other male heirs. Matthew was one of those who knew and he looked at his wife now, embarrassed to have included her son in his cover story.

But Eliza saw immediately that there was no danger to Henry and complimented Matthew on his idea. "No one in Ireland will be opposed to a leading Catholic nobleman seeking out information on agricultural improvements."

Matthew was to leave early on Monday. His clerks were busy drawing up lists and surveys, also complete sets of fictitious results from Dorset, Wiltshire and Yorkshire, to give some credence to his presence in Ireland. He was also presented with four large books on farming practices, a Catholic Bible and missal and a rosary.

"For I am to play an English Catholic, chosen by your son for this work. See my papers here, I am still a Matthew but with the name of Davies rather than Davenport, in case anyone makes the connection with my father as the famous Davenport preacher." It had been his selection of the temporary surname as his three pieces of personal luggage were all initialised 'M.D.'. He had thought ahead and Jacob had noted the intellect at work.

"It seems you have thought of everything, my dearest husband," Eliza replied, strangely numb to the fact that he was going.

"And you will go back to Bagber, my love?"

"I shall, sir." But she did not mention to him, because it did not occur to her until after he had gone early on Monday, that first she would take a diversion to Wiltshire to sort out some private business.

And Milly would accompany her as her young maid.

The association between Milly as lady's maid and Eliza Davenport, nee Merriman, as mistress, originated in early July 1689, on Milly's fourteenth birthday and just a few weeks after Eliza's fortieth. Before that, Milly had been a junior housemaid, given the most mundane tasks and little responsibility. Eliza had come to London with no personal maid since the decision that Sarah stay with her sister, Kitty, at Bagber to help look after Simon Taylor. She had told Sarah that she would make do until she found another maid in London. Sarah, not wanting to leave Bagber and her husband and children, had no objection, although she and Kitty were deeply attached to their long-suffering mistress.

Milly was delighted with her new position and held her head that bit higher when it was announced to the staff at Southampton Square. She blushed deeply the next morning when a young footman called Eric pretended not to recognise her in her new and elegant uniform with its lace cap and ribbons and starched white apron that was far too large for her slender frame.

"Who is the new employee, Mr Macclesfield?" he asked of the butler and got a friendly clout around the head for his cheek. But Temperance Ruddle, the elderly cook, noticed the way Eric Turner watched Milly as she left the room when the bell summoned her a few minutes later. She stored it away for future reference in the vast collection that was her mind.

Eliza and Milly left for Wiltshire the day after Matthew left for Ireland. Eric's hopes were granted when Macclesfield allocated him to be one of the two footmen that went with the coach; proud also when entrusted with a long pistol with silver scroll work down the barrel.

"Let's hope you won't meet any footpads," Macclesfield said, giving its pair to the other footman while the driver had a shotgun under his seat. "Better to be ready for them if you do."

Fredrich, 1st Duke of Schomberg, looked over the line of soldiers presenting their weaponry for inspection. He did not feel like enduring another long day inspecting arms but duty called, particularly as he was recently appointed Master-General of the Ordinance, alongside the Dukedom. He had also become a Knight of the Garter and been presented a handsome award of one hundred thousand pounds from Parliament. This was to compensate him for the loss of his French estates. He had thought to settle in France but life there as a Protestant, even for senior military figures, became more difficult each day.

And then the opportunity had arisen to serve with the Prince of Orange in his bid to become King of England, Ireland and Scotland. A Calvinist King needed a second in command to suit and Schomberg, without a hint of conceit, felt he was the man, despite being seventy-two when he enlisted into the cause.

Parliament had been generous in the extreme. It made the old general feel that maybe, after years roaming Europe from battleground to battleground, he had found a place to call home.

But not retirement, not yet. The Duke needed a triumph to close out his career. He thought back to the youngster who had first taken up arms in 1634; over half a century of fighting, so many causes.

He shook himself. It was time to inspect the troops then go on to look at the state of the cannon, powder and shot, not forgetting the carriages and horses for the transporting of the guns.

As he rode along the ranks, looping at the end to work his way back along the next row, he worked by rote; inspecting weapons, asking questions, making jokes in his poor English. His mind was not on the parade ground; rather it was back with William Orange, his king, in the last of their frequent discussions.

"My friend," the King had said. "I will rely on you for I cannot be in two places at once."

"Certainly, Your Majesty, both as to relying on me and the fact that even a King cannot be in two places at the same time." His joke had received a smile of acknowledgement from the King; quite an achievement from such a serious man.

They both knew that the second place was Ireland and that Schomberg was the natural deputy for William. James Stuart, King before his abdication, had landed in Kinsale in the south of the country and taken much of the island with a large and growing force. To Schomberg, it was like the Brixham landing of 1688 all over again; a fleet disgorging an army that quickly gathered support as it made its way through the countryside, building an unstoppable momentum.

Except there was one crucial and powerful difference. William had done it with the backing of a minor but influential country, his native Holland.

In the case of James, there was Louis XIV of France, undoubtedly the most powerful man in the world.

Schomberg had briefly been a French citizen before throwing his lot in with Louis' arch enemy. Now he would have to fight the French in Ireland and his very reputation as a commander would be put to the test.

All over again.

Chapter 12

Mr Prendegast looked out of his office window from his favourite chair, saved from his house when his wife had wanted to throw it out. The replacement furniture at home was elegant, fashionable and completely uncomfortable.

He looked over the London street below his second-floor office. The late October swirl of leaves, playing with sunlight to cause multiple sheens of orange, yellow and brown, made him shudder at the winter ahead. His bones were old and weary. He had built his publishing business from the tiny printing press his father had left him years earlier, when Cromwell ruled in his Godly, righteous way. Who, he wondered, would take it on when he breathed his last? He had no children; his wife had been unable to conceive. It had been a happy marriage in its way but saddened by the lack of offspring.

His firm was his offering to the world. There were no children to take over his work. Instead, there would be leather-bound volumes to last forever. He thanked the Good Lord that he had always insisted on quality in his publications. Now, they would be his legacy.

And, now, he had another gem to read. He had waited weeks on end for the manuscript and finally it was here, arrived this morning, sent by father rather than daughter. He had instructed for it to be brought straight to him and now it was here, lying on the table by the side of his chair. He poured himself a whisky and settled down to read, the pages chequered by the flashes of autumn colour from outside the window.

The day after the arrival of James Stuart with his large and loyal following, pitted against our puny walls, we found ourselves with two new Governors. Mr Henry Baker was to share the responsibility for our defences with Mr George Walker. We continued our defiance, shouting "No Surrender" from the walls and gates. But food was already short for there were many people in the town, probably 30,000 all told. Rationing was introduced at this time to ensure fairness all around. Very few people broke these rules and those few transgressors were punished accordingly. The rationing was largely adhered to as there was a common spirit amongst everyone.

We, inevitably, started to lose people to disease. You cannot crowd 30,000 people into a small area and not suffer sickness. Even at this early stage there were people dying. More died when enemy action thickened on May 5th. There was a battle at Pennyburn Mill when the Jaocobites attacked in force. They achieved little overall, save the death of one of their French commanders by the name of Maumont. I heard this directly from the man who had put a sword between his ribs and thrust up to kill. The man ran a laundry in normal times and had expected to live out his life in obscurity with his sheets and pillowcases.

But, on this very same day, a Jacobite General, Richard Hamilton, attacked also at Windmill Hill and took a small fort we had there.

Thus, the day of two battles ended with us losing a fort and our opponents losing a general. Perhaps the besiegers felt justified in their loss, for the taking of a fort is a serious matter and would undermine our ability to maintain the walls and keep the invaders out.

We were morose that evening but the common folk, me included, did not realise the plans for the morning. For on May 6th, we attacked Windmill Fort again and recaptured it amongst many Jacobite dead.

Seeing death so close is neither pleasant nor is it Godly to rejoice but we did rejoice for these people had come to us brandishing weapons and dragging cannon across fields and woods to conquer our town. We rejoiced, not so much in the death of our enemies, as in the wisdom of our commanders and the bravery of our soldiers.

And we resolved ourselves to continue the fight, although daily we look for ships bringing fresh provisions, as ours are nearly exhausted.

The skirmishing continues, causing much damage to our gates and threatening the inhabitants. Butcher's Gate lies on the long western wall and was the most damaged of all the gates. Bishop's Gate looks south and is on a short wall, for Londonderry's walls make a lozenge or oval shape for the town; two long walls east and west and two short ones north and south. Bishop's Gate is attacked frequently and is now damaged badly but remains a fortress to keep the Jacobites out.

It occurs to me' while waiting through these days and helping where we can with the sick and wounded, that there is no absolute in war. We are Protestants besieged by Catholics and feel keenly the injustice of it all. Yet, we are also Protestants come without invitation to a Catholic land. What could we expect? And do particular differences in faith make a reason to slaughter our fellow men? But then it occurred to me, just as a wounded young Jacobite dies in my arms on May 20th, that this has nothing to do with religion at all. This Jacobite was my age and we breathed the same air and drank the same rancid water. In happier times, no doubt, we would laugh at the same jokes and dance in the same formation. This siege is not about faith at all but about politics; politics and ambition have somehow harnessed God to their chariot to thunder down on the enemy.

The enemy who should be our friends.

So much, I say, for religious wars. I say look a little deeper and you will find, not faith but greed and spite and anger and all those things that came to Adam in the Garden of Eden when the world was new and shiny in its newness.

But I digress from my story for, shortly after the young soldier died in my arms, the enemy started doing big works on the river. It was at a place called Brookhall and we shortly learned that they were building a giant boom across the river to ensure any ships carrying provisions to us could not get through to the town. It was evidently quite a feat to accomplish as they spent many days dragging chains and cables across the water. Meanwhile, our hopes and fears seesawed. One minute we felt hopeful, the next full of despair. Spring moved to summer and we gently starved.

I say 'gently starved' for we still have some dignity born of pride. But, in truth, the ravages are terrible, especially to fever and other sicknesses. Every day, there are bodies to dispose of, trundled on carts as if the plague had come again, picking not London this time but its little satellite in Ireland.

Three days ago, hope rose to elation when the ships I previously mentioned were sighted off Culmore Point, just below the boom. They were our ships, laden, we were sure, with fresh food. But our high spirits plumbed to new depths when it became known that the boom was an effective barrier and our ships (for in our minds they belonged to us) could not reach us. And the night after the sighting of the ships, *we had six people die. It demonstrates how aligned the human spirit is with emotion. When hope left those weakened by disease, life left shortly afterwards.*

I have written furiously in the evening for three nights now and have caught up to the present. I cannot talk of events as a historian anymore for there is no gap in time, henceforth, between the happening and the telling. The next stage of this narrative will be a journal of the day's events. Then I propose to write a summary each week with general observations.

But for now, bed calls and a busy day tomorrow tending the sick. Except, one never knows what tomorrow will bring.

Just as I do not know whether this history and journal combined will ever be read by another or burnt in the remains of our wonderful city of Londonderry as the enemy enters and takes control.

But I sincerely hope someone someday will find my words and gain some insight from them.

Mr Prendegast sat back. There were lots more pages to the manuscript but they seemed to belong to another day. He was, at that moment, on the walls of Londonderry, taking a break from hospital duties, breathing in the fresh air and looking at the enemy.

And right beside him, perhaps sitting on the wall and dangling her legs as youngsters do, was Miss Browne, the narrator of the wonderful story of true events that happened earlier that same year just across the water. He moved back in time from October to July to be with her, looking out from those walls to a future they did not know.

In the city of Londonderry.

Chapter 13

The money starting flowing with the first bag of coins arriving at the new office of Grimes and Co on July 11th, carried in by an old man and his son. They insisted on handing it directly to Simon and then left immediately, never to be seen again.

Simon called Grimes into his office and poured the coins out on the table. Grimes counted while Simon read the note that accompanied it.

"This is a down payment, Grimes. It is no more than a good faith payment to start us on our way. We are to expect a similar amount every fortnight."

"Riches beyond our dreams, sir."

"Yes, and we must discuss two things this morning. First is how to make a start on our work to earn these payments."

"Our objective, sir, is to cause serious disruption to the Great Little Estate in order to drive the owners into bankruptcy? I suggest we achieve it this way, sir."

Grimes' plan was clever, making Simon convinced he had chosen the right junior partner for this endeavour. Grimes would ingratiate himself into the estate as a buyer of agricultural produce destined for London; meat and cheese in particular, for these were the two great staples of Great Little, but also wheat, barley, oats and horses for Great Little was starting to make a name for itself as a breeder of fine horses. But with everything he purchased after the first few items, there would be problems concerning quality. The goods would be rejected and the contract would have severe financial penalties for non-performance.

"That way we can tie up an entire year of produce and give no income for it."

"While also enabling us to place massive fines upon the estate. Yes, I like it, Grimes."

"At the same time, sir, it would not hurt for a few accidents to happen on the estate. In my capacity as visiting buyer, I am sure I can arrange such."

"Excellent, Grimes. Meanwhile, I shall be buying all the land I can around the area, with your persuasive help, of course!"

"Sir, you mentioned two things to discuss?" Grimes' eyes were alight with interest; he knew what the other matter was but had a different perspective on it.

"Yes, we must decide on your remuneration…"

"I don't want money, sir." That made Simon sit up; all the more for him.

"What, then?"

"Just resolving a matter of the heart, sir." Grimes looked like a young nervous man, twisting his hat in his fingers as he blurted it out. "I want to marry your daughter, Amelia, sir."

Two birds with one stone. Even three birds with the same stone.

The arrangements were made a few minutes later. Simon was to let Amelia know later that month and the wedding would take place in September when the weather was a little cooler.

Simon walked across his office and shook the hand of his son-in-law-to-be, rather relishing the announcement he would be making at Bagber Manor and the effect it would have on his family.

Grimes sent a letter of introduction to Lady Roakes, posing as the senior partner in Grimes and Co, wholesaler of agricultural products with new procurement offices in Blandford Forum. He received a reply a few days later and laid it before Simon.

There was a short and polite note from Lady Roakes informing them that her steward, Richard Tomkins, would handle all arrangements. A second note from Tomkins invited Grimes to a meeting the next day at noon.

The plan was under way.

And then the second payment came in six days early and Simon closed on another farm, this one nestling in the heart of the Great Little Estate. Grimes had a great deal to do with persuading the owner to sell to Grimes and Co rather than accept a more attractive offer from Lady Roakes.

When Lady Roakes heard the news, she shrugged and

commented that these things happen. She had a new baby to look after and not much else mattered right then. The infant, Sir Beatrice, looked exactly like her murdered husband must have at that age.

He brought both intense joy and abject misery to Alice Roakes; her husband lived on in his off-spring but the child would forever be a reminder of what she had lost.

Penelope Wiltshire looked at the baby and could not understand the fuss. It was a lump of pink, pulsating flesh with the lungs of a chorister.

"I cannot understand the endless fascination with the brat," she told Sally, her maid and lover.

"Pen, you must try and show enthusiasm, if only for Lady Roakes' sake. She is in raptures over the baby."

And so, Penelope, ever obedient to her maid, pressed the button marked 'enthusiasm' and made all the right noises, as if she cared.

Amy Tabard, as she now was, closed the front door as quietly as she could. It was very early but she knew her husband would wake soon despite his late arrival the night before. She wanted to get fresh bread from the baker's on the corner for his breakfast.

She planned his breakfast as she walked. There was sufficient coffee for a large cup for him. Then she would pour a glass of milk as well for she loved it when he drank milk and then looked at her with a temporary white moustache and a grin that spoke of love. She would do eggs, of course. He liked eggs. Today, she would poach two eggs in the shallow pan, add salt and a few flakes of cheese cut from the hard lump she had in the food cupboard, then cut two generous slices of fresh bread and warm them gently in the oven. The eggs and cheese would sit on top of the bread like island-fortresses guarding safe passage to the sheltered harbour below.

Just before she served him his breakfast, she would place the eggs and bread and cheese all back in the food cupboard, lest she be tempted to take for herself from their slender resources.

The cupboard was almost empty but the purse she had

hidden was getting quite full. Amy was determined one way or the other to get the capital Paul needed for his business. She often felt faint with hunger but struggled on, dreaming of presenting her husband with a purse that was so heavy it took both hands to hold.

But that day in late July 1689, she did not make it to the baker's. She stopped at the corner before and gripped the railings to a tall house that seemed to look down at her like an uncle at a small niece. She felt faint, needed to steady herself for a moment. Then she retched and retched again. But nothing came up for there was nothing to come up other than bile from the lining of her stomach.

All was quiet on that corner and the next; the one where the bakery stood, sending its sweet smells out to invade the early day. But, strangely, there was no smell of fresh bread on the streets that morning. Perhaps there was something wrong with their ovens and she would have to walk further for Paul's bread.

There was no one to watch her, except the tall house that stood like an uncle, or like Mr Amiss sometimes looked. And when she peered towards the next corner, trying to summon the will to move on, to be first in the queue for new bread, she saw no queue and the shutters still up. Even if there were problems with the ovens, you would expect the baker and his staff to be up and about. She would rest a moment longer and then go on. She closed her eyes, slumping against the railings of the stern but kindly uncle.

When next she opened her eyes, it was a different scene. The uncle had moved on, Paul stood over her now. There was nothing avuncular about the relief on his face.

"Paul," she said, then realised they were not alone.

"I am Dr Bostock," another man said, placing his large hand on her forehead. "Your father called me out in the night."

"My father?"

"Yes, dear." A fresh wave of concern swept across his face. Was his young charge delusional? He felt again her head; there was no fever. It was just as he thought. He would have to examine her later but he felt quite safely he could say his next words.

"Mr Amiss, you are going to be a grandfather." Then the doctor looked at Paul and said, "Congratulations, my boy and welcome to fatherhood."

Paul smiled in response; another one of his huge, face-splitting and boyish grins. He picked up Amy's hand from where it lay limp on their bed and brushed it gently against his mouth.

"Amy," he said.

Afterwards, while Amy slept, he went to the purse he had secreted on the top shelf of the food cupboard, too high for Amy to reach, and took out a half crown and two sixpences to pay the doctor, who promised to look in the next day.

Mr Amiss arrived back from the baker's, now just open. Amy had gone on her search for bread in the very first light of the new day, when even bakers were still wrapped up in bed.

Mr Amiss' housekeeper arrived and made an assessment of the situation.

"She needs eggs to build her up," she pronounced with the authority of long experience. "I'll cook some now."

Later on, Amy got up from her bed and immediately started to fret about the amount she had to do. Paul had gone into the office earlier, working towards closing a deal for a considerable amount of silk. He hoped to wrap up the sale and be back for Amy early.

She had washing and cleaning to do, his clothes for tomorrow to prepare and his supper to cook. She felt the weight of responsibility and tried to rise from her chair.

But that weight was too much and forced her tired body back onto the chair.

Mr Amiss came in and made her sit by the open window in their parlour while the housekeeper tidied up, tutting about the number of young girls who overdid things when they were pregnant for the first time.

"House proud, most of them are, Mr Amiss," she said several times over.

"What was that about being a grandfather, Mr Amiss?" Amy asked hopefully.

But there was nothing in it. "I am not your father, Amy dear, although more and more I feel like I am and wish I were. Dr Bostock just made an assumption from not knowing us well enough."

"Oh!"

"But we have become a family of sorts, have we not? And as your real father is not known, can I not act the role from time to time?" Perhaps he was her father, after all there was a certain look he recognised in her. But there was no way to prove it one way of the other.

"Yes, sir," she replied, as any good daughter would address her father.

Chapter 14

Thomas and Tristan crept from the priest's house. Father O'Toole had given warning that there would be a hardcore still seeking them.

"They'll be fuelled by ale and Sean Murphy, in particular, is not one to let things go. You should keep to the shadows until well out of Ballydalgagan."

"Why are you doing this, Father?"

"Let he who is without sin cast the first stone," the priest replied, as if expecting the question, and no more explanation was needed.

He fed them well and gave them bread, cheese, cold beef and ale for the journey, which they stuffed into their packs.

"Thank you," said Tristan. "We will be forever in your debt."

"Pay that debt by doing a kindness for someone in need one day, is all I ask."

Do unto others as you would have done to you.

They did their creeping from shadow to shadow, gradually relaxing their vigilance as, over the next two hours, they put the village of Ballydalgagan several miles behind them. Thomas found his ankle was sensitive but could take his weight. It was early morning now with the new day trying to make something of the persistent drizzle.

"Your country has the finest rain of anywhere," Thomas said, brushing a thin film of water from his jacket, wishing he had something more appropriate for the Irish weather.

"Everything is fine about Ireland," Tristan replied, chuckling at his joke.

"Even Sean Murphy?"

"He's no true Irishman, that's for sure."

"Hush!" Thomas stopped still so that Tristan, tramping along behind Thomas on the narrow footpath, bumped into him, causing Thomas to bend his foot again on a root.

"The Lord God in Heaven," he cried as another sharp bout of pain hit him in the ankle.

"Who's there?" The words came cutting through the rain. They knew that voice. It was Sean Murphy and he was mounted. They could tell because the horse's hooves kicked against the rutted ground and Murphy's voice came down at a slant to where they were crouched. Thomas thought the distance no more than twenty yards, judging by the trajectory of the voice.

But they could see nothing; all this was deduced by mathematics applied to the angles of the sound; geometry working in a practical application.

"Don't move," whispered Tristan, willing his words to travel inches instead of yards.

They stayed motionless for a long time. Rain ran down their backs, tickling as it went. They were soaked already but became drenched now. Thomas had a dull ache in his right foot; he desperately wanted to move it but dared not.

All this to the accompaniment of cries in the early morning.

"They're here, I can tell."

"I heard them."

"I'm sure I saw one of the miserable sods."

After a long time, the voices faded into the rain. Thomas stretched his right leg and placed weight on it, ridding it of cramp. Then he raised his body and tried to walk on his twisted ankle. The best he could do was hobble.

"I was lucky last time as no real damage was done," he said, slightly louder than a whisper, as if he had used up all his quiet words and now volume was breaking through. "But this time I think the injury is worse."

"We'll sort something out, Thomas. Never fear. Now, let me have your pack and lean on me. We need to move on."

Thomas did as instructed and the two of them moved on through the early morning, resting only occasionally. Both saw that every mile travelled from Ballydalgagan increased the size of the circle that Murphy had to cover in his search. Geometry in a practical application again.

They walked together through the morning, long after the

rain stopped and the sun turned the raindrops to steam. They stopped in the early afternoon, slumping down under some old beech trees.

"That one looks like my old man," Tristan said, pointing to a twisted and gnarled old tree.

"Well, look at that one. It is the image of Father O'Toole." Thomas was right. The tree had wrinkles parallel to the ground, indicating some stressful cropping in another age. It looked identical to the top half of the priest's head, rising, ridge after ridge, like an Iron Age hill fort. Tristan scrambled up from his slumped position to examine it.

"Yes, you see as you get closer it also looks younger, just like our friendly priest."

But Thomas, back against a giant grandfather of a beech tree, was not listening.

"Ssshh," he said, turning his head with urgency and placing his finger on his lips. "Someone's coming."

They were back into silent mode. The sound Thomas had heard grew louder and louder, such that they would have been able to shout without giving away their presence but they kept still and quiet; the only movement when Tristan scrabbled back to be beside his friend on the forest floor. Birds, frantic with worry, took off from the branches above them, squawking to each other. Then they flew up, towards Heaven, becoming dark specks in a deep blue sky.

"It is some truly monstrous thing," whispered Tristan. Thomas took the time from his panic to be amused on two accounts. His friend's formality of speech sounded incongruous in this natural surrounding where the ancient trees cast shade and sunlight in irregular blocks. And then there was the sound element again. Thomas had to cup his hand to his ear to hear Tristan's whispered words because around them was an ever-growing din.

It reminded Thomas of his friend, Big Jim, married to Plain Jane. Both stood out as incongruous. Big Jim was diminutive, yet his haulier's carts were enormous, towering over him. His wife, Plain Jane, dressed so ordinarily, shabbily even, yet was one of the most beautiful women he had ever seen.

Second only to Amelia.

But Amelia had broken God's law.

Not that that made him want her any less.

"It's some form of wagon. Look at those oxen." A team of four huge oxen had come into view, pulling up the slight incline, grumpily stepping over the beech roots that rutted the track.

Then Tristan was on his feet, denying all the secrecy they had so carefully generated.

"Whoa, sir!" he cried, addressing not the advancing oxen but the old man and the boy who controlled them from a seat high up on the heavy cart. "We mean no harm and are friendly," Tristan continued as the man called to the oxen and the boy put all his weight on the brake. They stopped the oxen just past the tree where Thomas lay with his twisted ankle.

"Friends, really?" the old man asked. Thomas was not sure whether the beads on his face were raindrops stubbornly remaining after the sun had come out, or perspiration from fear at the encounter with two strangers.

"Really friends, for sure." Tristan put on his best Irish accent, learned from his parents and learned well. It had a merry lilt to it that could be from almost anywhere across the country; it did not pay to declare oneself too early. "We're just two lads bored of farming and looking for adventure. We're heading north but it could equally well be south or east…"

"Or west," the boy chipped in.

"Now, how in the Heavens did you know what I was to say next, young sir?" Tristan teased but disguised it well.

"That was easy. You said north, then south and then…"

"Hush boy, let your old grandfather think for a moment." It was the grandson's turn to be interrupted.

But he was not to be hushed.

"We're going to Londonderry," he said. "We're taking this great big cannon to smash the defences and take the town. It's so exciting!"

"Are you to be a soldier, young sir?"

It was the best question Tristan could ask and was answered with a nodding head and a broad grin.

But the grandfather was thinking more practically. They had been commissioned to take this big cannon to Londonderry. His son, the boy's father, had won the contract and it paid handsomely. But the problem was the risk of enlistment on arrival; his son had just completed eighteen years in the army and nobody in the family wanted to see him go off to war again.

The grandfather and the boy had volunteered to go in his stead, knowing that there was no danger with an old man and a boy; also, there was little risk of theft for nobody could steal an article as big and heavy as this cannon. They had food with them and almost no money, to minimise their attractiveness to thieves.

But this had presented a problem the grandfather had not foreseen. When the cart carrying the heavy cannon got bogged down, there was precious little muscle to set it right again. They had spent what few coins they had on hiring help when the right front wheel slipped off the road into a ditch. The grandfather had been assured of help from the patriotic folk of Ballydalgagan by a man who called himself the happiest man in all Ireland.

Patriotic duty done and the cart righted again, Sean Murphy had explained that they would appreciate a donation towards the maintenance of their church's stained-glass window.

"It's a beautiful thing, perhaps the prettiest window in all Ireland. You must take a half-hour and come and see it."

It did not take half an hour, more like ten minutes, to extract every penny the grandfather had. There was lots of back-slapping and well-wishing as grandfather and grandson moved off through the single street of Ballydalgagan and Sean Murphy jangled the extra coins in his pocket.

"Will you travel with us, the two of you both?" The question came out slowly, as if the grandfather was still thinking through the implications. "There will be plenty of adventure at Londonderry," he added, thinking to sell the proposition he had just made.

"Well, the Heavens are smiling on us," Tristan replied. "For my friend, Thomas, has turned his ankle on a tree root and

87

would otherwise have to limp his way north. So, we will gladly accept your kind offer. But we must pay you, sir."

"You can pay us in labour should our wheels become stuck in the mud again. Thomas can drive the oxen from this seat and we can push with you."

The deal was done with quick handshakes and warm smiles. Tristan pushed Thomas onto the long bench where the grandfather and grandson sat and then jumped up to make a seat for himself on one wheel of the cannon, right behind the grandfather.

Thomas and Tristan had walked a third of the distance from Kinsale to Londonderry in a week. Now, their pace quickened for the oxen never seemed to tire, or else the grandfather was expert at driving them. They came off the road four more times over the six days to Londonderry. Twice, they managed to get the wheels back onto the road themselves. Twice, they had to seek help. One of those times it was done for free by a merry group of farmworkers spilling out of an inn to assist. The cost was just a round of drinks, which Tristan and Thomas stood and also purchased a barrel to take with them.

The other time they came off the road, they had to pay. But it was done upfront, price negotiated in advance, none of the sinister false friendliness of Ballydalgagan.

They said their goodbyes ten miles from Londonderry, Tristan explaining that they also wanted to avoid enlistment.

"Serving in the army does not count as adventure in my opinion," the grandfather said in agreement.

They hugged as they left, wishing the other party the best for the future. The grandfather planned to deliver the cannon as required, sell the oxen to the army for a premium price and then walk at leisure home with his grandson.

Thomas, having played the mute throughout the six days in order to hide his English accent, was eager to exercise his voice as soon as they were away from the cart.

"We need to find your cousins and take it from there," he said when the cart was out of sight. "Let's get a pint of ale and find out where they live."

"Halebrook Farm?" said the innkeeper as he poured two

frothy beers for Thomas and Tristan. "Why do you want to go there?"

"Because my cousins live there, or at least they used to."

"And you are?"

"Tristan Browne. My parents left here in…"

"Tristan Browne, you say?"

"Yes, sir."

"Then welcome home, lad. Every Browne is a friend to me. You must be Tristan's son? Tristan son of Tristan?"

"I am, sir."

"Call me Patrick. It's a wonder to behold. I remember when your mother and father fled all that time ago. They were newlyweds, I think not three months married and I was just a lad. Have another beer on me, Tristan and your friend." He turned to look at Thomas with an eyebrow raised in question.

Thomas decided he liked Patrick the innkeeper and would no longer be the mute, despite the risk of displaying his nationality.

"My name is Thomas Davenport and I am an Englishman…"

"I can tell, Mr Davenport, your accent gives you away for sure. What part of England?"

"Dorset, a beautiful county where I earn my keep as a builder."

"Ah, I might well have a project for you if you are interested in some work. But what brings you here so far from home and at such a difficult time?"

Halebrook Farm, home to the branch of the Browne family that had stayed in Ireland after the troubles of the 1640s, was no more than a mile from the inn they had stopped at. Patrick explained the story behind Tristan's parents' departure.

"As I understand it, Tristan's father as a young man was part of the Protestant resistance that formed after the Owen O'Neil uprising. It was a terrible time to be a Protestant." That last statement endorsed Thomas' decision to speak; he would not be betrayed by another Protestant. "He was travelling back to Halebrook Farm from a raid, looking forward to being with his new wife, when he was captured and imprisoned. This would have been around the year '46, when war was raging in your country too, Mr Davenport, such that our troubles over here are often overlooked. Anyway, young Tristan, no more than twenty years old by my guess, escaped and eventually, after a lot of adventures, got back with his wife; your mother, Tristan. They were in hiding for quite a few months but eventually got onboard a ship for the Americas. I understand there were a few letters from time to time and then nothing, as is the way of the world in all truth."

Tristan told the innkeeper about the deaths of both parents during a slave uprising a few years back.

"They had only the one child; me, that is. I was born late in their lives, in '67, twenty years after they left Ireland. Mother had many miscarriages before me, I am told."

"Well you will want to pass on the sad tidings to your Uncle Tobias I'm sure, but as to getting to Halebrook Farm, that is quite another matter."

"It's only a mile, you say, sir. Even with my poor ankle, I can manage that." They were so close now, Thomas could not accept that significant difficulties lay ahead.

"Ah, but it is quite the problem for a mile can contain a lot of soldiers, Mr Davenport."

"Soldiers?" They had not thought of that. Their confidence had grown as they had successfully evaded capture travelling up the country, not realising that as they approached the last Protestant strongpoint in all Ireland, the patrols and checks would multiply enormously.

"There is little chance of you getting there, I'm thinking. Every person travelling has to have a pass. It's a wonder you got from the main road into the village without challenge."

"So that is it, then?" Tristan asked.

"Far from it!" the innkeeper laughed. "'If the mountaine will not come to Mahomet, Mahomet will goe to the mountaine.' Written by John Owen, Calvinist theologian, whose several works I keep by my bedside. It follows a story from Sir Francis Bacon, a copy of which I do not have. Owen is my favourite theologian, although I am not a Calvinist myself. I just enjoy his way with words."

On reflection, it did not surprise Thomas that an innkeeper in the damp village of Frisk, some nine miles to the south of Londonderry, kept works by Owen at his bedside. Learning was getting everywhere these days; the common man could hold an argument with those that had the highest education, such was the beauty of the world they lived in. Then he thought about beauty in different forms. The Latin Mass of Father O'Toole had been beautiful for its tempo and lulling motion as it worked through the phrases by rote; so different yet equally full of beauty.

Thomas felt a shiver of excitement. He loved that chant for the sense of security it gave in such an uncertain world, yet loved the individualism that made so much of that insecurity. He had always been more relaxed about his religion than his sister, Elizabeth, and certainly his brother, Matthew, but he still had pride in the family beliefs, doubly so when Tristan spoke again.

"If you read sermons, you may have heard of Luke Davenport?"

"I have a copy of *Man Against Man* in my bookcase also! It is a fine work. But, no... you are of the same family?" Patrick turned towards Thomas.

"He was my father, sir, sadly deceased following his imprisonment by James Stuart." He would never again be King James to dissenters, in fact to so many of his former subjects; plain James Stuart would suffice. "He knew John Owen well. We have many letters from him to my father. In fact, when I was a boy, Mr Owen came to stay with us once and gave a sermon in my father's church."

Over a third drink, they discussed sermons and how they touched religion, delving into theological concepts. Tristan was bored and looked around the bar room. A few people lingered over pint pots, one person bent over a meat pie like a new-style scientist studying a beetle, prodding delicately with his instruments.

The door banged open for a troop of thirsty soldiers led by a sergeant with shrewd, pale eyes that seemed to linger on everything yet not stop moving. The innkeeper took them in with a glance and spoke in a loud voice.

"Well Major Browne, I am sure you and the captain will be pleased to be back in uniform after your long travels to get here. I'll call Lilly to show you to your rooms while I serve these fine gentlemen who look in need of a drop of ale."

It worked, at least for now. The sergeant snapped to attention, the soldiers in his charge following in some disorder.

"Good afternoon, sir," the sergeant said.

"Carry on, Sergeant, carry on," Tristan replied, following Patrick's wife out of the room.

Chapter 15

Penelope Wiltshire could not help her actions, slammed the new bedroom door to evidence her anger.

"Stewards are supposed to care for possessions, nurture them, make them increase like a gardener does with plants. They are not supposed to give them away recklessly."

"I wanted to talk to you about that, Pen. Tomkins has a lot of experience and Lady Roakes believes in him. But I think he is a little lost in these matters." Sally had picked up a lot from serving refreshments at various estate meetings when Penelope had attended. Penelope looked at her lover, as if looking anew. She was a remarkable person, both in mind and body. The once livid scar on her cheek was retreating each day, merging into the background as if whoever painted Sally had experienced a change of heart and now wished to rub away at it, a little every day.

"Yes, Sally, I agree. Also, don't you think he is putting all his mistress' eggs into one basket with this massive contract? Besides, I don't like Grimes one bit."

"You made that quite obvious, Pen." She referred to the meeting earlier that day, at which she had served coffee. Tomkins had been about to handle it on his own but Penelope had insisted on attending. They had met in the new orangery, a magnificent glass house attached to the long wall of the drawing room. There was no doorway yet from the drawing room so they entered through the rose garden below the terrace where Lady Roakes and Penelope had sat the night following the discovery of Sir Beatrice's body.

"He looks, acts and smells like a bad one, Sally. Do you not see it?"

"I don't like the look of him, for certain. Now, come and brush my hair, Pen. I want to look my best for you tonight."

Ever obedient to Sally's wishes, Penelope rose from the bed she had been lounging on, picked up the heavy silver hairbrush and stood behind her maid to brush her hair with short jabs to get through the frizz. She applied herself diligently, turning the mop of unruly hair into a neat bundle, finally securing Sally's little white cap and adjusting the long ribbons that hung from the cap down her back. She loved every bit of attention she gave Sally.

There was no one else in the room; just the two of them. But if there had been a third person, they would have been astonished by what happened next. Penelope, the Dowager Duchess of Wiltshire, moved her swirling, luscious skirts around to the front of Sally Black, her maid, and performed a deep and formal curtsey, skirts brushing against the long white apron that Sally wore. As Penelope went down in her curtsey, she saw again the small black hands folded neatly into the white apron and her whole body shivered with desire.

"Will there be anything else, Mistress Black?" she asked, struggling to keep her voice even.

"Yes, Pen. I am a little tired. You will turn down the bed and then change out of that ridiculous dress. Then you may warm me up."

Penelope Wiltshire did exactly as she was told. She always did when alone with Sally. Hence, when Sally said she was a little cold and needed human warmth, Penelope obliged by climbing into the great big bed in just her corset and underwear, removing Sally's dress, despite the declaration of being cold.

They kept themselves warm and afterwards Penelope did Sally's hair all over again.

"Tomkins has agreed to sell the entire annual output of the home farm to Grimes." Penelope returned to the subject foremost in her mind. "I tried to talk to Alice about it but she is too busy cooing over the brat... sorry, the lovely dear little baby Sir Beatrice."

"I don't think you will ever be a mother," Sally replied, hands inside Penelope's under shift and stroking her long, arching back. "At least, not a natural one."

"Well, with Mistress Black taking all my time and energy, I too think it unlikely. Ow! That hurt. No, don't kick me out of bed. I want to lie awhile."

"Get my evening uniform ready and then I'll let you back in for a while." Sally was further entertained by a ridiculously exaggerated curtsey from a giggling but beautiful girl in her underwear.

And that was all askew.

Penelope did return to bed after preparing her maid's clothes for the evening, laying everything carefully on a sofa in the corner of the large bedroom. Finally, as if dressing a doll, she went in search of the plain black shoes Sally would wear and placed them beneath the skirt of her dress as if Sally's soul could fly across from bed to sofa and slide into her uniform.

"Why do you take such care over little things?" Sally asked from the bed, not expecting the speech she received in reply.

"Because it is for you, Sal. My mother always said to take pleasure in the little things in life. I could not understand what on earth she meant until I first brushed your hair and laid out your clothes. It keeps a little part of me with you while you are in the servants' hall downstairs and I am eating with Alice in the dining room. And because it pleases me to think, however small my efforts, that we are really equals. You... sometimes... prepare my clothes and I always do yours." That remark was rewarded with a pillow across the room and a neat dodge to avoid it. But both were in more serious mood when Penelope climbed back into the big bed.

"What's to be done about Great Little?" Penelope asked.

"I spent almost two hours with Tomkins this afternoon while you were riding."

"You never told me that! What did he say?" Penelope was sitting up in bed now, drawing the sheet about her as if seriousness demanded modesty.

"He was reluctant to talk at first but later I think he liked to get things off his chest. The estate is in a mess, Penny dear. It is contracted this year and next to Grimes and the contract he signed is ruining Lady Roakes. I pointed out some economies we could make but they will have to be far more severe if we are to come through this."

"Will you continue to help, Sal? I feel useless in this regard."

"I will help gladly, my love, and you are far from useless, silly thing. Your job is to ride across the estate every day and be a living, shining example of optimism to the tenants and workers everywhere you go. I will happily work on the accounts with Tomkins, provided he continues to want to work with me, but it takes a push and a pull to get out of a rut in the road. I will push and you will pull."

Grimes reported back after the first meeting with a smugness that appealed to Simon, sending a shard of warmth to his heart.

Grimes was undoubtedly good at his work.

And Simon had had the foresight to recognise this and promote the man. He had been wasted as a gamekeeper, taking out his aggression on simple peasants. He now had some proper targets, thanks to Simon's command of the situation.

And, in turn, Simon reported to Parchman, travelling by coach to Salisbury four days later.

"It was easier than I expected. I coached Grimes carefully and, as a result, he performed adequately."

"There was no suspicion?" Parchman asked, his ferret-like face accentuating his shrewd eyes as the two of them sat in the rooms Parchman had taken in the Blue Boar.

"None whatsoever from Tomkins, as I understand. Only there was the woman there…"

"Mrs Beatrice?" Parchman would never call Lady Roakes by her married name.

"Who? No, the Dowager Duchess of Wiltshire."

"Oh her!" Memories of the pistol blast echoed in his ears. He rubbed his shoulder unwittingly. "What can the woman do if Tomkins has signed the contract? No, we have them for certain, Taylor. It is a good start."

"There's more," Simon added, smirking as he thought of the good news to follow.

"Well?"

"I've purchased a farm right next to the Great Little Estate."

"I thought I made clear that I do not want or need to know the details of what you do with your remuneration."

"But this farm has some significance to your plans, sir. It is upstream and there is a particular place I've identified where the river can be dammed."

"You mean?"

"Exactly, I can block all water to the Great Little Estate; at least everything of significance."

Parchman congratulated himself on the long journey back to London. He had for certain picked a good one with Simon Taylor. And he still had a particular weapon to play in that regard. He chuckled to himself as the coach bumped over the potholes and slithered around the corners. He had told the driver there was an extra ten shillings if he arrived at his destination before nightfall.

Of course, he had no intention of paying it. He would linger at the final stop but one so that they arrived just after the deadline. He would enjoy the denial as much as others would enjoy giving a reward for something well-earned.

In turn, he would need to report back to Candles, or Ferguson as he now called himself. That was the one fly in the ointment; that he had to report to anyone at all gnawed at him. But at least he would soon be able to delegate to his sidekicks, the oily Cartwright and the friendly but false Franshaw, and concentrate on the big picture.

And that big picture did not involve Candles or Ferguson, or whatever his real name was.

Mrs Matthew Davenport was also travelling by coach but heading in the opposite direction to Parchman. They almost met at Micheldever. Parchman had ordered a stop to change horses and was just pulling out rapidly when Eliza's coach came in at a more sedate pace.

"Careful, man!" called her coachman as he pulled back on his horses urgently to avoid the heavier carriage forcing them off the road. "You should take better care of your driving," he called after the disappearing coach.

But Eliza had caught a glimpse of the massive frame and small, pointed face of Parchman in the next coach. He was the man, after the previous Earl of Sherborne, most responsible for her wasted years. She had seen him once or twice around Whitehall or disappearing up some side street off the Strand. She felt outrage every time she came across him for he had gained immunity for his various crimes in return for some shady favour done for the King. He should be rotting at the end of a rope instead of being given free rein by the government to do its dirty work.

"How close are we to the village of Ashenham?" she asked the innkeeper as they took refreshments, Milly shyly sitting with her mistress in a private room at the inn.

"About twenty-five miles, madam. You won't get there today. Best to stay the night here, I'm thinking, and go on tomorrow. You can have the first-floor rooms, directly above here. If it pleases you, I can show them to you."

"That would please me very much, thank you. Can you find beds for my driver and footmen?" They climbed the stairs to inspect the rooms she would take.

"Of course, madam."

"And a spot of a space for my young maid?" The rooms were square with high ceilings, unlike many inns. They would suffice.

"I could put her in with my young maids. They are a kindly lot."

"Good. We will take the rooms. Milly will be ensconced within a happy family of youngsters."

"Very good, madam. If you excuse me, I will go and make the arrangements."

Later, as supper was laid in her dining room, she called for Milly again.

"I have no company to dine with, Milly."

"There is no one else of quality here, madam?"

"No, Milly, no one of that description. So, you will, I hope, agree to keep me company tonight."

"Me, madam? But I know nothing about the world or anything."

"Then it is high time you learned!"

They started early for Ashenham and arrived, tired and dusty, late in the evening. The main road was fast and easy. They did eighteen miles to the turning in under five hours, stopping first for lunch at a non-descript inn that could have been anywhere in the country.

The turning off the main road looked innocent enough. In fact, the road forked, giving the appearance of two substantial roads continuing into the haze of July heat. The left turn they took pointed a little more south than the other fork. It continued in this direction for three hundred yards and then disappeared around a bend.

"This seems remarkably fine for a country road," Eliza Davenport said to Milly. "We should be in Ashenham in no time at all."

But then they turned the corner, descended a long slope and hit the ford. The road narrowed and deteriorated; the first stretch had been the enticer, luring the traveller along its broad and even stretches to the difficulties beyond.

And there were significant difficulties. Several times, Eliza and Milly had to descend while the footmen pushed and shoved the coach back to more even ground.

They became aware in the mid-afternoon of a band of sordid looking men who circled like vultures when the carriage became stuck again. Eliza's driver, on his slanted seat with shotgun across his knees, pointed at the man who looked like their leader. The footmen, plus Eliza and Milly, pushed but the coach would not move; its right front wheel had slid off the rough road into a ditch and hung in mid-air with nothing to grip on to.

"We will have to unhitch the horses and ride bareback," Eliza said, looking at the seven men circling. "If they will let us through, that is." She started to loosen her skirts that she had tucked into her underclothes while pushing. Milly looked up from her position at the back of the coach and jumped forward to straighten her mistress's dress.

"Milly!" called one of the riders, the one they had supposed was the leader, although he had little to distinguish himself as their captain.

Milly stopped, shaded her eyes with her hand and squinted across the grass.

"Uncle John, is that you?"

"Who else would it be calling out from a bunch of strangers? Of course, it is your Uncle John!"

He rode forward, indicating to the others to hang back a bit. The driver raised his shotgun into his armpit and tracked Uncle John as he approached.

"No need for that, sir." He looked less sordid close up. His clothes were worn and tatty but once had been of good quality. His thick black hair was rough-cut but looked clean, as were his face and, Eliza noted, his fingernails as he loosely held the reins of his mount.

His voice also was far more cultured than Eliza had expected.

"Milly, it is good to see you but somewhat unexpected. I thought you had gone to a better life in London."

"This is my mistress, Uncle John, who is Mrs Matthew Davenport but once she was Lady Merriman."

"The Witch of Bagber?" He jumped off his horse and bowed. "I am honoured to make your acquaintance, My Lady." When he straightened up after the bow, he showed a warm smile matched by his crinkly eyes. Eliza liked him immediately.

"Are you Milly's uncle, sir?"

"Not a blood uncle, my lady. I am her godfather and a dear friend to the family. But we are all at sixes and sevens these last few years and I had thought Milly gone from here, and that being for the best. May I ask what brings her here again?" He spoke of his area of the country as if it was the least desirable place on earth. "But first, we need to get you back on the road." He turned and beckoned with his arm to his followers. They trotted in, nodded a greeting and, at his instruction, leant their shoulders to the wheel, which creaked back out of the ditch and onto the road.

Eliza returned the compliment by asking John Parsons, as he introduced himself, to enter the carriage and ride with them, so that both parties could facilitate explanations. Milly was despatched to sit alongside the driver and allowed to take off her bonnet and let her hair stream in the warm wind.

"Just make sure you tie it up snugly before we get to Ashenham," Eliza ordered, then watched enviously as Milly climbed up and shook her hair out. "I do not want to be explaining myself to your mother later today!"

Eliza went first with the explanations, hers being much the simpler story. She said she had employed Milly as a general maid in their London house, had closed down the house and was returning to Dorset. She had offered Milly a place in Dorset where they were going now.

"But Milly told me her story and I was moved by it. I wanted to see if I could help. I decided to divert to Ashenham on my way home."

"There's not much you can do to help unless you have a few hundred pounds."

"Milly had mentioned fifty pounds?"

"She has forgotten about the interest, my lady. Fifty pounds soon becomes a hundred with the interest he charges."

"I am somewhat acquainted with the Dowager Duchess and thought I could approach her if I make no headway with the Duke."

"The new Duke is as hard as nails, My Lady. He lived in penury all his life until suddenly inheriting when the previous Duke died in the fire at… somewhere in Dorset, actually."

"That was the Great Little Estate. The house burned down and the Duke was killed. I have a slight acquaintance with his wife, Penelope Wiltshire."

"I don't know her, my lady. She was only married to the Duke for a few months and was hardly ever here; mostly in London, I believe. I saw her once in her carriage. She is a beauty, like you. But, unlike you, she's a cold fish for sure."

"You are too kind to me and perhaps too unkind to her," Eliza laughed. "Now tell me why you, evidently a gentleman, are roaming the countryside like a highwayman."

Eliza Davenport already knew much of the story from Milly. But hearing it in full from an adult who had suffered through it first-hand made chilling listening. The old Duke, before he married Penelope, had trebled the rents of the whole village of

101

Ashenham, for no other reason than nobody had recognised him when stopping in the village for the first time.

It was the one and only time he visited Ashenham.

That had been in 1683, when Milly was eight and her father had just died; in fact, was lying in the parlour of their farmhouse with the growth protruding from his stomach like an outlying piece of granite in a washed-clean bay.

Milly's mother was a resourceful woman and managed for a while but there was the burial plot to pay for and her youngest child was sick all the time. She tried remedies and doctors, regardless of the cost. They all failed and the child became more ill, with fits that shook the foundations of the family. She paid the increased rent on their farm for a year, then fell behind, just as Wiltshire raised the rent again, only doubling it this time.

"It was a lovely farm and gave a good income in years gone by. The cherries they used to grow there were the best I ever tasted. Milly's mother borrowed to stay there. The loans were exorbitant in interest cost and there was no flexibility in repayments. I lost my farm as well but, thankfully, did not borrow."

"How do you manage, Mr Parsons?"

"My sister is an angel straight from Heaven. She married a grocer and moved to Salisbury. They did very well for themselves and she sends a small cartload of food every fortnight without fail. It feeds all the dispossessed. But there is no money to repay loans and that is the rub of it. Lots of farmers borrowed and are now in the same predicament as Milly's family; they have lost their land and, therefore, any chance of income to meet the loans. To make matters worse, I discovered that the loans were all made by the Duke so he cannot lose. He gets his money with high interest or he takes back the land and rents to another."

"What has become of the land, sir?"

"New families have moved in and, here's the rub, they have 'introductory' rates of rent at exactly the old level, before the increases, then rising in much more manageable steps. The whole sorry episode has been motivated by spite and a damaged ego. And the new Duke is even worse."

"And yet I must try!" Eliza Davenport replied grimly.

Chapter 16

Mr Prendegast sat in his favourite armchair, rug tucked tightly around him against the cold, despite the fire raging in the hearth. He seldom left his bed now, such had his health deteriorated, with a racking, hollow cough that marked out his decline. But twice a week, Mondays and Fridays, he would come into the office for a few hours. Most of the time was taken up in a series of brief meetings with printers, authors, binders, editors, and, most significantly, would-be general managers when he had gone.

Outside, there was a heavy and persistent November downpour, much the same as it had been last week. He could not remember when he had last seen the sun but it seemed a long time ago. Perhaps it had been when he was a boy; the sky is always blue and dotted with tiny, unthreatening clouds, when you are a child.

He read manuscripts whenever he had a spare moment between meetings. Mostly, he skim-read the doubtful submissions, pausing often to rest his eyes, rubbing at them for new life with his bloated fingers. These were the manuscripts rejected by his people but he had a rule that no offering was sent back unless two people had read it through.

"I'll be the second reader for the rejections," he had said when he had been forced by ill health to announce the new regime of two mornings a week. Then to the universal, but he suspected feigned, protest he added that it was a simple and unloved task that he could still perform for the good of the firm. "And you should welcome my willingness, for it is not a task anyone likes to do."

But today was to be different, for the final proof of *The Siege of Londonderry by a Woman of Some Education Who Lived through it All* was ready for checking. He was not to be the checker, for his weary eyes were not up to it. Instead, Mr and Mrs Frampton were present, both looking nervous at this change of protocol.

"Do not stand on ceremony, my pair of Framptons," he joked, "for I am not about to deal you a bad hand." But the joke went over their heads as to its significance, because Mr Frampton was a straightforward person and had taken a like-minded lady to be his wife. Mr Prendegast had often debated within whether this decision was right for there were so many more sophisticated fellows eager to lead the firm.

But none who had done such sterling work with the two key projects Mr Prendegast most favoured. One was *The Siege of Londonderry* but, even more important and more directed to his youth, was the work Frampton had done on Luke Davenport's Irish adventures, when both he and Luke had been young. It was not complete and Mr Prendegast was reconciled to not seeing it in print in this world but it would be a part of his legacy that he had instigated it and set the story on its way.

And the deciding factor behind his decision was that it was clear to him that Frampton had acted in the interests of Mr Prendegast and the firm rather than his own ambition. Mr Prendegast valued selflessness above every other virtue for it fitted his idea of how the world should be.

"Mrs Frampton," he coughed, "please be so good as to read a chapter or two of the book as I dearly wish to hear it again. Start, please, just after they first sighted the relief fleet. It speaks of such hope for the future, although recognising there are trials ahead. I think it is my favourite part."

"Of course, sir." And, unlike the others kicking their heels in the meeting room next door, she meant it.

"And do not mind if I interrupt from time to time as I have a desire to speak my mind on something of importance to me. Now, please, both of you, take chairs and do not stand on ceremony. Mr Frampton, you will not need your notebook and pencil. It is not that type of meeting."

Mrs Frampton cleared her throat, opened the new book and found the right page. Then she waited patiently for Mr Prendegast's coughing to stop. It seemed to her that he was very close to meeting his maker.

On 25th June, with our losses to disease and starvation mounting each day, our two governors sent someone with messages to swim the river and reach the ships waiting to relieve us. The boy who goes is the same boy that gave me a lift up on the wall to view the ships arriving last month; the day that caused such a seesaw of hope and despair. Now, our emotions are much grimmer, words such as determination and resolution, even resignation, come to mind.

It is certainly the same boy but I should not belittle him. He is a young man and a truly courageous one, a hero. His name is Alfred, or Alf to those who know him, but at first, I did not recognise him for he has grown so skinny this last month and with hollowed-out cheeks like a man risen from the dead, like the walking dead. I imagine he sees me and thinks something similar.

But we do not talk of such things; there is no point. Instead, he tells me he volunteered to go and I give him a kiss and a hug and tell him to watch out for himself.

And he is away. We can see him slink down to the river and wade in during the half-light of pre-dawn. The river will be cold at that time of day, even at the height of summer as it is, and there is no animal fat to keep it from chilling him. He looks back at me and blows a kiss and I blush and blow one back.

Soon after, despite the rising light, we cannot see him.

Later that day, a waterlogged head is catapulted across the walls by the besiegers. I hear people cry "It's a human head" and I know straight away that it is Alf, which is soon confirmed.

Poor Alf. Such a brave thing. I can still feel his arms against my body as he holds me up against the wall. I know he delighted in the sight of my ankles. But now he is no more, gone to Heaven and our hopes are dashed with his death.

The new hope now is that the besiegers did not find the messages our leaders sent, for they were messages of dire desperation, laying out that we could not hope to hold out much longer. And this will be music to their ears for certain.

As one hope dies, so we fall back on the next one.

Hope is all we have and our hopes are constantly shifting, like a large man on his backfoot, caught repeatedly off-balance. I believe that, whatever the level of desperation people find themselves in, having something, however small, to hope for makes it possible to face these *terrible things. Hence, we have our hopes and when they are spent we manufacture some more.*

"Mr Frampton." Mr Prendegast broke into the narrative. "Mr Frampton, I have been thinking on the future of this firm which has been my life's work to establish."

"I know, sir, it has been weighing on you dreadfully."

"How do…" But his question was lost to another bout of coughing, harrowing coughs that seemed to shake the very frame that his waxy flesh hung upon.

"Sir, I have seen you wrestling with it in your mind."

"I have an idea to…" Again lost, this time to a serious fit. Eventually, he managed to splutter for Mrs Frampton to carry on. He would return to his idea later.

Another surprising facet of human attitude towards difficulty became apparent in the few days after Alf died, we presume from drowning. Matters go from bad to worse each day, yet somehow each awful event renewed and strengthened our resolve. There is a comradeship in extreme difficulty that cannot easily be explained, other than relaying the facts that surround the phenomenon, which I shall now do.

On June 30th, our beloved Joint Governor Henry Baker succumbed to fever. He had been brought to the hospital where I work three days earlier. For much of those three days he had a raging temperature and gave great cries that he was full of sin and going to hell. We tried to soothe him but he seemed to burn up the cold wet cloths we placed on his forehead.

Mr Baker sat up suddenly on the third day and said, "I am leaving you but you will not fail. I die but you will live." We thought these were the cries of a feverish man, much deluded, but when he lay back down again he was dead. Was this a prophecy from someone who had seen the Lord or did we want to believe this against all reality?

We all cried at his passing, even some of the old men who helped us, even the surgeon and the physician, for whom this was a commonality born of long association.

But then another mood silently crept over us. Each person probably claimed it came to them first and they passed it on until it reached every ward and then out into the streets of the city. I think the truth

106

is no one was first and no one was last. We all suddenly knew that
God loved us and was behind our efforts to maintain our freedom.

Our determination that evening doubled and doubled again.

Hence this rule of humanity; extreme hardship does not weaken us.
Whatever the blows we take, we emerge stronger, more capable, more
determined, more in His image.

God has truly created a wonderful world.

Mrs Frampton paused. It was her first reading of the manuscript. She understood why she had been asked to accompany her husband that day. Or thought she did. It made sense to hear a woman's voice read a woman's thoughts. Outside, the rain thickened to be like stage curtains, cutting them off in a scene of their own. Mr Frampton rose and put two logs on the fire, creating an instant blaze in the room. It was a different world out there. They were safe, even from the November weather, reading in comfort about extreme hardship.

And the worst thing was it was not written after the event, when the author knew of her survival and the failure of the Jacobite siege. As she wrote each considered word, she had not known how it would end, whether she would be alive to greet the freedom they all stood for.

Suddenly, with all her heart, Mrs Frampton wanted to meet Miss Browne. She did not know how it would happen but she knew it would.

"You are my pair of aces, my dears." Mr Prendegast was talking again, although his chin was slumped on his chest and it was not possible to see whether his eyes were open. But he spoke without coughing, as if summoning every sinew for a great purpose. "With your two children, fine children I can verify, you make four straight aces in a row. A fine hand, a fine hand indeed, the very best." He seemed to be losing himself. "Read on, Mrs Frampton."

But then when she began the first words of the next chapter, he interrupted her as if he had never issued the instruction.

"Mr Frampton, please tell me the ethos behind my firm of Prendegast and Son." He was the son, following his father, but had no son to pass it on to. And now his time was close. Would he live out the year of 1689, now moving towards its final month?

"Why, sir, to publish the best and never to be underhand in any way."

"Well said, sir."

But there was no more from Mr Prendegast so after a few more vacant yet fully charged seconds, in which the Frampton aces started to realise why they had been summoned that day, Mrs Frampton read on.

Butcher's Gate was attacked heavily in early July. They brought up all sorts of hideous machinery to throw great stones at the walls and gate. One man was killed when a huge ball hit him directly, taking his head off cleanly so that it and the ball both rolled along Butcher Street. Each day saw fierce attacks and our leaders organised night-time work parties to mend the defences. The men fought all day and worked half the night and we women did the same, tending the sick and wounded, whose numbers kept growing, wheeling out the dead bodies, bringing water and thin gruel to the soldiers and the work parties. Day after day settled into the grimmest of routines and I dully thought this is a battle of wills. It seemed our slender resources, plus faith and hope were up against the might of the Jacobite army, reinforced with French experts and soldiers.

And then I considered how it must be for the attackers. Are they despondent that we have not capitulated yet? A great big army, so useful elsewhere, tied up in battering against a tiny force whose only strength is its stubbornness? Do their commanders worry that they will ever succeed in their objectives or do they remain supremely confident that the next push will be all that is required? We do not know their thoughts and they do not know ours.

"Sir," Mrs Frampton broke her narration, "there is an annotation here with a reference to the notes at the back. Shall I read that note?"

Mr Prendegast did not answer so she turned to the back of the volume and read the note.

It turned out later that the besiegers knew exactly how we felt for poor Alf had drowned in the river and his body had been washed up. They had found his messages and took great delight to read of our extreme discomfort. These messages were intended for the captain of the relief fleet and not for the enemy. This raises the question, if they knew we were on our knees, why not throw everything at us? Perhaps the new attack at Butcher's Gate marked the beginning of that final fling? In time, historians will understand more of the morale and motivation behind the decisions of the attackers.

"Now, sir, I will return to the main narrative."

"One moment, madam." Mr Prendegast tried to rise. Mrs Frampton rushed to assist, dropping the final proof on the floor as she rose. "It is alright, Mrs Frampton, I will be alright. Perhaps Mr Frampton could fetch the papers on the corner of my desk?"

Mr Frampton obliged. There were three documents. Mr Prendegast shuffled the three like the pack of cards he had alluded to earlier, Mr Frampton catching an escaping paper and handing it back.

"Thank you. I have three documents I wish to present to you. The first is my last will and testament." He was quite clear in speech and mind right now, as if making that final defence of his own little Londonderry, the publishing firm he had built up from a tiny print shop. When this was done, he could ascend or descend into whatever waited for him. "The relevant part is here." He thrust a page towards them, the loose one that Mr Frampton had picked up from the floor. "You will see that I leave a life interest in the business to Mrs Prendegast, who will receive exactly half the profits for her life. After she dies, title will pass absolutely to two people." He stopped, raised his head and they saw how clear his vision of the future was in his eyes. "You are those two people."

The second document was a simple recognition of a name change for the business. 'Prendegast and Son' was immediately to become 'Prendegast and Frampton'. The third document was simpler still and in one paragraph laid down the governing rules of the business, entitled:

To Publish the Best while Honouring the Public Good in All Respects.

It included the appointment of Mr Frampton as General Manager. The appointment was dated that day, November 12th 1689, witnessed by Mr Prendegast's attorney.

"Now, madam, please read some more of Miss Browne's splendid book." Mr Prendegast settled back in his old chair, as if he did not expect to leave it for quite some time.

The final effort to provide relief for us started on July 20th. General Kirke led it and, despite the fighting on land, the concentration was by ship for they held the provisions we required. Three ships came towards us. We could see they were low in the water with a telescope we passed around in our breaks from work and our hopes rose considerably. But then they stopped below the boom. They moved again the next day, reaching Culmore Point, but then stopped again.

Afterwards, it was clear that they were waiting for the right wind. But we did not know this at the time and had to wait out our frustration for a week.

I have now a confession to make. I did not write in my journal for eight days at the end of July. At first, I was too depressed and also had to concentrate on duties in the hospital, after which I just collapsed. In the latter part of this period, however, elation replaced despair, still keeping me from scribbling in my journal. What comes next is not a daily record but was written on August 1st and 2nd when we knew our fate. I apologise if the tone of this last section alters from living it to recording it after the event.

On 28th July, four ships set sail in the evening. They were called Mountjoy, Phoenix, Jerusalem and Dartmouth. Plus, alongside them, was a smaller boat, I later learned was the longboat from HMS Swallow. Mountjoy strikes the boom, bounces off, or so it seems, and runs aground. Mountjoy's brave captain, Michael Browning, was killed in the resulting firing from the shore. However, whether this created a diversion, or whether there were just too many ships and boats for the Jacobites to keep track of, the little longboat manages to cut the cables and chains. Thus, the smallest speck of a boat is the one that caused us to hope again and raised us from the despair we had offered to Our Lord as all we had left to give.

Suddenly, the boom is no longer. The metal wall that kept us in starvation has tumbled down. There are a lot of guns firing and many casualties but the big ships are towed up the River Foyle by rowing boats and arrive just before dark at Ship's Quay.

We were saved. We were provided for. The Lord God had heard our prayers and sent ships laden with provisions.

But we had to be careful. Some people gorged on food and their shrunken, shrivelled stomachs could not cope. There was much sickness as a result.

The Jacobites responded with a furious bombardment of Londonderry. It seemed as if they were more determined than ever to take the city. If it could not be done by starvation, they would vent their rage on our walls and send soldiers over the top to slaughter us all.

Then quite suddenly, the day before yesterday, they were gone. We saw flames everywhere that night and it was the besiegers burning their camps before sneaking off when dark.

In the morning, there was no enemy, no one around that wishes us ill. They had come in much force and fanfare and retired by slinking away under cover of darkness.

Thus, ended the Siege of Londonderry, which it has been my satisfaction to record. It was a terrible time. Many people lost their lives to shot and sword and disease. But in the end, our will proved the stronger and we, by the will of God, prevailed.

Mrs Frampton read the closing words with tears clouding her vision. She looked up from the book to see her husband staring, open-mouthed, at the slumped body of Mr Prendegast. Outside, the worst that late autumn could throw at them beat against the window, rattling the glass in its frame.

Ever the more practical of this pair of aces, she put the book on the floor, rose and went to feel Mr Prendegast's pulse. She then checked for breathing before turning to her husband.

"He's gone."

"God protect his soul," he replied. "He was a good man."

"And, husband dear, he has just put you in charge of the firm."

"It is a heavy responsibility."

"But one you will discharge with joy every day."

And Mrs Frampton knelt by the body of Mr Prendegast and, together with her husband, they bent their heads and told their Lord where Mr Prendegast belonged, asking that he be taken good care of.

Chapter 17

The announcement of Schomberg's appointment was well known before it was formally made. Everybody expected it as July ticked off its days. This took the shine off Parchman's foresight in Ferguson's eyes. He had half-heartedly attempted some resetting of facts with his deputy and co-conspirator.

But ultimately, as Parchman reminded him, it did not matter. What mattered was that their plan was working. And Ferguson was already getting richer.

"Sanderson and Sanderson were awarded another contract yesterday," Parchman reported. "This one is for the supply of boots, knapsacks and tents."

"How many contracts in total now, Parchman?" Ferguson asked. More and more he went by his real name as nonconformity became established. And the sins of his past could be forgotten, if not forgiven.

"A round two dozen, Robert." It was nearly always 'Robert' now while Ferguson used either 'Parchman' or 'sir', depending on his varying level of distaste for the man.

Parchman did not seem to have a Christian name.

Schomberg took leave of Parliament on July 16th and moved across the country into Wales. To get to Ireland, you travel west so from London you go to Wales and take ship for Ireland, making for the tiny village of Groomsport, close to the castle of Carrickfergus. The castle was held by the Jacobites. This was the logical first objective; relieve Carrickfergus and then march across Ulster to Londonderry.

Schomberg's army was well prepared. He had expected the appointment along with most of the political establishment and he had made preparations.

It was high summer and the task was to relieve Londonderry and free Ulster before winter, thus putting James' forces onto the backfoot. This was, likely, Schomberg's last campaign. He would retire, probably the following year if he managed to liberate Ireland by then. He had come to like the thought of spending his last years in England, winter in town, summer on a country estate. It would be a fitting end to a long, sometimes illustrious, career.

Yet even in this attempt at a final satisfactory seal to his career, he failed. Not through any character fault but because events moved more quickly than he could manage. Perhaps, on reflection, this is a character fault after all. Others, most particularly General Kirke, took the initiative while Schomberg manoeuvred and planned. Ultimately, there was no place for Schomberg in the history of the Siege of Londonderry. When, waiting to embark in Wales, he heard the news of the relief of the city, he knew he had passed over a magnificent opportunity, as was the mark of his career as the reliable organiser just missing the moment of glory.

History, like nature, is cruel; nobody remembers the runners-up.

Matthew moved through the near-empty streets of Londonderry, newly liberated and feasting on freedom and food. It was early morning. Most people were still in bed. He had an interview arranged with the Ulster agent of Sanderson and Sanderson, a reputable trading organisation that dealt mainly with government contracts. It seemed the perfect cover for his information gathering in Ulster, or espionage as most would call it.

As Matthew Davies, employee of the Earl of Sherborne, he had sent a series of letters over the last few weeks. They dealt with the quality and quantity of sheep wool by breed and other agricultural matters. Matthew had become an expert thanks to his diligent reading of the text books he had been given. It was surprising how much information he already knew, had absorbed over the thirty-four years of his life. But then, Sturminster Newton, where he had grown up, was a market town serving an intensely agricultural area and with a long - stablished meat market.

He believed his letters were convincing as to their

authenticity. But they were also riddled with clever coded messages; another reason to feel smug.

For he had worked out the code himself and was rather pleased with it.

Matthew had been given clear instructions and, so far, had carried them out perfectly. He was to report back on the Irish Catholic temperament. Then, when this was complete, he was to move north to Ulster and do a similar survey amongst the Protestants there.

All because the King did not trust the office charged with security over Ireland. And no wonder, when the whole country had risen against him.

Well, not quite the whole country for Ulster, although largely overrun by the forces of James Stuart, had remained loyal to the Protestant King William. Thank the Lord for that, for Matthew, no natural spy yet somehow drummed into it again, was tired of playing the Catholic and looked forward to being amongst his own again.

He entered the building. The main office contained only a clerk who flustered at everything.

"Good morning, sir," Matthew said, wondering if the clerk always stared with his mouth hanging down like the opening to a cave. "I seek Mr Paul Jensen."

"And you are, sir?" The clerk's jaw closed over the words, as if frightened they would turn tail and head back in there. Only when the words were clearly delivered did the jaw open again. And hang there.

"My name is Matthew Derwent." The old cover, being Matthew Davies in the employ of the Earl of Sherborne, was spent now and needed replacing. He was back in the familiar world of Protestantism so needed to be a Protestant again. He felt that he was coming home despite there being so many miles between Ulster and Dorset. He played with the two names in his mind, Ulster and Dorset. They had four out of six letters in common so must be cousins of some description.

In fact, he would soon be home. First, a week or two spent bustling around this part of Ireland, hopefully using the position with Sanderson and Sanderson to gain as much intelligence as he could. Then the neat resignation letter, stating that, on reflection, he found the job unsuitable. He would take a quick trip to Carrickfergus, where he had heard the Jacobites were still occupying the town and castle. That would also put him on the right side of the country to transfer to England. He would go by ship to Bristol and then overland to Bagber and his beautiful wife, who was waiting for him. He reckoned on three more carefully coded letters. Then his work would be done.

He would never offer himself for public service again; far better the pulpit on a Sunday morning with Eliza in the front pew.

His thoughts often turned to Eliza. He was amazed that she had agreed to marry him; could not quite believe it. They had married immediately, like two youngsters who cannot wait for anything, lost to hedonism, lost to everything but themselves. Then had come the summons to London. He could have declined it; no orders were issued, just the request.

London had been fun, setting up home together, entertaining and being entertained, his beautiful and clever wife hanging on his arm. But London had led to the request to go to Ireland alone for this important work.

And who could turn down the personal request of a monarch newly come to his throne? He had gone, of course, but soon would be travelling home, the ache inside him assuaged by the sight of her, by feeling her slender fingers on his skin, by the loving look from her eyes, her face, her voice, her everything.

And, yes, a voice could look, could give off an appearance when it wanted to.

"Mr Derwent, this way please. Mr Derwent?" The jaw clamped shut around the 'went' of 'Derwent', much as the gates of Londonderry must have shut before the invading hosts of Jacobites.

"You said, sir?"

The clerk had said it several times, raising his voice each time. Was this man a simpleton? Mr Jensen had said he was employing someone to help him in the office. The Lord knew he needed assistance to sort out this chaos. But was it to be Derwent?

"I said, sir, that Mr Jensen will see you now."

Paul Jensen was a huge man, squatting behind an inadequate desk in an office where Matthew had to bend to fit below the ceiling. It was clearly temporary accommodation, set up in a rush and with comfort the least concern.

"Your name, sir?" Jensen asked without looking up from the letter Matthew had written him.

"Matthew Davies."

"Davies?" This warranted a glance, more like a squint, then the eyes returned to the letter. "It says here…"

"Matthew Davies Derwent, sir, as I was starting to say. Davies is my middle name." Had he recovered from his slip?

"Ah, I see." He had.

"You will be working for Mr Caverns, who I believe you have met in the main office. He tells me he is overworked and much in need of an assistant."

"I understand, sir." The name, Caverns, was perfect, so neat was God's world.

"But first I must interview you as to some particulars. Please take a seat. Now, you state in your letter that you are a good Protestant. I wish to examine this a little."

Matthew's interview lasted an hour and consisted of a grilling on religion and morality, after which Mr Jensen gave his opinion that Derwent would do for the position. It seemed to Matthew, on later consideration, that the questions were genuine on religion but veered away on morality. Jensen appeared more interested in the boundaries to Matthew's principles than what they actually were. One question stuck in his mind as being asked particularly intently.

"What would your attitude be on discovering an irregularity in proceedings?"

"Do you mean dishonesty, sir?"

"Something of that nature."

Matthew's answer had been that he would report it to his superior. The peculiarity came when Jensen pressed him on this matter; how far up the chain would he go?

"I would assume, sir, that your judgement would prevail, hence I would mention it in a report to you." It seemed safest to imply he would go no further than Jensen, who ran this branch of the firm. It was the perfect answer, eliciting the only "Well said, sir" of the whole hour.

"You will start tomorrow, giving you today to find lodgings. Mr Caverns' wife runs a boarding house. I suggest you enquire with him on your way out."

"Thank you, Mr Jensen."

"Remember, just keep your nose to the grindstone, concentrate on the tasks set you and do not worry about the operations of the firm. Those are for your betters to concern themselves with."

"Yes, sir. I'll see you tomorrow, Mr Jensen."

Matthew, whether Davenport, Davies or Derwent, had no intention of seeking lodgings with Mr Caverns. He spent twenty minutes being lectured about his duties, noting the chaos the office was in, then left to wander the streets. He could stay in the inn he had stayed at last night but this would arouse suspicion for a clerk could not afford such as a permanent residence. No, he would have to find somewhere else to stay.

He wandered over to the Butcher's Gate, heavily damaged from the bombardment and fighting but looking so peaceful now in the August sunshine. The stone seemed to lap up the sunlight and radiate it back from walls and ground so that everywhere was an oven set on gentle heat. There were still guards on the walls but they were chatting and looking down at the growing number of inhabitants milling about. The guards and the residents shared jokes and mild insults as if it were a holiday. They were bound inexorably by what they had been through together.

Matthew felt hungry. He went into the butcher's shop on the corner and asked for a meat pie.

"Lamb, chicken, beef, duck or pork?" the good-natured butcher asked.

"Lamb for me. I suspect a fortnight ago there was a little less choice?" Matthew's jokes usually fell flat but there was so much good humour everywhere. They were looking for jokes, pulling them out of the air.

"Too right, sir, too right," Miles Denby chuckled, before

asking Matthew where he came from.

"I'm from London." Matthew offered a silent prayer for the lie. He supposed that strictly speaking he had just come from London. But that was not what the butcher had meant. "Do you know where a single man might find lodgings?"

"As it happens, I do." The grin continued. "My friend, Miss Browne, mentioned the fact this very morning."

"What fact would that be, sir?"

"Why, some rooms in her house are vacant as people return to their farms. She was just saying this morning that she doubted anyone would take them with so many people leaving for their homes. Take this stool and eat your pie and in ten minutes I will take you around there, if you like."

Matthew took the stool and the pie to a corner of the room and set up his spy station, spending ten minutes observing the huge joy in everyone. These were people who had won through a terrible ordeal. Soon they would, no doubt, settle down and grieve for the two thousand souls departed but right now the mood was born of gratitude and relief.

Matthew liked Bridget Browne immediately. The feeling was mutual.

"I am seeking renters for these rooms on behalf of the owners. Unfortunately, there were several deaths in the family during the siege, including the man of the house. I volunteered to try and rent the rooms to bolster their income a mite.

"That is very kind of you, Miss Browne," Matthew replied. What he did not know was that Bridget had continued to pay the rent for all three rooms, despite cutting her occupancy from three rooms to just one.

"Mind you, I can only let you take the small room as my cousin from Barbados is coming tomorrow with a friend. I only got note of this an hour ago."

"One room will be fine, Miss Browne. I'll take it if I may."

"Of course, Mr Derwent. Now, perhaps we should talk about the rent."

119

Chapter 18

The Duke felt the sunshine penetrate into his aching bones as he swung into the saddle. He had landed with 10,000 men at a tiny fishing village called Groomsport. He had heard the name meant 'grumpy servant' and could see the sense of it, particularly as 'Groom' rhymed with 'gloom'. Then he considered that it could be the other way around for a groom was a type of servant.

No matter about nomenclature. On arrival a few days earlier, he had reconnoitred and then decided to take the castle at Carrickfergus. He felt all action and decisiveness as commands were issued and soldiers everywhere moved into position. And now, having secured their landing, they were to move out against the castle held by forces loyal to James II.

He was too late to relieve Londonderry. General Kirke had sent ships through and the Jacobite army had withdrawn. Who knew what private disillusion the enemy had suffered prior to the decision to abandon their siege? It mattered not; far more important was that it delivered a huge boost to the morale of those, civilians and military, loyal to William.

And his job now was to build on that morale, bring it higher still.

He had rejoiced visibly at the news that Londonderry was free but secretly wished he, not Kirke, had been the saviour of the city. It would have been a fitting way to repay Parliament's generosity to him; to reset the balance of gratitude.

"Your Grace, we are ready to move out."

Schomberg responded by raising his arm in the air and bringing it forward and down. It was a symbolic order for most of the soldiers were too far away to see the detail but it would be relayed back along the ranks by a host of loyal officers, commissioned and non-commissioned.

But he grimaced to himself as the sweeping action of his right arm hurt considerably. Age ate into his bones. His body battled the elements that even a kind high-summer in Ireland put up against him. Only his will kept him going; will born of a desire for glory, for one last splendid deed to make the history books sit up.

Still, when he had finished this job successfully, he would retire and spend the days left to him writing his memoirs and reliving every modest triumph of the last sixty years. Perhaps, with a significant parting achievement, each event of his long military career would be magnified in a glorious aura of reinterpretation.

For Schomberg wanted to be remembered as a famous general and not as a pensioner, lapping up the generosity of an English Parliament enthralled with their new Dutch King.

Matthew expected the work to be tedious but found it anything but. Mr Caverns was disorganised in the extreme. There were papers stacked everywhere in any order and it took ages to find a particular memo or purchase order. Matthew immediately started organising the papers, finding several crates and designating one for each subject. Mr Caverns cared little what his new underling did, preferring not to be disturbed as he bumbled about the large office.

"All the purchase information goes over here," Matthew explained in the late morning when Mr Caverns emerged from a nap. "I'm sorting them by type of supply. Hence, in this crate goes everything to do with boots, while the one next to it is for ordinance. Eventually, they will be sub-divided by contract and supplier."

"I want you to organise everything while I go into town for a while," Mr Caverns said, refusing to acknowledge that Matthew was doing exactly that. "I suggest you organise it by subject matter and then, later on, by contract. I've been too busy with other operational matters to attend to this basic task and have told Mr Jensen repeatedly that I have need of a junior; someone very junior, I hasten to add."

"When will you be back?" Matthew wanted to know because he already had an inkling some things were not right around the office and he wanted a few hours alone. Mr Jensen had not been in that morning.

"An hour or two, I would think. Don't start imagining you can put your feet up. I want to see a substantial amount of work done when I get back from... well, never you mind where I am going."

"Of course, it did not occur to me to slacken at all, sir."

What Matthew had seen within the first few hours was clear evidence of malpractice. Whether this was carefully masked or carelessly ignored by disorganisation, he was not yet sure.

He noticed it first with the boots, the discovery being made by his decision to file papers by subject matter rather than date order. Thus, he soon had a small collection of paperwork on boots. The firm had purchased five thousand pairs at under a shilling a pair; cheap boots that could not be expected to last the winter.

That was bad enough – shoddy equipment was never excusable. But it got much worse for an hour later he came across a despatch note for 15,000 boots at nine shillings a pair. It could be an earlier order, of course, which is why he wanted the time alone. But, to add to his suspicions, he discovered that the contract from the government for supply of boots was dated only three weeks before the supply.

It helped that Mr Caverns tacked on a rather nice mutton pie and three pints of ale to whatever meeting he attended in town. He left the office before eleven and did not return until after three. He returned, slightly merry, to find Matthew in the latter stages of re-organisation of the filing system.

"I still have that pile over there to go through and then each category to sort into date and subject order but I do believe I have broken the back of the task... sir." Mr Caverns grunted in reply and retreated to a cubby hole he had made from bookcases and packing crates. Soon afterwards, there was gentle snoring, interrupted by occasional deep sighs and hiccups.

Matthew was free to continue his search yet found no other transaction referencing boots. This indicated that there was only one contract and the quantities purchased should, consequently, match those sold.

He did find, however, that ten barrels of gunpowder became one hundred, that rations for a week somehow only lasted a day and that there were almost enough coats to keep the rain off every person in Ireland.

And the prices were astronomical.

Jensen returned with the door banging open.

"What's this?" he thundered, seeing the boxes in a neat row along one wall. Order issued from those boxes, dispelling the chaos like smoke in a fresh wind. Mr Caverns was undisturbed in his slumber behind the packing crates.

"I took it upon myself to re-organise the filing, sir, and found some irregularities." Matthew offered the boot papers to Mr Jensen, thinking these the clearest evidence of something wrong. "Do you not think it strange, sir, that 5,000 boots were ordered and 15,000 sold on to the army? And the sale price seems discordant with the purchase price by a factor of…"

"What do you think you are doing, man?" Jensen threw the papers down on a nearby table without looking at them.

"I said, sir, I would report any discrepancies to you… is all I am doing now, sir, reporting…" Matthew's voice petered out as he perceived the rage of his employer, evidenced in a few choice words that Matthew had seldom heard and never used himself.

"Where's Caverns? Taking a nap, is he?"

"I believe he is indisposed, sir."

Dismissal on his first day but not a scrap of shame felt. For Matthew was convinced he had stumbled upon major corruption; why else had the rage turned suddenly to pretended indifference?

"Thank you, Derwent. You have done your duty in reporting to me. Now, please be so kind as to wash the floor in the main lobby. We have it cleaned twice a week but it always seems to need attention. Mr Caverns will show you where the bucket and mop are."

"But…"

"You will be doing me a great kindness, sir, if you would attend to this despite it being outside your normal duties. A great kindness, my man."

Matthew had done so, pushing the mop along the clean floor, wondering when he would be allowed back in the main office. The answer came a little later when Jensen visited him in the lobby, looking hopelessly embarrassed.

Or rather acting the role of someone hopelessly embarrassed.

"Mr Derwent, it seems I have made a miscalculation as to funds. We are not very profitable at this newly opened branch and, on studying our monetary projections further today and meeting with my advisers, it seems that we cannot presently afford a second clerk. I am going to have to ask you to leave."

"I can happily reduce my wages, Mr Jensen, if that helps."

"I'm sorry, Derwent. This is the decision we have arrived at. There is nothing else to be said on the matter." The fact that Derwent offered so readily to cut his wages proved that he had other motives for working in the offices of Sanderson and Sanderson. *The quicker he goes, the better,* he thought. "I think it best if you leave now." It was rotten luck that he had taken on this man the week that Cartwright and Franshaw were visiting. As branch manager, he was the senior but Cartwright had the ear of the boss in London, meaning Jensen had to impress.

"I see, sir." Matthew made to take the bucket and mop back to where he had found it.

"I'll take that." Instinct was now screaming at Jensen to get Matthew out with no prospect of returning.

"Well, sir, there is just the matter of my wages." Matthew was suddenly all presence of mind, seeking one moment back in the main office.

"Wait here and I will send Caverns with the money. Two shillings a day, I think we agreed?"

"That is correct, sir, but I have taken lodgings at five shillings a week and owe that at the end of the week."

"Very well, wait here."

It was much easier with Caverns. Matthew simply said he had to get his hat from where he had put it down in the main office and Caverns let him back in.

Matthew hurried back towards his lodgings, feeling the boot papers pushed against his shirt, quickly stuffed from view. His plan was to write a coded letter that evening and send it the next day with whatever ship was leaving for England. His mind was working through the encryption as he walked, lost to his surroundings.

He would not send the boot papers as there was too much risk of them being lost. He would summarise the content within the coded letter and mention that he had the originals to prove his case.

Matthew's mind continued to work on the code as he walked. The journey was a simple reversal of the course he had made that morning; through Shipquay Gate into the city and then along a short way, turning right just at the start of Butcher Street into the narrow lane where Bridget Browne's lodgings were, one room sub-let to him. His mind was on auto-pilot as to direction, too absorbed to take in the pair following him, both of whom he knew.

And neither of whom he wished to see again.

But even his coded letter composition was forgotten when he bumped into someone at the corner of Butcher Street. The other person recovered more quickly.

"I'm sorry, sir... oh, Matthew. What on earth are..."

"Thomas! What in the Lord's name brings you here?"

It was clearly time for explanations. The two brothers had not only bumped into each other on a street corner in a town neither of them had been to before in another country entirely but also were lodging with Miss Browne in rooms beside each other.

They had come to Ireland along very different routes but, perhaps, were fated to meet in the stronghold of Protestantism; the one city of consequence that had defied James Stuart and sent his generals away to find other, easier targets.

Chapter 19

Eliza Davenport had, unthinkingly, introduced herself as Lady Merriman, her maiden name.

"Ah, the Witch of Bagber," the Duke of Wiltshire replied, his frame stooped and a pot-belly protruding as evidence of sudden addiction to new carnal pleasures. He loved expensive sweetmeats and had had his remaining teeth removed a month earlier so as to be able to indulge without risk of pain. He now shone a set of polished wooden teeth, specially made by a surgeon in London who dealt in realistic-looking sets.

"I offer the bite without the pain," he had said several times until the Duke had told him to work in silence.

"I was known as such," Eliza replied, thinking maybe a reputation as an oddball would assist a little in her efforts to get justice for Milly's family; for a whole village, in fact.

But it had not worked. The Duke snorted when Eliza mentioned Ashenham.

"Bunch of no-goods," he said, after enjoying the sweet and polite reasoning presented to him. "They are a waste of space and you won't persuade me otherwise, madam." Yet he had allowed her to continue for twenty minutes, without any offer of refreshment, not even one of the sweetmeats he picked at constantly.

"Regardless of the right and wrong of it, and I concede they were hugely disrespectful to your predecessor, Your Grace, can I not appeal to your generosity?"

"I don't have any."

"Surely, Your Grace?"

"Madam, I've lived sixty-four years on this earth with never a care for any other fellow. It is a practice that has worked exceedingly well." He pointed towards his tray of sweetmeats as if they offered all the evidence he needed. "Why would I vary it now?"

"I bid you good day, Your Grace." Eliza rose and curtsied automatically, then wished she had not. He did not deserve such respect, particularly with the leer he wore when looking at her.

Outside, she shook herself, turning her face towards the sun, wanting to be rid of the Duke of Wiltshire. She climbed into the carriage, head shaking towards Milly and John Parsons. It was enough for them to know that Eliza Davenport had failed.

She had tried and failed and now had to fall back on the alternative plan.

Which was going to be an awful lot more difficult because of where Penelope Wiltshire had chosen to live.

Or rather, who she had chosen to live with.

The coachman drove the horses hard, sensing that his mistress wanted to be back in Bagber Manor that evening. They made it as the day was drawing to a close with long shadows giving a patchwork of light and shade like an elongated chessboard. As they pulled up to the front entrance, the horses had to be dragged to a stop, as if they were fixed on a fast trot and feared any other pace. Two footmen rushed from the door to hold the horses, while Sarah and Kitty helped the passengers down.

"Welcome, My Lady," the sisters said. To them, Eliza Davenport would always be Lady Merriman. "We are so glad to have you back home." Standing right behind Sarah and Kitty, as if the two servants had a greater right to their Lady Merriman, were Elizabeth and Amelia Taylor, waiting their turn.

"Hello Lizzie and Mealy." They kissed and hugged, then stood back to take each other in before embracing again. "Please meet my new lady's maid, Milly, who travels with my guest and Milly's godfather, Mr Parsons."

"Welcome, sir. Welcome, Milly, I hope you will be very happy here."

Milly loved Bagber from the moment she saw it. The fields all around belonged to the estate and were bathed in the rich, departing sun of an early August evening. The stone-built house seemed to lean kindly into the introductions, noting carefully her name for future reference. For long reference, she hoped, for she knew instantly that she wanted to live in this house for the rest of her days.

"No silly, you don't need to curtsey to us. We're staff, just like you," Sarah said, taking the slender hand of this slender girl and giving it a squeeze. Her own chubby hand was three times the size of Milly's.

"Silly me," Milly replied.

"Silly Milly," Kitty laughed. And they all did.

"What is the joke Sarah... Kitty... Milly?" Eliza asked, turning around from her catch-up with Elizabeth and Amelia.

"I've just been given a nickname is all, Miss."

"Silly Milly," said Kitty again and, this time, their mistress could not help but join in.

"Have the coach ready tomorrow," Eliza ordered when the laughter subsided. "Mr Parsons and I will go to Great Little after breakfast. Silly Milly, you will stay here and take instruction from Sarah and Kitty as to your duties at Bagber."

"Yes, Miss, I mean My Lady." This time she did curtsey, blushing at their kindly-meant teasing.

"Who's here?" Penelope asked as she tried to dress herself while Sally looked on languidly from a chair.

Sally moved across to the window, then opened it to lean out.

"I do believe it is Lady Merriman as was, now Mrs Davenport. She's with a stranger, a big man with a bushy beard. I wonder if this means more trouble." Sally had witnessed the attempted reconciliation between Alice Roakes and Eliza Davenport a few months earlier. It had not ended well, with Mrs Davenport leaving abruptly.

"Can you do my hair please, Sally, so we can go downstairs and find out?"

"In a moment. I just want to see her dress. It's gorgeous." She opened the window further and leant right out.

"Careful, Sal."

"It's peach coloured, would look perfect on you," Sally replied, turning to Penelope. "Of course, I'll do your hair, my love. That's what I'm here for, isn't it?"

"No!"

"Really?"

"You're here because I love you to the ends of the earth. If you were just my maid, you would have been dismissed months ago for being incompetent. No, don't throw that book at me. No! That hurt!" Sally's throw had been accurate, hitting Penelope on the small of the back as she turned away.

Quite a bit later, Penelope Wiltshire made her way downstairs. She was dressed of sorts, in that nothing broke the rules of modesty, at least not too excessively. But her hair fell untidily over her shoulders.

She did not care.

Eliza was prepared. Her plan was simple and it should have worked.

Except she could not have known what chaos she found at Great Little.

She had not wanted to come, for any association with Lady Roakes, Mrs Beatrice as she had been, was painful in the extreme. There were too many memories she did not want to bring back. Time is a great healer, they say, but that is a misnomer for time only facilitates the healing which has to come from within people.

And how could there ever be healing for the theft of her youth?

But she had to see the Dowager Duchess of Wiltshire, and she now lived at Great Little, the home of Lady Roakes.

"Mrs Davenport, what a surprise."

"Lady Roakes, forgive me for calling."

"You are always welcome, Mrs Davenport." They edged around each other for a few minutes, trading platitudes which clanged against the armour they wore.

Alice Roakes answered the inevitable question as to how her estate fared with the standard response that things were well. She was not going to parade her deep worries in front of the one person who had suffered so terribly at her hands. It was just not something one did.

Mrs Matthew Davenport was not ever going to be a salvation for her problems; far more likely that she brought fresh problems of her own to lay at Alice's feet like sick tribute in an upside-down world.

"What brings you here, Mrs Davenport?" Alice asked, moving the conversation on because someone had to.

"I would very much like to have a word with the Dowager Duchess." And at that moment, Penelope burst into the room, as if she had been hanging on the end of a string with her name on it and Eliza Davenport had yanked that string.

"Penelope, your hair!" Alice cried, looking at her hair and her dress; ribbons hung loosely as if pulled by a spiteful child, while her overskirt rode up one side. "Are you feeling unwell?"

"No, I have never felt better, Alice, my dear. Hello, Mrs Davenport." She spoke as if their next-door neighbour had come to tea. In actuality, they were neighbours in a fractional way for Alice's land touched a farm recently purchased by Eliza on the slopes of Okeford Hill. It gave them a sixty-yard-long shared boundary on the lower eastern slope of the hill, where Alice's land petered out into woodland dotted with several small fields used to house rams and bulls during the summer months.

"Well, I shall leave you to your discussion," Lady Roakes said, rising from her chair. "If you need me, I shall be on the terrace with my son."

"Of course, I meant to congratulate you on the birth of your son, Lady Roakes. Do forgive me, it went clean out of my head."

"There is nothing to forgive..." Alice Roakes almost said 'Arkwright', just stopping in time. It was the name Eliza had come to her with nine years earlier, given to her by Parchman. "Mrs Davenport, there is nothing at all to forgive."

But their eyes met at this point, having avoided contact before. And Alice's eyes said there was something to forgive, something terribly important.

But the forgiveness was sought by Alice, not offered. It was the other way around.

Eliza looked away first; the moment was gone; the question of forgiveness was put away again.

Perhaps it would be brought out another day but it was too soon right now.

All this time, John Parsons sat quietly by the window while

the trio of ladies tried to cope with emotions he could not hope to understand. He just knew that Eliza Davenport and Lady Roakes had a history. He had heard something about captivity but had put as much credence to it as tales of the Witch of Bagber. Now, he could see there was something to it.

But how could it help Ashenham?

"Lady Roakes, might your steward be so kind as to show Mr Parsons around while I discuss a private matter with the Dowager-Duchess? Mr Parsons had a good-sized farm in Wiltshire before some underhand moves took it from him. I believe he understands farming."

Lady Roakes nodded in agreement, not trusting her voice. It was Penelope who called for Tomkins and explained what he should do.

"I don't understand why you've come to see me," Penelope said, having caught sight of herself in the mirror above the fireplace and tidied her hair a little while trying to listen to the sad story of Ashenham. It was a battle between hearing out Eliza Davenport and dreaming of spending the day with Sally.

"I thought you might have influence with the new Duke, Your Grace."

"I have none, madam, none whatsoever." Penelope snapped out her reply, then told Eliza of her last meeting with the Duke. "I negotiated a pile of money and took my clothes and jewellery but the Duke made it clear he never wanted to see me again. But this needs money, this problem of yours, not influence."

"How so, Your Grace?"

"Please call me Penelope. Reference to my title brings back unpleasant memories of my late husband."

"Then please call me Eliza, Penelope." Was this progress? Was it familiarity, the start of a journey that might lead towards friendship, even? She was a strange fish, this young Dowager Duchess. There was a directness, and an honesty about that directness, that stood politeness on its head. It was like a child brought to the dinner table to entertain the guests. Once there, the child told the absolute truth, regardless of how that truth would be received. "How is it about money, Penelope?" The name had four even-length syllables, four neat stepping stones into the upper class, given her, no doubt, by a doting mother. Eliza knew something of her father, too. Sir John Withers was elderly and ill but had made a vast fortune in property after selling his initial business servicing rich households with the removal of shit by handcart, sold on as fertiliser for the fields he later purchased and turned into houses.

Property, of course, was how the Roakes had made their money. It seemed that people made fortunes in the city and then came to the countryside to spend them. But key to this was buying, alongside land and houses like the Great Little estate, an acceptability and position in society.

"You need to buy the village from him and then you can charge whatever rent you please, Mrs Davenport." She had addressed her formally. It was not the beginning of a possible friendship but merely a dislike of her own formal address. There was something hostile yet endearing about this woman, who still had her hair somewhat dishevelled and her overskirt riding high, revealing a series of petticoats. There was something, also, about this woman's maid. She remembered seeing them together last year when she came to Great Little and could not stay after the discovery of who Lady Roakes was.

Or rather, who she had been and what it had meant to Eliza.

But then, she remembered, Penelope Wiltshire had displayed some true nobility at that time. She had begged them not to go far and then came out that dark winter night to plead Lady Roakes' case. She had brought her little black maid with her.

That was it; they were lovers. Mistress and maid together.

"That would cost thousands. I don't have that much. I would have to mortgage Bagber and that I could never do. Do you think Lady Roakes could help?" What she meant was, did Lady Roakes feel sufficiently guilty about her past to invest the several thousands.

"She might have been interested but…"

"Yes, Penelope?" Eliza wanted to persist with the informal; even if every step she took forwards was matched by Penelope taking one backwards; at least it was movement.

"Madam, she is destitute."

"How so? I mean, she is so wealthy. The building works going on here?"

How much did she owe Thomas' firm of builders for the work that was still going on? Could it really be that Alice Roakes had overstretched herself? How would Eliza feel about that? Just a few months earlier, she had wanted to buy Great Little just to see the woman homeless.

But Hate has only one offspring and that was More Hate, generating itself again and again and multiplying its ferocity with each generation.

And now that she had heard this news about the person who had stolen five years of her life, she felt no triumph, not even a sense of the wheel turning and fate dealing what Alice had dealt to others.

There was no joy in misery and Eliza Davenport, nee Merriman, had promised herself much joy in this world now she was free again.

Penelope was animated now with the subject involving her and those she cared for. She told of the devastating contract signed with Grimes and Co. "I never liked that Grimes from the very beginning. We have not been able to fulfil the contract quantities because of several terrible accidents on our farms. He is demanding huge penalty payments under the contract."

"But the London properties? Surely…"

"All sold to pay for this." Penelope raised her arms wide to indicate the house that was less than half-complete but would be magnificent one day. "There is worse to come for we also have an obstinate farmer who has dammed the river and cut off our water. We've had to rent new fields and take our cattle there to keep them from dying of thirst."

"Good Lord, this is a run of bad luck." But was it bad luck? The name, Grimes, was vaguely familiar; there was some connection to Bagber but she could not place it.

"I have stopped all building work in Alice's name," Penelope said.

"But the debts to the builders?"

"They are all paid from my own purse, except some stone I have asked the quarry to take back at a discount." She puffed out her chest in preparation for the next remark. "I negotiated to buy it back at the exact same price if it has not sold by the time we require it."

"That was a good move, Penelope. But what are we to do about these problems? I need thousands to buy a whole village and surrounding farmland and your host, Lady Roakes, needs sufficient to tide herself over from this disastrous contract and to restart the building works. That adds up to a lot of money that we simply do not have."

The door opened and Sally entered. Eliza looked at her as she served coffee in silence, noting that Penelope started breathing more heavily and then blushing when Sally brushed her hand against her mistress' arm. What was it about this girl that held such fascination for Penelope, who could take her pick of husbands at any time? Sally was slight, a little bigger-boned than Milly. Her skin was dark, varying from jet-black to light brown as she moved from shade to sunlight; the sunlight showed a nasty scar on one cheek, jagged and rutted yet doing nothing to detract from her pretty looks.

She compared Sally to Milly, her new maid. Milly's skin was snow-white. Sally moved more fluidly than Milly, yet, essentially, they performed the same tasks with the same movements. When finished pouring the coffee, she stood behind Penelope's chair with her hands neatly clasped and her body completely still. Milly would fidget so when not tasked.

Why, Eliza wondered, did she feel just maternal love for Milly when Penelope obviously had raging passions for her black maid? Such that Penelope had left society and was happy to live out her days in Great Little with her lover. She just could not imagine feeling like this for any woman. It was the way she felt about Matthew and had felt for Henry, her first lover, who the old Earl of Sherborne had forced to marry another. After their cruel separation, she had never seen Henry again and it had taken almost two decades to find her son, also Henry and now the Earl of Sherborne, provided the secret of his birth remained so. But here was a lady who clearly felt that love for another woman, against all the laws of God and man.

She desperately wanted to ask Penelope what this was all about.

But their relationship did not allow for such questions. Eliza sipped her coffee instead, trying to turn her mind to the problems they had aired. Solutions were not coming that day and finally, as Penelope sighed her inconvenience at Eliza's presence, she took her leave, wishing Penelope the very best.

Chapter 20

Amy Tabard was sick of being pregnant; sick of the nausea, the tiredness and the urges to eat everything that seemed expensive. She was determined to save every penny for Paul and was furious that continued weariness kept her from working and earning something to put towards the capital they so desperately needed.

And to make matters worse, Paul was away often, selling silk across Dorset and even into Somerset. He had gone again early on Monday morning and she had not seen him since and now it was Tuesday already.

"You must calm down, my dear," Mr Amiss said, worried that she would worry away the tiny child within her.

"I can't, Mr Amiss, I'm all a fluster, that's how I am, sir."

He ached to say *call me Father,* but could he? And should he? He thought of the first Amy Barratt he had known over twenty years ago. The timing certainly worked as evidence of paternity. She had come to the Red Lion the week he had bought the inn. He had been full of enthusiasm then, wanting to run the most successful tavern in Dorset.

She slid behind the bar when the barmaid did not come to work, turning her hand to pouring drinks and collecting plates of food from the kitchen with her natural good humour. It made customers talk about the place as somewhere to go. They had slept together that night and many nights after. But she was too restless a soul to stay in one place. Something drove her onwards, as if licensed to spend only one season in each place.

It had been a long summer that year, 1665; the year in which Charles II, the likeable rogue of a king, had presided over the worst tragedy in living memory as the plague returned to the capital. Everyone who could left London and Amy Barratt ended up in Dorchester.

The summer was long enough for Amy to discover she was pregnant.

But not long enough to see the baby born, again timing working as evidence of paternity. In all likelihood, she had not been pregnant when she had arrived at the Red Lion.

Amy Barratt just disappeared one night, driven on in her restless state.

The baby was born in 1666, the year the Great Fire purged London of the plague. Mr Amiss had heard from a traveller that Amy Barratt had given birth to a girl a month or more premature in a hospice in Poole. The mother had died from complications in childbirth, leaving the baby an effective orphan.

It had taken most of what he had saved to persuade a farmworker to take on the child. "Just until she is fourteen. Then send her back to me."

And Amy had arrived at the Red Lion fourteen years later, seeking answers where no answers could be given.

For Amy Barratt, the mother, had been a whore and who could tell which of her many clients was the young girl's father? They gave the baby her mother's name, Amy Barratt, for want of any other name.

But Mr Amiss believed it had been something more between him and Amy than a commercial relationship. Yes, he had paid, but there had been something special between them from the start.

He felt sure of it. And he liked to think the baby was his. It was just that he could not be sure.

And there was no possible way in which he could tell young Amy the circumstances of her birth. That meant, whatever he felt and thought, he could only tell her flatly that she had arrived at the Red Lion seeking work and shelter when she was about fourteen. Mr Amiss had taken in a stranger and that was all there was to it.

Leave Dorchester and its own worries now and travel north and west. Travel fast, like a bird in flight, for there is a long way to go. Like a bird, look down on the weather; the August heat of Dorset and the West Country gives way to heavy cloud over Gloucestershire. It breaks into rain showers over Herefordshire but you do not get wet for you are flying above the grey turrets of clouds that make castles in the air. You make it to the Welsh border and, as the hills and mountains rear up, so the air cleanses itself, becoming thin and pure as it dumps its water on the ground below.

You fly lower now, enjoying the shafts and blasts of air that whistle around the mountains, feeling the surge of power on your wings. Your eagle-eyes see the Irish Sea ahead and your feathers sense another change in weather coming. For the Irish Sea is stormy, dark, thrashing about. Your instinct is not to go there but you must. Perhaps you are a mother eagle, ranging far and wide for meat for your chicks. You have no choice but to fly straight through the storm.

You emerge the other side. Some birds do not make it; heavy, waterlogged wings become exhausted and unable to stay airborne any longer, dipping ever towards the water and then plunging down through it and drowning in the choppy depths. But that is not your fate for you do not rush and, in not rushing, you arrive before the other survivors of the storm. You pause first on a cliff top on the Welsh coast. You eat and rest and then have the strength to fly high above the weather, where there is no storm at all; just the peace of God as you come near to His Kingdom.

You expect storms in Ireland but, strangely, you see none of it. There is a sweet purity about the air, as if it has been dredged of all contaminants. Down below are the grim fortifications of Carrickfergus, tempting you to land and rest again on the sharp stones of the castle walls. But you are a wise bird and hear the guns popping in the still air. An eagle would not be their target but a stray musket ball will not discriminate. Besides, you have an overriding urge to get to Londonderry because in Londonderry there are some brave young things in mortal danger.

And your job is to beat your wings, send harsh cries onto the light wind of Londonderry and warn these young souls to flee while they still have life in them.

For what is alive one minute can be nothing but a bag of bones the next.

And a city full of joy at its liberation can also house evil things that would chop the innocent down for their own ends. People survive the most incredible hardships and then drop down dead the next day. They lived but are no more.

Cartwright and Franshaw tried to emulate Parchman in creeping through the streets at night. They could not hope to be as professional as Parchman but were not too noticeable. Certainly, the young group ahead did not seem aware of their presence. There were four in the group; two Irish and two English. They knew the English and the English knew them, for Franshaw had arrested them the previous year and Cartwright had questioned them before their escape from the burning prison in Shaftesbury.

But capture was not in their minds that night. They had learned the hard way that arrest can be followed by freedom and did not want to risk that again.

"It's only Matthew we need," Franshaw said at the table by the window of the inn. They had pushed a drunk out of his second home so that they had a good view of the other inn across the street, where the Davenport brothers and the Browne cousins were catching up on each other's tales while eating beef stew washed down with beer.

Cartwright, in their own inn opposite, ordered similar food and also brandy against the fear that dug at his stomach. Mr Jensen had asked them to silence Matthew and anyone he may have talked to.

Cartwright just hoped that Franshaw would do the knife work, leaving him to report back their success.

"What's the name of the inn they are at?" he asked, thinking of that report.

Franshaw craned his neck to see the sign opposite.

"The Eagle and Child," he said. "What's more, Mr Cartwright, there's a dirty great big bird perched right on top of the sign."

You've done your work, flyer to the heights, and may rest now for you have come a long way.

Chapter 21

They called in reinforcements. Not Caverns; he was too idle to be any good in a fight. Instead, while staying away himself, Jensen sent four heavy types he knew from a previous career as a provider of protection to small businesses in Londonderry. With Franshaw, they made five, plus Cartwright who would direct affairs from a little way behind the main force.

"I'll be lookout as well as project leader," he told them, as if dividing up roles in a children's game.

"Shouldn't be a problem, this job," the smallest of the four grunted. Franshaw felt puny standing next to him, like a miniature dog entered by mistake in the big dog class.

"I doubt any problem whatsoever," Cartwright said, trying to find a way to stamp his authority on this band of oversized men.

"Leave it to us," leered the largest giant. "We know what to do."

"We'll need to get all four," a middling giant said, as if reading lines from a script.

"No!" Franshaw cried, a little too loudly. "Four murders at once is going to cause a real stir."

"It will cause a stir, Franshaw, but my judgement is that it has to happen. Matthew Davenport will have talked to the others, without doubt. If we are to keep this quiet as ordered, we are going to have to nip all four budding blooms at one time." Cartwright announced his decision which had already, in truth, been made by the four heavies because they liked the thought of a quadruple bout of violence.

"I'll take the girl," said the smallest giant, licking his fat lips.

But they all wanted the girl so Cartwright said they would draw straws for it, winked at the smallest and ensured he got the one short straw. One clever move and he had regained control and found an ally amongst the heavies.

You would never imagine that four men, the lightest at seventeen stone, could move so quickly and quietly. And with so much co-ordination. It was as if they had pooled their brains, knowing they would always be working together. That pooled brain floated between them and had invisible ropes twitching the nerves of each of the four to achieve that perfect co-ordination.

Within seconds, two had darted down a side alley, appearing silently ahead of the two brothers and two cousins as they made their way back to their shared lodgings.

"This looks like trouble," Tristan said, seeing the evil, fake-friendly grins planted on their crooked faces. "There are two more behind."

"They've got knives," Matthew added, indicating towards the glint of metal in the moonlight, held low for an upward thrust.

It was Thomas who saved them. Looking around wildly for an escape route, finding nothing, for the murder-to-be scene was well selected on a short stretch of street with no roads branching off, he reached up suddenly and pulled a long length of gutter from a low-hanging roof. It came away in two pieces. He handed the smallest piece to Tristan and struck the larger part on the cobbles. It conveniently broke into two so that Matthew now had a weapon.

"Get around Bridget," he hissed. They formed three points around her like three turrets surrounding a citadel. Bridget bent down to the ground and picked up a ten-inch length of gutter that had broken off when Thomas smashed the long length down.

"Just so I have a weapon too." Her voice sang out into the night. They instinctively realised with the noise of the gutter smashing on the cobbles, that silence was their enemy and noise, the bigger and louder it came, was their friend.

The four giants hesitated, not because of the arming of their prey; that did not concern them at all. Rather, it was the ringing of smashing gutter-pipe on the cobbles. Their modus operandi was menacing, smirking silence and the loud clanging broke into their confidence, made them that bit uneasy. Then,

Bridget's loud voice ate at the darkness like flames in a fire. In an upstairs window a lantern was lit, then another and a window was opened.

"What's going on down there?" came an authoritarian voice.

"We're being threatened with knives, sir." Tristan, sensitive to the sudden change in their fortunes, made sure his voice was loud and clear.

"Call the guard," the voice of authority from above the street-scene returned in equal measure of volume. "Call the guard," was taken up from top floor window to top floor window and the cry sailed and echoed down the street as if there was a special plane of communication above their heads at second story level.

Matthew looked around, his concentration on the ground, for that was where the evil was planned.

"They've gone," he cried. But he did catch sight of one person as a lantern swung above his head, illuminating him perfectly. "Franshaw!" he cried but his voice was lost in the clamour and then even Franshaw, slower in reaction than the others, relying more on bluff cheerfulness for survival, was gone, taken up by the night.

The guard came soon enough. After several minutes of questioning, they were escorted back to their lodgings and safety.

"It was definitely Franshaw," Matthew said to Thomas. "The man who arrested us both last year, I saw him as clear as anything in the lantern light."

"That means Parchman is behind this," Thomas replied. "And that means you have stumbled upon something big, brother."

How safe were they, even in their lodging? Two soldiers were to remain outside the house for the rest of the night, front and back, but they could not stay permanently.

"We've got to leave Londonderry," Thomas said, as they drank chocolate into the early hours.

"But how? They will be watching the house for any sign of movement."

The chocolate was long gone. They were without a solution; four minds worked through the possibilities, jumping into ideas only to realise the deficiencies of them.

"Let's go back to the beginning," Thomas said. "We know they are probably watching the house." That conjecture was later proved to be correct. The would-be attackers had broken into the house opposite, tied up the elderly couple who lived there, and now had a perfect view of the front door. The door at the back was watched by the quietest of the large men, who could rival Parchman in his ability to be somewhere without being seen. "They know we went in here so all they have to do is wait for us to come out again. We cannot spend the rest of our lives in here!"

"And they know the guards cannot stay indefinitely," Bridget had a twang to her voice that made the word 'indefinitely' seem delightful to Thomas. He looked at her again. She was plain, tall and angular. But a spirit shone out of her that made those angles of body and face somehow magnificently attractive. Her hair had fallen down to her shoulders when she had taken her hat off and put on her pinafore automatically on entering the house. It was as if placing the pinafore around her dress calmed the mood, making their collective rapid breathing slow down. It was she that had suggested the chocolate and she that took them to the kitchen to drink it, one on each side of the kitchen table, making a neat square; cousin opposite cousin and brother opposite brother.

And Bridget next to Thomas.

Her loosened braids made her head seem too large for her body and accentuated those angles with the natural sweep of the hair. It seemed like a diagram he remembered from his studies in Dorchester, with curves meeting triangles. That had been geometry and something to do with how to calculate the volume of an irregular shape.

He liked the idea of slipping away into the countryside with Bridget Browne; practical, educated, strangely attractive Bridget Browne. Then he thought about Amelia and a wave of guilt swept over him. Mealy seemed so far away suddenly; she was in another country. But it was not that. It was the choice she had made in turning away from him and choosing to lie with another woman, thus turning away from God too.

He could not imagine Bridget Browne lying with another woman. But he could imagine lying with her himself.

"You seem lost in thought, Thomas," she said. And then the idea came to him.

It involved some preparations. Rather than go to the guards outside, they called gently through the door.

Opposite, eating the roast beef they found in the old couple's larder, the watchers noted one guard entering the house. Then, minutes later, he came out and spoke briefly to the other guard at the back before marching away.

"I think we're starting to get movement," Franshaw said to the giants. They ignored his comment, swatting it away like a fly.

But the opposite happened for half an hour later a whole troop arrived and all entered the house. Were they to defend the house against attack; a miniature version of the Siege of Londonderry all over again? The smallest giant felt uneasy again. He had survived over forty years of dirty street-living by trusting his instinct. At first, he quelled it like fighting the urge to vomit but instinct is instinct and it gathered in potency as soldiers moved in and out of the house.

"Let's withdraw," he finally said.

"What?" said Franshaw, again ignored. And where was Cartwright in all this? Thinking back, he had not seen him since the street scene. Could he be busy reporting back when there was nothing to report?

Nothing except abject failure.

The last thing Franshaw saw, lingering behind the others, was the big body of troops; all troops, in fact, moving off again.

"There's no guard left," he called after the disappearing hulks of his fellow conspirators. But his cries did not penetrate even the thin morning air to reach their ears; he was left alone with an impossible task.

It was much later in the day that his mind turned to mathematics. Not the fascinating geometry of Bridget's face but simple arithmetic.

"Two plus twelve is fourteen," he said to Cartwright, back again now that all prospect of violence had passed. They had watched the house all morning and into the afternoon but there had been no movement at all.

"It is, Franshaw, but so what?"

"Don't you see, Mr Cartwright? There were two guards overnight. One entered the house in the early morning and left again. He came back with twelve others so that is fourteen in total."

"We've established that much."

"Well, at the end, eighteen guards left. I remember thinking it a longer chain as they marched in pairs but it did not mean anything to me at the time."

"You idiot," Cartwright admonished. "They played out their plan right in front of your eyes and you did not notice it."

"I'm sorry, Mr Cartwright. Yes, it is my fault."

And so, ended the second Siege of Londonderry, with an equal lack of success to the first.

Chapter 22

Paul Tabard had one more stop to make; one more house to sell silk to and one more chance to make his bonus for the month of August. He rode an old horse that had seen finer days, sold in its old age to plod around the countryside leading a donkey piled high with silk.

It was a puzzling house at the end of a long, winding drive. He had seen glimpses of it; teasing snatches; one a grand vista, the next a building site frozen into immobility. As he got closer, he noticed the lack of any builders and wondered what terrible dispute had led to them downing tools and leaving the site.

The truth was worse than he could ever imagine.

"We cannot afford any silk, young man," Tomkins sat heavily in the chair.

"I could leave a few samples for another time, maybe." Paul could see the weariness of defeat on his grey features. Even his words sounded grey. Grey was the colour of imminent death. It was not the colour of death itself. That colour changed constantly; a kaleidoscope of the most vibrant to swirl and snatch the unsuspecting soul. But it was proceeded, in most cases, by the relentless growth of grey; skin, voice, mannerisms, optimism, demeanour, all with a creeping grey pallor, until there was nothing left of the old, colourful self.

"It would be a waste on us and would just tease our senses terribly. There is little point in leaving samples, young man."

"What has happened here?"

"You don't want to know."

"I do, Mr Tomkins. Perhaps there is something I can do to help."

"There is nothing anyone can do to help. It's too late for that now."

"Who do you have there, Tomkins?" The rich aristocratic voice sailed down the half-complete staircase; the structure was there but no stair rail and no decoration, so that it seemed the

146

surviving depiction of the Littles at their ancient feast was at risk of toppling into the grey nothingness of new plaster all around. Paul looked up the staircase from the hall and saw the scene for the first time, his eyes drawn by the contrast of vibrant colour as the Little family of old made merry.

"Just a representative of a silk merchant from Dorchester, Your Grace. I've suggested he leaves as he is wasting his time here."

"I would like to see his offerings if it is not too much trouble." Penelope was now down the stairs, followed by a young black maid a few steps behind, with a long, fading scar down one cheek, raised like the furrow in a field. Penelope turned to that maid and asked her if she would not like to see a little silk to brighten the day?

"Oh, yes please, Your Grace," Sally said, arms clasped in front of her and eyes fixed reverently on the floor, as if she knew her place very well indeed. But Paul picked up on another side to this scene immediately. There was something about the way the aristocrat talked to her maid. If this lady and her maid was so true and proper, why the dishevelled hair on the lady and the crooked, un-ironed apron on the maid? It was as if they had both been in their beds and then rushed downstairs to see what the new arrival brought. Yes, both were breathing too heavily; he could hear it across the hall now that they were downstairs.

"I would be delighted to show you some of the new imports, Your Grace."

"Come then, sir." A small procession formed. The Dowager Duchess led the way to the library, followed by Paul a few steps behind. Sally only started moving when a reasonable gap formed between her and Paul. Mr Tomkins came last.

"Mr Tomkins, I am sure you have things to do and will not welcome the distraction of some silly girls drooling over silk samples." Penelope looked at her maid as she said 'silly girls'. The mischievous look was supposed to be private but Paul caught its tail end and the full facial response from Sally.

"Yes, of course, Your Grace." He turned to leave and Sally jumped to hold the door for Tomkins.

"Would you like me to bring some refreshments, Your Grace?"

"Go quickly, Sally dear, this is to be your treat as much as mine." Then she turned to Paul and said "You do know, sir, that we are unable to buy today but would welcome a short viewing in the hope of happier times to come?"

Quite why Paul responded as he did, he would never know. It was not his stock to give away and would have to be paid for out of his slender savings. "I would happily give some small samples in exchange for an understanding of why your circumstances are so… well, I mean to say…"

"You mean to say, reduced, sir, reduced to poverty and despair." It was a statement rather than a question.

Paul blushed and took his eyes, like Sally's, to the ground, expecting to be dismissed from the room for insolence. But his eyes, in their downward movement, met Sally's on their way up. Both sets locked. Paul saw lots of things in that instant. He saw the superficial shine of excitement at the prospect of viewing the silks. He was used to that anticipation. He saw a cheeky, irreverent stance that most would understand as cocky. But deeper, far deeper, he saw a strength of character that surpassed anything he had seen before. She was everything rolled into one: frivolous, cheeky, excitable, calm and robust.

Her character bounced around inside the body of a demure maid whose tasks were to keep her mistress' clothes in order, prepare her bath and brush her hair. And, at that moment, Paul knew he had done the right thing to make the offer. He also knew that Sally, whatever the peculiarities of her relationship with her mistress, had significant influence over the Dowager Duchess.

They sat a long time in the library. First the two girls went over the silks, exclaiming at the beautiful colours and soft feel of the luxury material. Penelope was tempted to buy something for Sally but knew it would be rejected as an unnecessary expense. Sally, acting through Tomkins, had been the main cutter of the household expenses, suggesting time and time again that they could do without a lot of the things that Penelope considered essential. It was Sally who, despite her playfulness when alone with Penelope, had gone over the figures and told her mistress

148

to pay the fines imposed under the contract from her own pile of cash as Alice could not meet the bills.

"And so, we have settled our immediate debts but the Dowager Duchess has only twenty pounds left in the world and Lady Roakes has nothing between herself and the poor house. If you give us a sample in exchange for the explanation we have given, I will have it sold in Blandford. We will only get sixpence on the shilling but another sovereign will assist us no end."

Paul sat back and stared at the maid, standing with her hands still clasped yet demonstrating enormous determination.

"What can I do to help?" he asked, then thought that was exactly what Sally had wanted to hear.

There was a considerable amount, it turned out, that Paul could do. Although still not yet twenty-five years old, he had spent all his working years developing his skills in contract law. His help started with the obvious.

"I could look at the contracts and see what possible avenues there are to escape the fines. I don't hold out any hope but it is worth a look."

"We cannot pay you, sir."

"Your Grace, I do not require payment, just..." Here, thought Penelope, came the crunch.

"Just what, sir, do you require?" said with a sharpness even she had not intended.

"Just the satisfaction of undoing a crooked contract, Your Grace, nothing more. Believe me, I have my reasons to want to undo wrong." Paul told them a sanitised version of the takeover of Sanderson and Sanderson, gliding over the extreme violence that had resulted in the death of his old master. Sally sat down during this recounting without being asked, then took hold of Penelope's hand, confirming what Paul had increasingly suspected.

But, like Lady Roakes and several others who knew their secrets, he did not care what they did so long as it did not hurt others. His morality sat oddly with established religion and seemed to be spreading to others like wildflowers.

Or weeds, depending on your point of view.

Tomkins was called back in and asked to get the contract. Paul spent three hours alone with it, quill and paper to hand, making notes, sometimes furiously. At other times, he sat back pensively and stared out of the open window so that Penelope, on checking on him, wanted to remind him of his chosen task and duty.

But she did not.

Tomkins also waited patiently, sensing that some good unwinding might come from this young man.

Which in time it did.

Chapter 23

They arrived at the priest's house in the middle of the night. They had chosen this time deliberately, hiding in the woods, not wanting to risk detection despite their magnificent disguises.

Four donkeys carried them from Londonderry to Ballydalgagan. Four tired donkeys carrying three monks and a nun. They knocked on the door of the priest's house at half past two on a moonless night with heavy clouds adding to the darkness.

All four of them felt like secret agents, sneaking around in the dark.

They had, apparently, outwitted their pursuit. Five men they now recognised easily had galloped past them on the second day. The only action Bridget took on seeing them was to pull her habit closer down over her face, then bend her head down as they pushed past, as if in prayer. On flicking her eyes halfway up, she noticed the other three doing similar; Thomas and Tristan were even fingering rosaries while simultaneously controlling their reins, as if born to Catholic rites of prayer.

Franshaw was the fifth of the bunch and he looked thoroughly miserable. He trailed the others by thirty yards. Every so often he spurred his grumpy horse into catching up.

Franshaw slowed as he drew level, letting the four giants on their heavy horses charge further ahead.

"Have you seen any Protestants, three males and a female? They would be travelling fast, no doubt."

"No, sir," Sister Mary Bridget replied.

"No, sir," said Brother Tristan, then added that there was no point waiting for the other monks to answer as they had both taken vows of silence. He did not add that he had imposed those vows just moments before lest their English accents give them away.

"You know, the four we seek were both brave and intelligent.

I admire that in people. They were about your age and build too, I would say. I can't predict whether we will ever find them but try we must."

"We will pray for justice for all involved," Bridget said, inspiration chasing the words out of her mouth.

"I am sure you will, now I must get on my way and catch up with the others. If they are left alone, who knows what they will get up to. Remember that I am the voice of reason and restraint within this unhappy party."

"Then we will pray doubly for you, my son."

Franshaw kicked his grumpy horse forwards, turned back as it accelerated.

"I really can't say if we will ever find them. Even four devout Protestants can lose themselves in this sea of Catholics. I did not counsel for these steps. I favoured reason and restraint."

"Go with the love of God, Mr Restraining Reason," murmured Thomas under his breath, thus breaking his vow of silence within minutes of taking it. But the wind that blew spatters of rain in their faces, took his words and lost them in his habit so only odd syllables escaped and they scattered in harmless directions.

The donkeys had stopped when Franshaw reined in his horse to talk. They remained motionless until Franshaw's body blended with his horse in the far distance.

"He knew," breathed Tristan quietly, as if the enemy could hear over hundreds of yards of field and copse, along roads and over streams.

"He knew," said Matthew. "And I will pray for his soul despite the evil he committed against us last year."

Cartwright was distinctly lucky in his unluckiness. He had failed to silence Matthew Davenport and his friends yet had persuaded Jensen that he was the best one to go to London and explain what had happened.

This was doubly lucky for it gave him the entire voyage to put together his story. The essence of that story was that he was entirely surrounded by idiots, whose incompetence had ensured failure from the outset, despite his very best efforts.

A chain is only as good as its weakest link.

"If it were not for my careful planning and diplomatic skills, there would have been a public outcry when Davenport and his cronies were attacked. I don't believe that throwing brute force at the problem will work. You need a combination of aggression with careful planning."

"And you think you have those skills?" Parchman asked.

"Undoubtedly, sir."

Too late, he realised his mistake, tried to backtrack but sounded feeble in his insistences.

"I want you to take over in Ulster. I'll draft a letter dismissing Jensen. You will take that letter back and run the operation properly. Give him fifty pounds from the company's chest; we don't want sour grapes spoiling the wine!" Parchman started to write on a clean piece of paper, then thought better of it. "I'll need to give Jensen's letter some consideration. I need to find a way of keeping him content despite his dismissal, there's too much at stake here for continued failure." Cartwright assumed his employer meant the money, which was flowing in nicely, but Parchman was thinking of something much more important.

He was thinking of the work Simon Taylor was doing so brilliantly. And then he thought of Alice Beatrice becoming destitute. In his fantasy, she came and begged from him and he tossed scraps of his dinner for her to gobble up like a street dog.

He stopped listening to Cartwright's insufferable whine, despatching him to his London lodgings, wherever they were, with an instruction to return in the morning and be ready to sail back to Ireland. His attention was taken up with stage two of his plan. Stage one, bringing down Alice Bloody Beatrice, was well advanced, so it was logical to move on to the next objective.

Cartwright left Parchman's study, thinking more than ever that his employer was going mad. He had a fixed stare and a dribble down the right-hand side of his chin that fell, drop by drop like a melting stalactite, onto his collar.

He also thought he was lucky in his unluckiness for another reason. He was being sent straight back to Ireland when he had hoped to resettle into London life. But, he was being sent back in charge, replacing the indolent Jensen. He would enjoy walking him out of the branch office of Sanderson and Sanderson and then doubling the income of the business in no time at all.

Father O'Toole was a heavy sleeper. The knocks on his door woke the housekeeper who lived next door. But the knocking made no impression on him. He had to be roused by the housekeeper, who had a key to the presbytery, and thought the world was coming to an end.

"Not a word of this to anyone, Mrs O'Keefe."

"Of course not, Father." But they both knew it would be around the village before most people had eaten their porridge and shoved on their boots for the new day.

"We don't have much time." Father O'Toole may have been hard to wake but, once so, he was all alertness. "Mrs O'Keefe, please come back in here." He called her from the hallway into the dining room. "These brothers and sister have travelled a long road to tell me of the illness of my brother…"

"I did not know you had a brother, Father." Her eyebrows raised to emphasise that it was a statement rather than a question. Father O'Toole noted it with a wince; she was going to be hard to keep quiet. Then she moved into question-mode. "And, dare I ask, Father, why send a nun all this way, indeed, why send four religious when one or two would suffice?" They were a pair of very good questions. Father O'Toole chose to ignore them for the greater interest was at stake. He was about saving lives through building bridges between Catholic and Protestant. He could not understand why everyone sought to tear those bridges down.

"I have one brother. He is Abbot of St. Joseph's. I believe it is a half-day's ride south of Rouen in Normandy, although I have never been there. He is dangerously ill and I have to leave immediately. Would you be so kind as to make some breakfast for all of us and then we must be on our way. There is no time to spare if I am to see him again this side of the afterlife." He had just lied, inventing a non-existent brother, so had no reason to expect to meet him in any afterlife, still less in Heaven.

Father O'Toole played it as cleverly as he could. He had recognised Tristan and Thomas immediately, seeing through their monkish disguises. With Mrs O'Keefe in the kitchen preparing a grudging breakfast, he ushered the others out to their donkeys, tethered to a bush by the front door. "Go due east," he said, pointing into the night sky. "You'll come across an inn called the Sleepy Hollow in about six miles. It's in a hamlet called Hotherington. I'll meet you there for breakfast and further planning."

They slipped away while Mrs O'Keefe fried eggs and slices of ham. She dreamed of being the centre of attention, relaying news about the four strange people who had come in the night, knocking on the door of the presbytery with some tale of a sick brother never mentioned before.

Mrs O'Keefe's suspicions were, inevitably, magnified when she carried two heavy trays to the dining room to find nobody there except the priest.

"I sent them on early to get good horses to take us westward for a ship for France." But he could not meet her eyes as he spoke another mistruth.

Father O'Toole had one more weapon to use; that of time. And this needed precise calculation. How long would it take four people on tired donkeys to cover six miles? And how long for him to cover the same distance on a fresh horse? How long would they wait for him before deciding to go on alone? Or would they – perish the thought – come back for him, thinking him detained and in need of rescue?

There was another time calculation to consider. When would Mrs O'Keefe deem it acceptable to go to others with her tale? Subjectivity crept in here. He doubted she would dare wake the likes of Murphy so she would probably wait until breakfast was on the table, maybe 7am. He checked the clock on the mantelpiece and made his decision after considering the angles and lengths of the triangles in his mind.

"Mrs O'Keefe, thank you for getting up at night and cooking this sumptuous breakfast. I've reconsidered and decided that there is little point in hurrying. I shall go back to bed while they travel westwards on their donkeys. I will easily be able to catch them in the morning on my horse. I arranged for them to wait for me at the big tavern in Rhiannon by the river. That is fifteen miles and will take them all the rest of the night and into the next day." He looked her over, concluded he had not satisfied her, but his next words went down much better. "Moreover, perhaps I will see things a little more clearly in the morning. I must admit, the shock of all this happening has thrown me."

"Quite so, Father."

"I never was much of a one for sensible thought when woken in the middle of the night. Why, they might be criminals out to kidnap me. Or they might even be Protestants trying to travel through Ireland without being captured."

"They were not Protestants, that is for sure. Two of the brothers never stopped fumbling their rosaries."

"Did they now? You see, I missed that and was starting to think they were. I'll tell you what I shall do, Mrs O'Keefe. I shall go to bed now, having partaken of your delicious breakfast. Then, in the morning, I shall walk up the road and consult with Mr Murphy as to what is best to do." He noted the nod of approval from his housekeeper; round one had gone to him. "There is one other thing," he decided to press his luck. "I do not believe Mr Murphy will be happy should news of this get out prior to his being briefed by me."

"Mr O'Keefe will want to hear why I was roused in the middle of the night, Father. I am surprised he is not banging on the door right now, demanding to know why his wife is called upon at such an unearthly hour." The truth was far from her conjecture; Mr O'Keefe was not inclined to bang on any doors at three o'clock in the morning. He had rolled over and fallen back to sleep the moment Mrs O'Keefe had left the bedroom. Father O'Toole suspected this and sensed round two within his grasp.

And it was the best of three rounds, he decided that moment, while standing up and stretching to make his point that the discussion was almost over.

"Mrs O'Keefe, perhaps you would consider accompanying

me to Mr Murphy's house after I've caught up on some sleep. You are clearly much more observant and perceptive than me in these matters and I am sure will be able to aid Mr Murphy in his decision-making more ably than I."

Mrs O'Keefe let herself out of the presbytery a few minutes later, chest puffed and head full of what she would tell Mr Murphy in a few hours' time. She did not try and sleep, Mr O'Keefe would now be taking up the full bed anyway. Instead, she went to her kitchen. To the rhythm of his snores echoing through the floorboards from above, she opened the basket she had brought with her and set about resurrecting the priest's largely uneaten breakfast for her husband later that morning.

Waste Not and Want Not for the Lord Giveth and the Lord Taketh Away.

And today the Lord promised considerable excitement drilled into her dull life.

Chapter 24

"Milly, I have been foolish."

"No, miss, I mean My Lady."

"I have, indeed." Eliza Davenport took Milly's tiny hand in hers and guided her towards the woods that bordered the lawn circling all four sides of Bagber Manor, her ancestral home, the centre of her estate, although that description, she contemplated, was more figurative than accurate; her land originally had Bagber Manor as the centre but recent purchases had been skewed towards the south and the east. This year alone, Simon Taylor had acquired almost two hundred acres just beyond the delightful village of Okeford Fitzpaine and another two small farms on the other side of Okeford Hill.

Was she deliberately stretching out towards the Great Little estate? Or was it coincidence that no land had become available other than in that direction? She did not choose the land; Simon was in charge of acquisitions.

Which brought another matter to mind; yesterday she had had a strange conversation with Simon Taylor. He had seemed distant in explaining why the cost per acre had risen so dramatically.

"Eliza, we have to pay market rates and these have risen dramatically. You have asked me to continue acquiring land…"

"But not at any cost, Simon. You have used up most of our liquid capital on recent purchases, leaving me nothing to improve the land you have purchased. This is contrary to our arrangement."

"Far from contrary, Madam, I have stuck to the letter of our agreement and require the commission as promised. If you do not have the money, you will need to borrow it." Was he talking about borrowing to invest in the land or borrowing to pay his five percent?

And where had his slurred speech gone? He was fluent and

coherent, like the slick lawyer he had been before. The only thing that marked him out as an invalid was his chair with the smooth wooden wheels on either side

"Who did we buy the Okeford Fitzpaine land from, sir?"

"I do not recall, Eliza. I will have to look it up next time I am at my desk." As he spoke, Eliza turned back from the window with its view of the woods beyond the stream. Did she see him raise his eyes to the ceiling? Had their relationship suddenly deteriorated? Was that hate he was now struggling to contain? She knew much of both contempt and hate. She wished that Matthew was here, or Thomas or Henry or her father even, back from the grave for his little girl. She was determined to fill the second part of her life with lighter things; fun and laughter, friendship and love, yet here was a great weight of hate thrown straight at her.

"Please do, sir." Her voice trembled. Could it really be that he did not remember who the seller had been? Why hide it from her?

They had left the conversation there, Eliza wanting to control the next steps, feeling wounded at Simon's turn against her. As his capabilities in speech and reasoning had improved, it appeared that his old ways were returning. She had thought him changed.

As Eliza and Milly walked, mistress and servant, towards the woods, she squeezed the hand she held, for a moment thinking it was Matthew's and wondering how his hand could have grown so small. She had not heard from him in weeks, just a quick note from the port when he had left for Ireland. He had said he would be two or three weeks but that time had passed. Was he lying in some miserable ditch, body rotting to make food for the crows?

Was he no longer, this sudden love of her life? The man who she had chosen to be a partner?

"You are crying, My Lady. Does something trouble you?"

"Nothing of any consequence, Milly my dear, except my foolishness."

"You are never foolish!" Milly broke away from Eliza's grip impetuously, as if she needed to break the manual bond in order to stress the emotional one of admiration. "Sorry, miss, My Lady, I mean." She sprung ahead on the path, for they were in the woods now, having left the Bagber lawns behind. She turned in order to look into her mistress' face; her earnestness was just as weighty as Simon's hate had been the day before and was sent with just as much force.

But Simon had had two weapons; hate and contempt. Milly had just the earnestness of her love; shield and sword against shield alone.

"Milly, I don't think you will ever get the way to address me correct!" Eliza smiled, her eyes shining like a watery rainbow through her tears. "I'll tell you what troubles me, seeing as you did ask."

Eliza told of a problem third on her list of worries; the reason, she supposed, for taking Milly's tiny hand and steering her into the woods. Topmost was concern for her husband. Second was her financial problems; these had grown up almost overnight. One minute she was wealthy, the next short of cash.

But these were not problems to share with a fourteen-year-old girl in her employ. Instead, she spoke of what she imagined was top in Milly's mind and third in her own: rash promises to do something with Milly's family's situation. She had stepped in to help, certain she would manage something. But she had drawn blanks from both approaches.

"The Duke had no interest in helping whatsoever, while the Dowager Duchess wanted to help, I believe, but is hopelessly ensnared in her own problems, or rather the problems of Great Little. Why do you laugh, Milly? Has something I've said amused you?"

"No, miss, it's just such a funny name. How can something be great and little at the same time?"

"I don't know, Milly, I really don't," she laughed back, turning her tears to steam. "Unless, I suppose, you could have something great in some aspects and little in others. For instance, a fast horse that wins lots of races is undoubtedly great but if it develops a weakness, say… a fear of jumping… then it becomes little. It is great at competing on the level but a disaster at the steeplechase or across the farm where there are hedges everywhere."

"Yes, I see, miss."

"But what troubles me, Milly, is I just cannot see what to do about your family's problem. It would take a few thousand pounds to buy Ashenham, in fact my interjection on behalf of your family has probably increased the price markedly."

"Something will turn up, miss, it always does. If you do the right thing each day, God will take care of things for you, My Lady."

Wise words from a sapling of a girl.

The harvest was excellent at Great Little that year. The sun and rain co-operated beautifully to give strong yields from the middle of August onwards. They all worked hard, Alice Roakes first among them; she was a city girl, having spent all her life in Bristol before meeting Sergeant Roakes at Sedgemoor and then moving with him to London. But she learned quickly. Her spirits rose with each cartload of grain despatched to the barns. She did figures and extrapolations in her head as she worked, checking them with grim-faced Tomkins or Penelope who, despite no farming background, seemed to understand the essentials innately.

"If this keeps going, we might be able to trade ourselves out of difficulty," she panted, as she threw herself down under an oak that had provided shade for countless generations of harvesters.

"I'm hot, tired, itchy and irritable!" Penelope flopped down beside her friend, standing again as soon as Sally came around with cold water and a basket of fresh cherries. Penelope made to take the load from her servant.

"Sit down, Penny. If you jump up every time Sally comes on the scene, someone out there is going to put two and two together. I am sure that Sally can serve us with cherries and water quite independently of any help."

"It's just that I thought she might be tired, is all."

"I'm fine, Pen," Sally said, while doing an exaggerated curtsey for the benefit of the farmworkers stretched out under various duplicate oaks that dotted the huge field. Even with so many working from sunrise into the night, they would be a week in this field.

But it would be worth it. The price of grain was high and the quantities were surpassing anything heard of in recent times.

"Lady Roakes, might I have a word?" Sally and Lady Roakes had been assigned by Tomkins to load the cart with bushels of straw, newly separated from the ears, like parents whose children had been taken from them. They had quickly devised a way to handle the heavy bundles and were working to a rhythm; bend using the legs, for the back would not last long at such a task, grasp the bushel, spring with those legs and add to the momentum by swinging the arms upwards and forwards just before the legs reached the peak of their thrust. The bushel would leave their hands and sail upwards, over the rim of the cart, and land roughly in the correct place. After an hour, they had the nuances just right and could position the bushels exactly with tiny movements of their feet to change the direction of travel.

Penelope had the job of tying up the bushels ahead of the pair who swung them into the cart. She had time to look back at her friend and her lover working together. Sally was wearing her old red dress that seemed to reflect the sun in two ways. It shone a red hue down onto the wheat stalks she worked on. But it also, mysteriously, changed patches of brown skin to make them almost purple in the sunshine. Penelope's blood rose. She dropped the knife she had to cut the twine, fumbled for it and was behind in her task; she inadvertently broke the rhythm of the swingers. Alice looked at the sun ahead, shielding her eyes and shaking her head.

"We will break for lunch. Yes, Sally, you may have a word."

Penelope found her knife amongst the stubble and straightened to see Sally and Alice walking towards the stream, where a nurse held young Sir Beatrice. She had three more bushels to tie but she wanted to be by the stream, with Sally.

You are mine, Sally Black, all mine.

She meant it doubly so. Sally was her lover. But nobody but Penelope knew that she was also her slave, bought and sold like the ears of corn torn from the stalks that had borne them.

She had the paperwork to prove it.

Alice took the baby and Sally cooed over it, marvelling at the contrast between skin colour as she took his hand and traced her finger up his arm.

"Lady Roakes, I have been assisting Mr Tomkins with some matters of the estate."

"I heard so from Tomkins."

They were talking through Sir Beatrice, rather than directly between themselves, as if the baby boy could absorb their awkwardness and radiate back calm to each other.

"Such a pretty baby, Lady Roakes."

"Yes, quite so." *And he may have no inheritance due to my mismanagement of the fortune left by my husband.* "What did you want to say, Sally?"

"I've also spent some time with Mr Tabard, going through the contract. It seems watertight in most regards." Paul Tabard had been to Great Little four times in the last few weeks, poring over the documents and going away again to beg his firm's lawyers for use of their library. The fact that he had sold more silk than the principals in the last two months helped them tolerate his absences but their patience was strained. "There are one or two points he is following up on but it seems like we will have to honour the contract this year and next and then will be free again. I've done a calculation, Lady Roakes." She hesitated, placed her hand in her pocket, started to withdraw it and then placed it back again.

"Please show me your calculation, Sally, I would be pleased to see it."

She read it after the harvest work that night, three candles glowing in her bedroom. When she got to the part about economies, she got out of bed and blew out two of her three candles.

Sally had plotted a way through. It involved enormous economies but it could be done; provided prices maintained their recent highs there would be just enough. She blew out the final candle and let the darkness take her tears of relief. Sally had put an enormous amount of work into her plan. Alice had been lost completely as to a way forward and now Sally Black had presented her with one. She snuggled into her bed, feeling hope for the first time in months. The harvest was half in and Tomkins said prices were remaining high. Grimes and Co would have to dig deep in their pockets for the grain; that would be their saviour.

That was the night the main barn at the home farm caught fire. It held half the grain they had harvested. The Harris family and all the workers on the estate worked through the night. Penelope was woken and said not to wake Lady Roakes. She went down with Sally and the household servants to help. There was nothing they could do. They saved a portion of the harvest but not enough.

"Our profit is gone," Tomkins reported gloomily.

"Then, Mr Tomkins, we will just have to work harder and economise the more carefully." Sally seemed a part of the night with her dark skin blending into the black and reflecting the flames as they were gradually brought under control.

The next morning, Alice came downstairs for breakfast, wondering where the servants were, thinking perhaps Sally had sent them all away in the night to make a start on her economies.

She heard the news from Penelope, waiting at the bottom of the main stairs where Sir John Little of old toasted his wife or mistress or someone with a long lavish wimple and a fair face, other than the piece of glass missing that made her right eye. Being one-dimensional, she had no left eye so was effectively blind, relying on the sounds of the feast to know what was going on around her.

Alice sat on the second-to-bottom step and wept. She had woken so full of hope and not even managed the stairs without it being dashed from her.

"Lady Roakes, we will get by, see if we don't." Sally had come quietly across the hall, her dress smudged with water stains, torn in places, smeared with dirt where she had scrambled countless times with pails of water. "Mr Harris thinks we have saved one quarter of what was in the barn."

Penelope sat on the step next to Alice, placed her arm around her and told her to weep.

"Later, we will assess the situation and decide what to do. Now, let your grief spill out for a while." She took Sally's hand in her other; both had burns that brought to mind the house fire at Great Little a year ago. They shuddered to think such could happen twice in so short a period.

The barn was ashes, as was Great Little itself last year, but from the ashes rises the phoenix, splendid and terrible, magnificent and fearsome.

For only those who know the depths of despair can know the power of hope.

Later on, while the servants and workers slept, Alice, Penelope and Sally saddled three horses themselves and rode to Home Farm. The ashes were still red hot, steam rising following the vast quantity of water thrown on the flames, but all three wore sturdy riding boots and could walk amongst the rubble and embers, although once Sally's dress caught fire at the hem and Penelope had to bash it out with her riding crop.

"Everyone came out to fight the fire?"

"Everyone, Alice, except your nurse who stayed with little Beatrice."

"Why did you not call me?"

"Because we wanted to save the harvest for you, or as much as we could, Lady Roakes. We decided that you had too much to worry about, too much weight on your shoulders, and we want to help share the burden as much as we can." Sally spoke the words that Penelope could never find. She looked at her lover, standing in her burnt dress with her frizzy hair loose and wild. Sally had a way with words, making them smooth with rounded corners but full of meaning. When Penelope tried to express herself, the words were sharp and angular, full of attack and vim. She sounded proud whereas Sally sounded humble. Was that what being a slave was about? But that made no sense for Sally thought she was free. She had no reason to behave like a slave.

They wandered a few more minutes; all three were lost in their own thoughts. Penelope kicked what had been a metal bucket. It rolled along the cobbled yard, turning a half-circle, due to one circumference being greater than the other. Maybe that was what it was like to be a slave; the bottom of a bucket. The slave went where the mistress, the larger circle, dictated and turned and span at twice the speed just to keep up. Yet it was always the overlooked one. Nobody fills a bucket by turning it bottom-side-up. Penelope looked across at Sally, who caught her eye and smiled gently. Sally was her base, her foundation in life. She was the stand the Dowager Duchess rested on. She was the strength while Penelope took the attention.

Maybe that was what it was to be a slave to someone like Penelope.

"Together we will build something both great and little," Alice said into the silence of the smouldering ruins.

"What do you mean, Alice? Great and little at the same..." But her voice faltered as Penelope understood what her friend meant.

What they rebuilt from the ashes would be great without being arrogant. It would be good for them but also good for the everyday people who lived and worked on the land. It would be a haven against cruelty and prejudice.

It would be Alice's redemption.

And it would be the making of Penelope.

Chapter 25

Some things work out completely as planned, some not at all. But most fall into a middling range, working out in part.

Father O'Toole's plan was in that middle range.

It worked in that it kept Mrs O'Keefe from running straight to Murphy's house, blabbing out her tale to any early riser she found on her way. If she had done so, a party would, undoubtedly, have left in pursuit of these strangers much earlier than they eventually did. Murphy, the organiser of most things in Ballydalgagan, was too aggressive behind that pretence of charm to do anything but strike out for a rapid capture. He would worry about the legalities later.

But it did not work because Father O'Toole had not taken the weather into account, surprising for an ex-sailor. The light rain of the previous day had intensified into the night. It stopped in the early morning for a few hours' catnap, just as the four fugitives were sent on their way to Hotherington, before resuming with force and weight at eight o'clock, moving slowly eastward.

But that gave enough time for Murphy to hear out the priest and his housekeeper, to wonder why O'Toole had so obviously delayed, then to inspect the scene for tracks. Those muddy tracks were still visible at a little after eight in the morning, despite the new rain just starting.

"It's clear they went east, not west," he said, pointing to donkey tracks in the mud around the presbytery.

"How do you know, Mr Murphy, that these are not the donkeys arriving?"

"Because the Lord God can do many wonderful things but I have never heard of him making donkeys walk backwards."

"We will go east," Murphy decided. "We will head for Hotherington and see what we find there." He gave Father O'Toole a long stare as he spoke. The priest found interest in a loose button on his coat, twisting the thread until the button broke free.

Murphy had collected an unofficial posse comitatus of willing volunteers, including the two who had guarded the door to the church when Thomas and Tristan had made their dramatic escape. "You, Father, will come with us."

"Why...?"

"Because you never know when they might have need of a priest, especially when we invite them back to share in our hospitality."

As is common with middling plans, Father O'Toole's had bought them a precious few hours. Those hours should have made all the difference.

The four travellers arrived at the Sleepy Hollow, to find it aptly named. The river Hother took a tumble down a steep hillside, rocks protruding through both grass and water, to the hamlet below, notched into the bottom. On the other side and all around, the hills rose even more steeply. The river, little more than a stream, bounded around with youthful exuberance. When it reached the hamlet, it turned abruptly back on itself and headed out the way it had come, veering to the south slightly where the lower land lay; it seemed to take one look at Hotherington and decide it was not a place to stay. In truth, there was nowhere else for the river to go for Hotherington was at the bottom of a vast bowl of steep-sided rock. The way the river went in and out again and the single road following the river, made that bowl like a saucepan, cooking up who knew what?

There was only one road into Hotherington, which meant the same road out again. The far side was too steep for anything but a mountain track. For a moment, Thomas thought maybe Father O'Toole had sent them into a trap. Block the road and there was nothing but sheep trails to choose from.

But, as they descended further and the steep hillsides rose like prison walls, he came to appreciate something else. In fact, it was Bridget who suggested the advantage first.

"Nobody on a horse could ever get over those hills." She indicated the vast natural amphitheatre with the hamlet at stage centre.

"There's only the road we're on," said Tristan.

"We have a good friend in that priest," Bridget commented.

"You mean that anybody pursuing us on horses will get left behind on those steep banks?" Thomas said. "Why, they're almost like little cliffs."

The hamlet of Hotherington had fourteen houses. At the centre was the inn, the 'Sleepy Hollow on the Hother' said a worn sign that did not swing in the wind, for in that hollow there was seldom any wind.

"Except when it comes down Road Hill," the innkeeper told them as he arranged a simple breakfast of cold beef and bread with a variety of pickled vegetables in large jars with ladles that barely fitted inside the neck of the jar. "Then it blows a veritable gale, funnelling down between the hills on either side."

"Is there another way out of here?" Thomas asked.

"You'd be okay on your donkeys. Maybe a sturdy little pony that was used to mountain tracks could do it but not your average horse."

Murphy and his troop of twelve posse members came on average horses. They came mid-morning, just in time to see four donkeys scrabbling over the loose stones that made the far slope.

"Halt!" shouted Murphy and the echo of his voice wound up the mountain. "We are friends… are friends… are friends… friends…" chased after the initial cry. They were dismounted now for even the donkeys struggled on the last part of the climb.

Tristan stood on a large loose stone, so as to be as high as he could be. He waved vigorously at the 'friend-figures' below, smiling broadly until he slipped off the stone and tumbled down the hillside. His head hit the scrubby ground with a crack but he continued his tumble down and down, limbs limp and floppy.

There was nothing to break his fall so he rolled a long way towards the bottom. Nothing to break his fall except Matthew and Thomas. Instinctively, they threw themselves down the hill in formation on their falling friend, one to the right and one to the left.

Down below, Murphy's mob had assimilated what was happening and were moving up the hillside on foot, using large daggers to grip the ground. They were fifty yards only from where Tristan came to a halt and making thirty or forty yards a minute, speeding up as they perfected their dagger-led climbing technique.

Matthew got to Tristan's still body first but Thomas slid to a stop seconds later. They both felt for a pulse.

"I've got one," Thomas panted. "He's alive."

"But unconscious."

"We're going to have to carry him, take turns." The thought of the four hundred yards' climb to the summit was enough to take hope away. Thomas turned; their pursuers were approaching fast and looked anything but friendly. Eleven men scrambled up the hill, each hoping to be the first to get there, each working on how to cover the ground the quickest.

Competition is a wonderful spur to invention.

Two figures remained at the bottom of the steep incline. Thomas was sure that one was Murphy and the other was Father O'Toole.

Was he friend or foe? Deliverer or executioner? At that moment the priest, slightly behind Murphy, waved at him frantically, urging them back up to the summit and safety. When Murphy turned around, sensing movement behind him, Father O'Toole turned his frantic wave into an elaborate stretch, then pulled his horse around and walked it slowly back to the inn.

But it gave Thomas the answer he needed and took away his doubt.

He hoisted Tristan over his shoulder so that his arms hung limply down to reach Thomas' ankles as he leaned into the climb. He did ten yards quite rapidly then collapsed, exhausted. Matthew quickly did another ten.

But they would not be able to go on like this. Murphy's eleven were now just twenty yards behind and below them. Sensing success, they spiked their daggers into the ground and heaved themselves up another foot in what had become a never-ending rhythm.

The rhythm of death, of disaster, of despair.

"Come on laggards," came Bridget's voice wafting down the hill, as if they were choosing a place for a picnic and getting hopelessly distracted by silly little things. They looked up, then both blinked and looked again. Bridget had brought a donkey down with her and was twenty feet ahead.

But the pursuers were now only twenty feet behind.

"Get his legs," shouted Thomas, grabbing the shoulders and lifting. Tristan's head lolled backwards, as if it might snap off his body and roll down the hill to give something to Murphy after all.

They manhandled Tristan between them, falling, cutting, scraping, but always up again for another yard. Bridget and the donkey were at the top of a five-foot cliff, with no way for them to get down. Thomas looked back as they reached the foot of the cliff. Murphy's men were only ten feet behind them, getting closer by the second.

Dagger in, test it, haul yourself up, turn to wrench the dagger free, dagger in again. They were like eleven moving parts of a giant machine, clicking and clacking as they ate up the ground.

"Matthew, lift now!" They lifted and Bridget leant down to add her desperate strength to their mission. She hauled while they pushed. She scraped her hand badly but did not stop. Tristan's body moved and moved further. Thomas and Matthew had their shoulders under the body now for extra shove.

Only their feet kept slipping on the rubble-like stones that littered the ground they were on.

One final effort and they had the inert body over the top of the five-foot cliff. Thomas scrambled up after him and dragged Tristan to the donkey, throwing him over its back with the last of his strength.

Matthew was a little less adept and paid for it with a nasty dagger slash on his left leg that bled profusely. Bridget hauled him up.

But it was not over yet. The men below, as if long rehearsed, started to pool their hands together to make a human pyramid. Four along the bottom so that two could stand on their cupped hands. That would allow one to scramble up and stand on the middle two. Then another and another. They would surmount the mini-cliff easily.

Only, their feet also slipped on the stones and when one collapsed the whole tower came down. Bridget, leading the donkey, looked back to see the chaos below. They now had fifty yards' lead and were increasing it with every step.

The men below tried a more thorough approach, clearing the stones first with their daggers and boots. Then they built the pyramid again and, this time, easily cleared the cliff.

But the lead now was substantial. They were safely at the summit. They mounted the other three donkeys and went clattering down the other side; then a long, gentle slope down, up and down again, ideal for horses, but Murphy's men were on foot and had no chance.

"How do we get around the hills?" Murphy asked the innkeeper.

"Oh, that's easy, sir. First, you go to Ballydalgagan. What's the matter, sir? Did I say something?"

They were on a plateau above the world, it seemed. They rode in a hurry for a mile and then Bridget, leading Tristan's donkey, came to a halt. Together, Thomas and she lifted Tristan off and laid him on the dry ground for the rain had dumped itself on the steep slopes and had nothing left for the plateau. Tristan opened his eyes, smiled at them and said, "I must have dropped off."

"Yes, Tristan, you certainly dropped off," Thomas replied.

Bridget pulled some biscuits and a flask of watered-down wine from her saddle bag and passed them around. Thomas walked over to Matthew and examined his wounded leg while Matthew stayed on his donkey.

"You'll live," he said with a brotherly grin and a slap on the donkey's rump so that he jolted forwards and almost made Matthew tumble off.

"We made it," Thomas said.

"I wonder," said Matthew, pointing at a cloud of dust in the distance ahead of them. Once he had straightened himself, he had the advantage of a donkey's height over the others. They watched as the dust cloud became visible to those standing on the ground and then grew. Horses were cantering towards them.

"Could they…?"

"No, the innkeeper was adamant that the only way around on horseback was to go back by Ballydalgagan. It's a three-hour trip at least. Perhaps these people are neutral, about some other business."

They were not. As the dust cloud formed into figures, they could make out, first, five people on horseback, then the size of four of them.

"It's our friendly giants," Thomas said.

"And Franshaw in the rear," Matthew added.

Five minutes later, they were circled by the four, Franshaw trying desperately to catch up by slapping his heels against the horse's sides. His horse seemed to play with him, trotting a little faster and then slowing to a walk. It would have been comic if the threat of the leering giants had not been right before them, circling like great birds of prey, or lions who knew their business and enjoyed it time and time again.

Bridget's intuition was probably the more advanced of their party. Certainly, she went through the following emotions over the sixty seconds before Franshaw acted: fear and apprehension gave way to a calmness that spoke of joy, of placing one's fate in the hands of God. But also, it smacked of tables turned and deceit or double-dealing. Then, seconds before he pulled the pistols, she sensed malevolence; evil, even.

"I've got two loaded pistols and two more in my belt," he said. At first no one was sure who he was talking to. The largest giant grinned and it spread to the others. "I want you brutes to get off your horses and let the reins loose. Drop your own weapons on the ground and take six steps to the west."

Nobody but the giants and Franshaw had horses. It dawned slowly on the giants that they were the target. Turning slowly, they saw the pistols aimed straight at the largest two.

But nobody moved. Nobody got off their horses. A moment of doubt swept across Franshaw's face. The smallest giant read it and reacted, yanking on the reins then charging his horse forwards.

Pistols don't go bang, they go pop. But the lighter sound is no less deadly. And Franshaw's aim was true. And a ball will enter a larger man, just as it would a smaller.

The giant who led the charge rolled off his horse and fell, dead, on the ground.

The other three froze, then dismounted with gathering motion and did exactly what Franshaw had told them to do.

"Mr Davenport, will you be so kind as to walk forwards and gather the horses' reins? I believe you will find these fine horses a more comfortable ride than your tired donkeys."

Thomas, too, did exactly as he was told. There were still pistols pointed at men and he did not want any other deaths.

Franshaw was polite and courteous; the public face of evil?

"Why did you do this?" Matthew shouted at Franshaw as five horses left the scene at a canter. Matthew had pushed his horse up to draw alongside Franshaw, who was streaking ahead.

"Let's just say I dislike rude and obnoxious people," he replied with his famous grin.

But a little later, when nine or ten miles separated them from the giants, he stopped his horse to make confession.

"I've been a bad person all my life. I just wanted to be on the other side for once."

"What will you do now?" Thomas asked.

"I don't know, Mr Davenport. I might go to America and try my luck there."

"Go there, Mr Franshaw," Matthew spoke up. "But remember your experience here today. Listen to your conscience for that is the Lord talking to you."

"Sure," replied Franshaw. "But it is hard to teach an old dog new tricks."

"It's the trying that counts," Tristan put in as Franshaw turned his horse to face south.

This time, when Franshaw kicked his horse, they did not watch until he had disappeared amongst the scrubby vegetation. Instead, they cantered on for Dublin and a ship to take them to England.

Chapter 26

Grimes was like Parchman in one particular aspect. Of course, he was a good match in the delight he took in cruelty or the total disregard for his fellow human beings, but where they fitted together even more closely was having only one name. There was minimal difference in their nomenclature, nothing of significance. Parchman had a name but did not use it, ever. Grimes very likely had a name but did not have the slightest idea what it was; maybe his parents, whoever they were, had never given him one.

He could have gone through parish records to find the entry of birth, except for two factors. He had no idea where he had been born, nor when. He supposed he was in his forties. He could remember Cromwell dying when he was a lad in the streets of London, shovelling shit for a living while others grew rich off the proceeds. Sometime after that he had been in a fight in Shoreditch. Someone had died and he had left London on a stolen horse, letting the horse run in order to get away as soon as possible; it seemed to know in which direction to go. It had come to Bagber Manor. He knew this to be the Merriman home for the saddle had a plate stating it to be owned by Lord Merriman of Bagber Manor at Sturminster Newton in Dorset.

He turned the horse in, claiming he found it on the road to Salisbury. He asked for a bed for the night and any odd jobs that needed doing. Lord Merriman had given him half a crown for returning the horse and offered him a position as undergardener.

He knew the year of the next great event in his life for it had been just after news of the Great Fire of London filtered into rural Dorset. It had been September 1666 when he had next killed a man. And that man was Lord Merriman, who had both employed him and housed him.

It was the first time he had met Parchman. He knew he was still young at that time, for Parchman had called him 'young man' repeatedly, almost in a fatherly way, although Grimes knew nothing of fathers.

Take that last statement back, Grimes, for you have watched Simon Taylor and the way he treats his daughter, Amelia. That was what had given Grimes the idea, the ambition, to wed with her and then he would be free to treat her in the same way. He cared little for money. If a windfall came his way, he spent it quickly, gaining entry to the dog fights or, on his day off, going to a seedy house in Dorchester, where everything was very much behind closed doors.

His wedding represented the deeds of ownership on a woman he could then treat exactly as he pleased. She was middle class and a Puritan; both of these made the prospect of marriage more entertaining. There were no limits with your own wife; property was protected by the law.

And now the time was rapidly approaching. The date was set and Taylor had been gloriously adamant that the wedding would take place. In a week, on September 5th, Grimes would be a married man.

This thought gave him great pleasure despite, or perhaps because of, the virulent cries of protest that shook the very foundations of Bagber Manor. Taylor had remained deaf to their anguished pleas; indeed, he had taken Amelia away to their town house "in order that I might get a bit of peace and quiet."

"Where will you live, Grimes?"

"In my cottage, of course." Grimes had never considered domestic arrangements.

"How many rooms does it have?" Simon would enjoy this conversation.

"It has two upstairs, sir. Then downstairs there is a small front room, a kitchen and a scullery at the back."

"She is used to living in a mansion." He ran his tongue around his mouth twice, clockwise then anti-clockwise, aware that he was short of breath. Amelia had become so confident of late, so superior since his stroke. It would be excellent to see her returned to total dependence on another.

"I know, sir." They both smiled, both anticipating the pleasure to come.

Eliza Davenport had refused to hold the wedding at Bagber. They would be married, instead, at St Gregory's in Marnhull and hold a brief reception at the Crown. From the Crown, it was a short ride by carriage or cart to Grimes' cottage on the northern fringes of Bagber Manor. Simon wondered what transport Grimes would think to arrange.

Elizabeth pleaded, begged, argued, shouted, nothing would work to change her husband's mind. She considered taking Amelia away and spoke endlessly to Eliza about it. They would have done so had they been able but Amelia was in Simon's town house and they could not get near her.

"Sir, could we not help her prepare for the wedding?"

"She has all the help she could desire," Simon answered. "I have hired a maid to help her." He knew exactly what they planned and would have none of it.

"What of her dress, of flowers and bridesmaids, sir?"

"She has a dress, no doubt. You ladies may decorate the church if you want to do something to make the scene pretty." The word 'pretty' was laden with contempt, his sentence spat out between closed teeth. There was no question of him being a stroke victim any longer. His diction was fine, his command of vocabulary likewise. He no longer pretended to need his wheelchair and had drawn satisfaction from smashing it to pieces with a sledgehammer.

Elizabeth prayed for relief for Amelia. She prayed that Simon would change his mind. She prayed that, God forgive her, a thunderbolt would come down from Heaven and strike Grimes dead. Then she prayed, her last forlorn hope, that Thomas would return and, forgiving the past, claim Amelia as his bride and take her far away.

Thomas did come back, but he came the day after the wedding. He and Matthew arrived on September 6th. They had landed two days earlier in Bristol after crossing the Irish Sea in a fishing boat well past its best. But the weather had treated them well. For their last six days in Ireland, rain had poured down constantly, heavy and unremitting with a wind that reached gale status.

"I think the wind is driving us out of Ireland," Thomas joked but it was a perfect wind for a quick crossing to Bristol.

On arrival, Matthew had used his remaining cash to send a fast rider to London.

"Make sure you report only to Herr Avercamps," he said. "Bring any message back to me at Bagber Manor in Dorset. Go to Sturminster Newton and ask for me there."

"Yes, sir." And the rider was away with a pouch containing Matthew's latest coded letter. Matthew kept the purchase and sale documentation for the boots, still unwilling to trust a stranger with the evidence.

Thomas went to his home in Sturminster Newton, the Browne cousins with him, while Matthew rode on for Bagber Manor and Eliza, his wife.

When the facts came out, Matthew immediately sent for Thomas. Thomas did not come at first, thinking it a ploy to get him back with Amelia. But the second messenger got a better response for it was Elizabeth herself. She strode into the Davenport family home that was part hers. After an introduction to the Brownes, she started the speech she had rehearsed during the ride over. It condensed all her thoughts since the spring.

"Thomas, you need to listen to me and you need to put all prejudices to one side."

"I saw what I saw."

"You saw what you saw, but not what the real situation is."

"I won't hear of depravity and…"

"Thomas, you must listen to your sister." Bridget Browne cut across him. "I can see she is much distressed."

Thomas listened, stunned into doing so by the command of someone he had come to respect considerably. At first, his attention was grudging towards Elizabeth then, quickly alarmed, he did put all prejudice aside.

Elizabeth covered events calmly and quickly; this lack of drama added to the drama, simple words creating horrific pictures in Thomas' mind. She told of Simon's mistreatment of his daughter over the years and of the gradual reinstatement of

178

her confidence after her father's stroke. She told of how lonely they both had been, restricted by Simon's twisted notions of ladylike behaviour. They had naturally rebelled and a part of that rebellion had been to bathe together, because they had known that Simon would disapprove. They had stripped to underclothes to bathe, partly practical and partly an enormous sense of freedom gained from shedding corsets, stays and petticoats. She told the truth about their temptation to lie together but how they had backed off and decided it was not for them. Both of them had then felt that, with the temptation faced and conquered, they were free to swim half-naked together whenever they wanted.

"It gave us a type of freedom, taking off all but underwear and lying in the dappled sun and shade by the edge of the stream."

Then, Elizabeth moved on to recent events, the sudden announcement that Grimes was to marry Amelia. The reaction to it and the unshakeable way in which Simon resisted all pressure to end the marriage contract.

"Two things struck Eliza and I about his approach and they conflicted somewhat. He seemed determined not to weaken in any way lest it prove the breaking of the dam, we suspect."

"And the second thing?"

"He seemed to enjoy it."

Finally, it had happened the day before in Marnhull.

"She cried all the way to the altar, throughout the service and back up the aisle. She was carried off in a farm cart after Grimes had several beers in the Crown. It was pulled by a plough horse! She turned as they trundled away and the look she gave me was agony."

"She is wed?" he spluttered, unable to take it in. "She is married?" Despite his recent anger, he had always assumed they would spend the rest of their days together.

"Yes, and the worst of it is he is a vile person who leers at her and has taken her from Bagber Manor to a dingy cottage on the estate that my husband arranged to be Grimes' home. I used to visit old Mrs White in the cottage next door and it is a miserable place indeed."

179

"Why would your husband...?"

"To get back at me, at Eliza, at you, even to spite his own daughter."

"It's utterly despicable. I've got to go and see her."

"You will not get in the cottage when Grimes is there. But you do need to see her, to comfort her and to tell her you finally understand that she is innocent of what you suspected her of." Elizabeth had been frank with Thomas in explaining the first time. But now that it was out in the open, she could not mention the alleged sin again; perhaps her acknowledged innocence put the thoughts they shared beyond words, to be skirted around. "It will not change her marriage status but it will give her considerable support to know you are no longer her enemy."

"I was never her enemy!"

"No, you are correct, brother. You were not her enemy but your own. And she is a victim of the war you held with yourself. She deserves all your pity and love."

"Your sister is right, Thomas," Bridget spoke for the first time since the explanation had begun. Tristan, from his place on the window seat, nodded his agreement.

"Then how do I visit her, sister?"

"Grimes travels often on business. You will have an opportunity very soon. Come with me back to Bagber and consult with Eliza also."

The sun shone brilliantly that day but brother and sister saw only grey as they rode the few miles to Bagber, the Browne cousins coming in support. They saw different things, but all washed and watered to a dull grey. Elizabeth saw Amelia's face, looking back in despair on the wedding-cart, silent pleading for someone; God, she supposed, to wind back time to before the fateful words:

Until death do us part.

I declare you man and wife. You may kiss the bride.

That first kiss had been terrible. She had struggled at the force of it, struggled more when he gripped her arm and pinched it between his fat but strong fingers. His breath had smelt of cheap brandy and the horrendous pipe-tobacco he was always smoking.

Thomas could see nothing but her thigh, fixed in his memory since the day he had gone to Bagber and got the wrong evening for church. If only he had checked the day, before setting out for Bagber.

But he had not, nor had he listened to Amelia's explanation. If he had, perhaps none of this would have happened.

Chapter 27

Parchman was excited to have cracked the code within an hour. He wanted to brag about it but he had sent Cartwright to Londonderry. Ferguson was not interested; had brushed him aside with a comment that he was tied up with his writing.

All Robert Ferguson wanted to do was to become more famous than Luke Davenport, the Presbyterian minister who had died in 1685 in Winchester Prison. He had been the father of Matthew, the man who had signed this letter he had just decoded. Not that the letter was signed in his name; even the signature was a clever manipulation of letters.

What had Luke written to make Ferguson so jealous? Some tedious stuff concerning man against man. Well, Parchman was a man set against most other men; perhaps he should have featured in Davenport's book of sermons.

What Parchman did not realise is that he did feature. Not in name but in type. And the type was not depicted in flattering terms.

But then Parchman would not have cared. He was an island. There was a causeway on the Island of Parchman. It reached out to the mainland only occasionally; limited contact for absolute essentials.

For instance, he would have to communicate with Taylor now in order to speed up the attack on Eliza Davenport, the wife of the author of this letter.

It was a neat world. Parchman copied Matthew's handwriting and used the code to write a new letter stating that Matthew had examined the operations of Sanderson and Sanderson in Londonderry and found them to be all in order.

'In their patriotic duty, Sanderson and Sanderson apply incredibly fine profit margins to their activities. I would recommend the Government increases their margins to make their business more sustainable. A twenty percent increase in prices should suffice.'

He chuckled at his inventiveness. A half of his share of the twenty percent would go to Simon Taylor for services rendered.

Vengeance is mine said the Lord.

No, thought Parchman, *vengeance is mine.*

Paul Tabard scratched his thinning hair and stood and stretched before returning to his task. He had begged half a day off work in order to make one last attempt to discover a loophole in the contract Tomkins had signed on behalf of the Great Little Estate. The senior partner had called him into his office to explain his frequent absences and Paul could only say that this was important to him. He did not know why. He was acting on instinct.

He had brought Amy with him. She had gone on a tour of the estate and would be back soon. He had hoped to find the answer to this contract on this last visit.

"Any luck, my love?" But Amy's question was met with a shake of the head. "If you want, we can go through it together. We will need to leave soon for home." It was a twelve-mile ride to Dorchester. In a carriage, it would take over three hours.

"Are you not too tired, Amy? Would you prefer to leave now and get back a little earlier?"

"I am tired but would prefer to rest a while here before travelling." He could not tell whether she meant her words or not. They were at the stage of loving when the other person's comfort or enjoyment was of absolute importance. Later on, they would move to telling the complete truth and their marriage would become all the stronger. But for now, they both put the other before themselves every time.

He rang the bell and tentatively asked Sally for coffee. Increasingly, she came when the bell was rung. Sally was eager to help out around the house as Lady Roakes had been forced to dismiss several of the servants.

But most of the time she worked with Tomkins on the great record books of the estate and reviewing practices to see where economies could be made.

"I tell you what," Amy said, trying to break the sombre mood she had found her husband in. "I'll read the contract out loud. You keep your eyes closed and say whatever comes to mind.

"You mean a game?" he asked disapprovingly.

"Yes, dearest, a game to lighten the moment but you never know when something might come of it. Sometimes the lightest things in the world produce the heaviest outcomes."

"That sounds very philosophical. Can you remind me where you got your education? That's right, it was the Red Lion, was it not?"

That got him a pinch on the arm, rapidly followed by a kiss on the same spot, just in case she had really hurt him.

But the pinch closed out the gloomy mood, like the book being snapped shut at the end of the story.

Paul drew back a chair for his wife, checking on her comfort. Then he sat himself and slid the contract along the table-top towards Amy.

"Close your eyes, now."

"But I can concentrate…"

"Just close your eyes, husband, or witness my terrible wrath."

"Yes, ma'am, sorry, ma'am." The fake humour revealed their desperation. In Paul's case, he was desperate to make a discovery, while for Amy it was desperation that her husband should be happy again.

Both made silent little prayers before Amy started reading.

"I'll start from the top."

"You can skip the first bit. It's pretty standard stuff. The detail starts in the third paragraph."

"I'll start from the top."

Amy could read, was used to reading receipts for deliveries in the Red Lion and several times had settled down with a book belonging to Mr Amiss but had never finished one. She stumbled over some of the complex phrases, such that Paul opened his eyes to assist several times.

The Parties to this contract, The Great Little Estate (hereafter Great Little) and Grimes and Company (hereafter Grimes) state and warrant to the value of the contract plus reasonable damages incurred by the other party that they and their principals individually and severally, are of good standing with regard to observance of the law in every regard save minor offences; furthermore, the Parties explicitly infer by entering into this contract that…

"What is it, Paul? Tell me what it is." Paul was standing, clearly in a state of transition. Was he moving towards elation or another level of despair?

"That's it!" he cried. "That's it, that's it, that's it!"

"What's it, Paul?" Amy had read the words, concentrating on pronunciation and flow, ignoring the meaning. She read them again.

The Parties to this contract, The Great Little Estate (hereafter Great Little) and Grimes and Company (hereafter Grimes) state and warrant to the value of the contract plus reasonable damages incurred by the other party that they and their principals, individually and severally, are of good standing with regard to observance of the law in every regard…

"That's it, Amy!" Paul stopped the little dance he had begun on the second reading and gave his wife a huge kiss on the lips; those were the lips that had read the words of hope.

Are of good standing with regard to observance of the law.

"You mean…?"

"Exactly, all we have to do is prove some serious breaking of the law at some time in the past and we can sue for the return of all money under the contract and damages such as legal fees. I'm not a lawyer, Amy, but perhaps we can even claim for damages incurred by the estate. I skipped the opening two paragraphs, considering them to be standard stuff. This is precisely what I have been searching for all this time and you, Amy, have brought it to me."

They were still kissing when Sally carried the coffee in five minutes later.

"Sir, you are celebrating. Have you discovered something of use to our cause?"

"Yes, Sally, I do believe Amy has turned something up." It was evidence, again, of the first stage of a loving marriage when everything was offered up to the other party with pure joy. New lovers were not interested in balance. "Could you be so kind as to call your mistress in."

"The Dowager Duchess?"

"Sorry no, I forgot. I meant Lady Roakes but the Dowager Duchess too, of course."

"Yes sir. I'll get them straight away."

On an afternoon in mid-September, Eliza and Elizabeth met, by arrangement, on the large slab of rock that overlooked the Divelish, tributary to the Stour that ran through Bagber Manor. It had been a dry summer and the river had reduced to a stream but still housed in the banks of a river so that it looked like the world was drying up.

"He's insufferable," Eliza complained of Elizabeth's husband. Since the wedding, he had moved back into Bagber Manor as if it was his own. He had ordered rooms rearranged and taken Eliza's favourite sitting room to be his personal study. "He's upset everyone in the house and dismissed two servants because they were not pretty enough. The worst thing is, I cannot do anything about it."

"Because of me?"

"Because of you, but do not think it your fault. No responsibility lies with you. He knows that if I complain, he will take you, my last friend, away to some awful place as he has done with Mealy."

"And with Matthew away in London and Thomas watching the Grimes house, there is no man able to stand up to him." Matthew, growing impatient at no message from the court, had decided to go to London to report personally. He should, perhaps, have gone at the start, only he had been so keen to reunite with Eliza that he had entrusted his letter to a messenger at Bristol docks. Now his impatience had caught up with him, forcing another absence from Eliza.

"Thomas told me that Grimes has barely left his cottage in the ten days since the wedding. And, do you know who comes to him?"

"No, Eliza, who visits him?"

"Why, your husband has been there almost every day, often for short meetings of a few minutes but twice for over an hour."

"Why on earth?"

"I don't know, Lizzie, but we must find out."

Thomas was deeply surprised by who had offered to help him watch the Grimes' home. The house was remote, situated with a matching cottage that once had housed old Mrs White but was now deserted. Nobody wanted to live so far from others and, latterly, nobody wanted to live where the only neighbour was surly and uncommunicative; plus, people remembered Grimes as a particularly hated gamekeeper appointed by Simon Taylor in 1680 and only dismissed five years later. Gossip made him out to be a sinister monster who had manipulated Taylor into marrying his daughter for some peculiar motivation they could only guess at.

It did not occur to those gossips that Simon Taylor did it out of greed; by giving away his daughter, he saved a fortune in salary and bonuses for Grimes.

The cottages were at the end of a long field that had been harvested several weeks before and its bareness sat like a stark reminder of the bleakness of one's intended destination, assuming one found a reason to make the trek to Grime Cottage, as it had started to become known.

Behind the pair of cottages was a small copse on a hill. This is where Bridget set up her 'Observational Station'. She worked out a rota between herself, Thomas and Tristan to watch the cottage day and night. Realising she needed more people, because it was best to have two observers at any one time, especially at night, she asked Thomas who he knew in Sturminster Newton that might help.

"Well, Matthew is off to London." He started with the obvious. "Eliza is deep in her own problems and Lizzie is kept at home the whole time by Simon." It sounded difficult to get the numbers up but then Thomas thought further. "I'll ask Big Jim and Plain Jane."

"Who?"

"They're good friends. Grace and I met them in Bristol. Grace is my other sister. She's the Countess of Sherborne. Big Jim and Plain Jane moved to Sturminster Newton and set up a very successful hauliers' firm."

They ended up with four new recruits. As well as Big Jim and Plain Jane, who were very small and exceptionally beautiful respectively, Grace and Henry, the young Countess and Earl of Sherborne, heard about the venture and joined up.

"We can discuss theology while we watch," Bridget said with a grin when she learned that all four of the newcomers were Catholics.

And they did, endlessly. The rota Bridget set divided up the watchers by overlapping their duties so that Thomas would start a session by joining Plain Jane, who already had been there a while. When she left, Tristan would replace her and then, two hours later, Henry would replace Thomas.

The rota cycle went on but with little to report other than the belief, gradually holding sway, that it did not matter what religion you wore, the important thing was tolerance of others.

And here views differed markedly for Bridget and Tristan, being essentially Anglican and, therefore, the established religion, felt tolerance was in an abundance.

"That's a typical view of the establishment," Big Jim, easily the most ardent Catholic in their band, said time and time again. "But try living life as a minority religion. We are excluded from office, from the army, from becoming a Member of Parliament or a judge."

"That's largely because James Stuart would go to all lengths to promote Catholics into every office. It's a backlash."

They agreed generally that it was a backlash, also accepting the view that James II had been the worst King of England since John.

"I know it's not religion, but look what happened in John's reign, the Magna Carta." Thomas veered the conversation away from theology out of a sudden observation. "And then, while not quite in James' reign, we have the Bill of Rights because of James. It seems a weak king is actually good for us common folk."

In quieter, less combative moments, when Thomas was alone with one of the Catholics, he would ask about their religion intently, feigning general interest but actually captivated by the beautiful Latin chant he had heard back in Ballydalgagan with Father O'Toole leading the proceedings.

And then, late on the fourth day, something did happen. Simon Taylor turned up. He stayed only seven minutes but he came early the following day and stayed over an hour.

"What does he want with Grimes?" Thomas wondered out loud.

"He used to employ Grimes, you dolt," replied Big Jim. "He was gamekeeper here, I've heard, when Taylor was the 'owner' of Bagber Manor." It had been an unhappy time after Eliza, the ancestral owner of Bagber, had apparently exchanged the valuable manor for a remote pig farm in Yorkshire, owned by the Roakes family. Roakes' parents had refused to sell but had mysteriously died one Sunday afternoon during an infrequent visit from their son, who was then a private soldier in the army and recently introduced to Parchman. This and the sudden death of Lord Merriman allowed the exchange to go ahead. Roakes had not owned the manor long, selling it by pre-arrangement to the old Earl of Sherborne, Henry's grandfather and the fountain of all this hate, stemming from the affair between Lady Merriman and the Earl's son.

The Earl had leased Bagber out to a series of tenants, not realising in 1680 that the new tenant was actually Eliza Merriman, the real owner of the property if the fraud was set aside.

Eliza lived there blissfully that summer, making friends with young Grace and Thomas, who used to play truant until they were both sent away to different boarding schools. But, before they were despatched, Lady Merriman suddenly disappeared. The manor was given to Simon Taylor for services rendered and he legally owned it for five years until Thomas and Grace found Lady Merriman and brought her back to claim her inheritance. Simon had employed Grimes as gamekeeper throughout that five-year period. Simon did not know it but Parchman had pushed Grimes forward, wanting his own man in the place.

And, as far as Parchman was concerned, Grimes had been a very useful plant.

But, as to what Simon wanted with Grimes now, nobody had the slightest idea. As far as they knew, Simon had dismissed

Grimes back in '85 at the height of the Monmouth Rebellion, for capturing him riding bareback on a donkey and hiding in his own woods. Grimes had enjoyed parading his master through the estate but had paid for it with his job.

Only, nobody knew that Grimes' real employer was not Simon Taylor but Parchman.

Chapter 28

Jacob Avercamps stroked his beard as he re-read the letter from Matthew Davenport. He could not say he knew Matthew well but had trusted him in the past and had a good feeling about the man.

But something did not ring true with this letter. There was something missing, or was it something extra? Or was it just different? He unlocked the drawer to his desk and pulled out the other three, laid them out in order of receipt on his desk, first to the left and the latest one to the right.

He looked first at the handwriting; all four letters looked identical. The paper differed but that was to be expected. Matthew would have picked up paper wherever he could on his travels in Ireland. Next, he examined the layout, word spacing and then the phraseology, the way the author put the words.

After twenty minutes, he sat back in his chair. Why did he have suspicions over the fourth letter in the series when close examination showed it to be exactly like the others?

He rose from his chair, feeling tired and homesick. He came from a small farming village in Holland, an obscure place that would not even have existed had it not been for the land reclamation that had made his father's fortune and given him and his brother an education. It had served him well but his younger brother had not been so fortunate. He had died a drunkard seven years earlier, having squandered his side of the fortune and then quite a lot more. Jacob had harboured his wealth, gradually increasing it, but with no real interest in business. Instead, he had gone into public service and worked his way up steadily, becoming a trusted adviser to William of Orange, now King William of England, Scotland and Ireland.

Now the trust placed in him was demanding an answer from these four letters and yet nothing came to mind.

He, probably like so many before him in that office, went to the window, seeking inspiration, seeking answers written in the glare of the late-September sun before it went below the buildings that circled the palace like a maze offering no way through.

Why was he doing this? He was quite young but could afford to retire, buy a house in the country and live off his capital. He would be careful, as he always had been. It had been a childless but happy marriage; perhaps it was not too late for his wife to have a child at thirty-six.

With a deep sigh that matched the setting sun, he returned to his desk, gathered the four letters and placed them back in the drawer. It was late, too late to worry about it. Perhaps tomorrow would bring an answer.

Michael Frampton, personal assistant to Mr Prendegast, had passed the manuscript from Miss Browne immediately to Mr Prendegast, sending it by an office boy to his home rather than waiting for one of his twice-weekly visits to the office. Then he turned to the letter, sent by Tobias Browne, her father. It was dated August 20th so had taken over a month in transit from Ulster to London.

Dear Mr Frampton,
I am the father of Miss Bridget Browne and am acting on her written instructions in communicating with you. These instructions were found in her lodgings in Londonderry by her host and handed to me during a visit to see our beloved daughter, much missed and worried over during the siege of the city about which she has written and we are now in correspondence.

It was a well-written letter by a man with education and a considered approach to life. Mr Frampton could see where Bridget got her calmness in adversity from. But the question in his mind was over the other facets of her emerging personality, the exuberance and the longing to give; were they part of her youth or another gem of her upbringing? He read on.

My daughter was not at her lodgings. My good friend who had housed her all these months had succumbed to disease during the siege but his wife informed me that four giants of men had descended upon their house and ransacked it. They sought any evidence of where Bridget had flown to with her "evil friends". They were led by a bluff red-headed man, who would have seemed quite well built had he not stood right by the giants. He looked remarkably like the old King Harry and made several comments about this likeness, as if proud of the fact; as if appearance alone rose him to the ranks of royalty. I say the giants were led but it seems they did what they pleased and caused much destruction to the house.

My friend's wife had spotted Bridget's instructions before the giants arrived and, as they broke down the door which was, incidentally, open already, she hid them behind a loose brick, itself behind the stove.

I will get to the point, sir, for I know your time is precious. The instructions said two things. The first is the simpler. If I heard from the firm of Prendegast and Son regarding publication of her account into the Siege of Londonderry, I was to send whatever was requested. Hence, enclosed with this letter is the original manuscript in full. I have taken the liberty of reading it and am very pleased with my daughter's work, although her suffering during the siege gives my wife and I considerable sorrow.

You are right to be pleased with her work, Mr Frampton thought, for she is clearly a product of her upbringing.

That sorrow is magnified and mixed with extreme concern by the second point she raises. She explained that a Mr Matthew Davenport had been sent by our King, no less. His mission was to assess without fuss the mood in Ireland and to examine the function of government in regard to the supply of the army loyal to the King; this latter task because the King is much concerned about corruption Lacking direct evidence of malpractice or fraud, he commanded Mr Davenport to either find it or clear the names of those involved.

Mr Davenport apparently landed in the south and made various reports back as to his findings. When he had finished examining the Catholic strength and disposition, he moved to Ulster, changed his *false name for another, and decided to take a job with a government contracting firm. He then sought lodgings in one of the rooms my daughter had latterly rented, having cut her occupancy from three rooms to one to make more space for others. By coincidence, the third room was to be occupied by my long-lost nephew, Bridget's cousin, Tristan Browne who had travelled up Ireland under some difficulty with a friend he met on his way, surprising us all for his parents had left Ireland forty years ago during the troubles and we barely knew of their son, having latterly lost contact with them.*

This friend of my nephew was the brother of Matthew Davenport, by the name of Thomas, hence the substance behind the assertion of coincidence. Bridget writes, somewhat cheekily, that Thomas is exceedingly handsome and spends some time looking at her. I suspect that my daughter is guilty of the same crime in reverse but I digress from the main point.

Mr Frampton, here the story hots up. The four of them, including Bridget, had to flee because Matthew Davenport had discovered some terrible corruption at a government contractor by the name of Sanderson and Sanderson. I have never heard of this firm and suspect they are new to the area. I would beg you to lay this before the King or his closest advisers. I stress closest advisers for it seems the bad practices emanate from London, where the main activities of the firm are. They very likely will have connections within the government in the capital. I am considerably worried about my daughter and would beg you to look out for her. She has promised to get word to me when she is safe and yet I have heard nothing. She said in her letter that she would try and get to England and that the Davenports were from the county of Dorset. I have never heard of it but have looked up Dorset in the atlas we have and see that it is in the south of the country.

Please Mr Frampton, do everything you can to find my daughter should she be in England. And, once found, for the good of King and country, please help in exposing this corruption.

I am, sir, your obedient servant in all matters,
Tobias Browne.

Immediately after reading the letter through the second time, Mr Frampton wrote a short note back to Tobias Browne, stating that he would do all in his power to assist and would, that day, leave for Dorset to find the Davenport family in the hope of getting information about Miss Browne's whereabouts. He sent another boy as a runner to Mr Prendegast's house, begging his employer for a short period of absence from work but not giving any information in case he made the old and very sick man worry too much.

He left the office, went home, hiring a strong, fast horse from the stables on the way. He explained to his wife, said he would be gone ten days, packed clothes into two saddle bags and took the road to Salisbury, thinking he would start at the top of the county of Dorset and work his way down.

Riding hard, he made it to Salisbury in two days. Saddle-sore and with an exhausted horse, he rested a day in the city but spent no time in the famous cathedral. Instead, he asked in every inn and every shop for news of the Davenports.

At half past six, he was close to the end of Fisher Street. There was a large house towering above the shops. He had enquired at the butcher's and the tailor's and that left just a tiny florist on the corner. No one in all his enquiries had heard of the Davenports.

"There was a girl here once, sir, I mean upstairs of course. It's a kind of school for young ladies. They learn how to be pretty adornments to their future husbands, so I understand, sir. I believe Mrs Ferrow had a cousin of sorts from Dorset who went by that name and his daughter attended the school some years ago. Would you like me to pop upstairs and ask? Very well, if any one comes in please say I will not be a minute."

The shopkeeper took eleven minutes, by which time Michael Frampton had served four customers and taken over fifteen shillings in orders.

"How did you know how much to ask?"

"I buy flowers for my wife every Saturday after work," he answered.

"But at the prices you've charged? You must come from London, sir." She did a calculation in her head, running her eye over the missing flowers. "I would have charged only six shillings and threepence for what you have sold for fifteen shillings!"

Mrs Ferrow was tiny but every bit as equal a talker as the much larger lady in the florist's below. She was the type whose age could not be determined, which Mr Frampton found a little disconcerting. More so, when she asked a series of penetrating questions, the answers to which would be circulating around Salisbury's middle-class circles within a quarter-hour of his departure.

But Mr Frampton held his own, sticking to a story he had prepared during the long ride down. He was an attorney seeking the Davenport family to inform them of a small legacy being held in London for safe-keeping. He reasoned good news was more likely to turn the family up but decided to keep the legacy small, in order not to encourage imposters.

"Grace Davenport attended my school here for five years. She is the daughter of my second cousin, Luke."

"Luke, you say? Luke Davenport? The famous sermon-writer who died in…" Mr Frampton was suddenly alert. He had not made the connection before.

"Winchester Prison in '85, a martyr to the cause of true religion, sir." As she asserted his martyrdom, Mr Frampton looked around her elegant drawing room. Nothing spoke of the Puritan persuasion. Mr Frampton would have put Mrs Ferrow firmly in the mild-Anglican stable.

"Of course, madam, as you so aptly put it." Luke Davenport had died awaiting trial at the hands of Bloody Jefferies. He had done nothing more than write and preach about what God expected of the people he had created while they spent their time on earth. Mr Frampton had long wanted to seek out his family for a particular purpose and now, it seemed, fate had given him exactly that. If Matthew was the son of Luke and he had been in Ireland, he must know something of Luke's Irish adventures forty years earlier, this being the information Mr Prendegast had long sought. Perhaps there were documents stored carefully?

"Where might I find the family, madam?" It seemed incredible that he might be able to make a connection and please old Mr Prendegast in the last few weeks of his life. For there was no doubt in Frampton's mind that Mr Prendegast would soon depart this world. It was now late September with the weather turning. Mr Prendegast had never liked the cold and Michael doubted he would see the winter through.

"Well, Grace was always excitable when with us but she did do very well."

Two and a half hours later, after tea and sherry, he declined the offer of supper and took his leave. He had the information he needed. Matthew Davenport had lived at Bagber since his marriage to Lady Merriman: "A good match indeed, if I am any judge," while Thomas resided in Sturminster Newton nearby. "He became a fine builder and took over the firm from Milligan when the older man retired. He started as headstrong as young Grace but turned out just as well, although he remains a bachelor."

Frampton's destination was less than a day's ride if he started early. He thanked his hostess, edging backwards as she talked. Finally, he reached the door. "Goodbye and thank you again, Mrs Ferrow." He was free to retreat down the steps to ground level.

As he made his way back to his lodgings, his head was full of that joy at possibilities unearthed that only the selfless can know.

Chapter 29

The first leaf to fall landed on Bridget's hair. It drifted down with no announcement. It was a chestnut leaf, large and floppy, so it looked like a new hat on Bridget's head; she had taken her own off and shaken out her long, black hair. Still green mainly but tinged with orange and brown, the leaf made a fine fashion statement according to Thomas, who was her companion on watch at the time.

They laughed about it, Thomas at twenty-two a little more subdued than the giggles of the nineteen-year-old.

Thomas leant forward on the groundsheet they were sitting on and adjusted the hat to a different angle, giving it a current-fashionable look.

"There!" he said. "Just right."

Bridget then leant forward and kissed Thomas on the lips. The edge of the leaf came down over her right eye, at an angle. It left the stalk hanging off her right cheek and it lightly scratched Thomas's chin as she moved into place for the second kiss.

They sat back and looked at each other. The world was utterly still, as if every creature was holding its breath to see what happened next. Even the wind stopped teasing at the thick block of leaves overhead, stopped its worrying at them and bent at the waist to have a closer look at Bridget Browne and Thomas Davenport, alone together in the copse one field north of Grime Cottage.

Would that wind later claim to have had a role to play in this scene? Or was it just the means by which some higher power unlocked something between two people? How much did God involve himself in every little detail of the stage he had built with his own hands, and the cast he had selected so carefully? Or were they just actors endlessly rehearsing for the Grand Performance on the main stage, way above their heads, where God lived with all the souls he had collected around him?

Only time would bring answers to those questions but right now it was the now, not the why, and the now did not care to give answers.

Very slowly, brown eyes locked on blue, they moved together again for a third kiss. This one was longer, as was the way with a man and a woman.

Bridget had said nothing since the leaf fall, Thomas just three words. Words seemed unnecessary. Words made questions and questions required answers. And answers needed more words, or else they hung there like sharpened scythes to poke at the unwary stumbling in the dark.

It was now. Now did not need words.

But no man is an island. Even Parchman, who thought he was an island, riding that moment up to Grime Cottage, had that causeway, that frying pan handle, to the rest of the world.

And if no man is an island, it stands to reason that no woman is either. In fact, women are generally more connected and more in need of those connections than the average man. They will build bridges whereas the man will wait for low tide and strike out across the sandbanks, knowing there is a risk of being caught as it floods back in.

Into their quiet, hushed scene, in which they made the only noises, came a signal to both of them, passing easily through the still air. They turned from each other, still holding hands, left on right and right on left, and looked towards the cottage they were watching.

"Good Lord, it's Parchman."

"Who's Parchman?" Bridget asked. She broke both hand contacts and moved to adjust her leaf-hat. Like a child with a paper hat, she wanted to keep it on as long as possible and that required little adjustments.

It was the first time in half an hour that they had no contact with each other. It felt strange, making them conscious of their own bodies, their own personalities. Bridget went from sitting to kneeling, then levered her legs like a hinge to stand up. Thomas followed her example, to better see the cottage and who was arriving.

"There's Simon Taylor," Bridget said. "They must be having some type of meeting."

They did indeed have a meeting for both visitors went inside after nodding at each other as they hitched their horses to the gate.

They were in there a long time. Outside, the wind picked up, a fly and a sleepy wasp came to buzz around, beetles, voles and rabbits started moving about the place again, perhaps stretching muscles kept still for so long. Birds contributed to the general noise, calling urgently about departing this world for warmer habitats to the south.

They were the normal noises of early autumn but after the recent stillness it seemed to Thomas and Bridget to be like market day, held strangely in the copse overlooking Grime Cottage below.

Where Amelia was held very much against her will.

Henry arrived to take over from Thomas but Thomas did not leave, explaining that something was going on. The trio now watched the cottage, with its trail of thin smoke rising from the rearmost chimney. Inside, Amelia was the cause of the thin smoke for, try as she might, she could not get the ancient stove to light properly. Grimes, annoyed at her incompetence, shoved her aside and tried himself.

"Get beer, bread and cheese instead," he grunted when he could do no better. His nominal boss, Simon Taylor, and his real boss, Parchman, had come to talk and would not be served beef stew but bread and cheese instead.

The watchers and waiters were rewarded then with sight of Amelia Grimes. She left the back door and walked around the house to a stone hut, returning with a large jug of beer. Then she appeared a second time, carrying a round cheese from the same stone hut. This time she looked up, a sweeping glance across the horizon but resting ever so slightly on the copse where they were hidden. Thomas, seeing this, walked out in front of the tree line and waved at her. She dropped her cheese and waved back, both arms high in the air. But it was only a moment. She bent and picked up the cheese and made for the back door; once at the corner of the cottage, she turned and looked again but Thomas was gone, pulled back by Henry.

Plain Jane arrived to take over from Bridget but Bridget did not leave, did not even turn her gaze from the cottage. The four stood like trees, slightly swaying as muscles stiffened and weakened from the strain of stillness.

The door opened as the sun fell down the western sky, dragged by its own deep rays clutching the earth and winding it down, invisible hand over invisible hand. They seemed to leave in seniority order, Parchman first then Simon Taylor after twenty minutes.

Another half an hour passed. They heard a horse moving through the copse from behind, turned their attention away from the cottage to see Elizabeth, dodging branches that threatened her head. She wore long gloves and an elegant, tall hat that made her branch negotiation tricky; it was the way Simon Taylor liked his wife to dress and she was taking no chances in risking his displeasure over something as trivial as her attire. She was taking enough risk as it was, riding out here when he had left her at her tapestry.

"My husband left after breakfast," she gasped, eager to play some part in their efforts. "Why are there so many here? I thought it was only ever two."

Bridget explained while the others turned back to the cottage to see a man on a horse disappearing around a bend in the track.

"Is that Grimes? It has to be."

They watched the cottage another ten minutes, as if not believing their luck. But further confirmation came when Amelia came out of the front door this time, shaded her eyes against the slanting sun to check her new husband had really left, then made windmills of her arms towards their hiding place.

Elizabeth got there first for she had her horse and the others were on foot, having left their horses tethered in another wood half a mile back to avoid detection.

"Mealy, my dear!" Elizabeth cried, sliding down and holding

her dear friend in her arms. "Let me look at you, Mealy, you poor thing."

Amelia claimed to be fine, to be bearing up well, but she could not hide the bruises. She could not hide them but glossed over them.

"The worst thing," she lied, "is the lack of intelligent conversation." The worst thing, in truth, was the cruel pain inflicted on her for Grimes' amusement. They went inside the cottage after Henry said he would take Elizabeth's horse back to the copse and tether it there.

"That way, if anyone comes we can leave by the back door and sneak through the outbuildings and up the slope to the cover of the trees. A horse would be an immediate give away that Mealy has company."

Amelia, against whom much wrong had been committed this last fortnight, gave freely and gave doubly over the next hour. Her giving was not the normal hospitality of the hostess; nobody cared for food and drink, nor for the comfort of their seat or the type of amusement offered. She gave freely and doubly in other ways.

First, she had quite a lot to offer in terms of information. Perhaps Grimes' big mistake in fact, Parchman's too, for he was the organiser in the shadows, was to choose a highly intelligent woman to share Grimes' bed. Enquiry was integral to her character and deduction followed right behind.

"I've worked some things out," she said. "Grimes and Simon are in league together and this man, Parchman, who you know well, Thomas and Lizzie; oh, and Henry too, is the brains behind it. Their scheme is much to do about land and most of it is directed against the Great Little Estate, which lies the other side of Bagber."

"We know Great Little well," said Thomas. "In fact, I am building the new house there following fire last year."

"Exactly, well they try to keep things from me but I listen carefully when summoned for more ale or food. They congratulate themselves for the most hideous things, laughing like madmen into their beer. Yesterday, they spoke again about a fire at a barn that destroyed much of the bumper harvest. They spoke in mocking tones, saying what a tragedy it was, all that hard work gone up in smoke. But they were laughing to belie their sorrow. Apparently, the fire would have been put out more quickly except for some stubborn new land holder who has dammed the river and made a drought of the home farm. I saw your husband, Lizzie, wink as he stressed the words 'some stubborn new land holder'. I think that man is Grimes."

"But how could that be? Grimes does not have money for land purchases and my husband always complains about lack of cash," Elizabeth broke into the account.

"Maybe that is where the third man comes in," Bridget said. "What did you say his name was?"

"Parchman. He is something to do with the government. He was involved last year in our arrest; Matthew's and mine, I mean. He also played a major part in Eliza's kidnapping. He is a bad sort, for sure." Thomas' blood boiled at the thought of what the man had done to those Thomas cared for. "He was Keeper of the King's Person to James Stuart and sold him down the river, literally!"

Parchman had organised James' second flight by boat down the Thames, declaring he would follow his Sovereign into exile and work unceasingly for his restoration. Instead, he had made his peace with King William, gained immunity from prosecution, and obtained some important position in government. "He had no intention of following James into exile and, in actual fact, caused the legal loss of his throne when Parliament decided James' flight was abdication. Not a good person to count amongst your friends."

"Being in government, he would have access to money." Bridget's observation made perfect sense.

"But how does all this connect together and why target the Great Little Estate?" Thomas wanted to know.

"It must have something to do with Lady Roakes' past," Henry said, remembering how shocked his real mother, Eliza, had been to see Lady Roakes last year. She had some dreadful responsibility for…

"That's it!" he cried suddenly, interrupting his own thoughts.

"Parchman was the architect of my mother's kidnapping and Lady Roakes, who went by some other name at the time, was merely the jailer. They have fallen out in some way and this is all about revenge."

Thomas witnessed the doubling of Amelia's kindness amongst adversity for, before they left, she called Thomas to one side.

"Miss Browne is a fine lady," she said so that no one but Thomas could hear.

"Mealy, what is to be done?" He spoke a little too loudly in reply, becoming conscious of it and ending in a clumsy whisper.

"You must forget me and find happiness elsewhere."

"I cannot and I shall not."

"So, you want to make me even more unhappy?" she said sharply, her intellect working on the problem; she had to use herself as the angle to get Thomas to think beyond her.

She was dead to this world.

"Miss Browne is a fine woman," she said again, sensing something between the two of them, something that could be built on. "And, Thomas, you will make me happy if you live your life to the full. That means fill it with love and generosity and advantages taken. I want you to live your life for me, Thomas my dear." She put herself on tiptoes and kissed him full on the lips. Her lips were warm and wet; no, that was because of the tears streaming down her face. She pulled back, controlled her emotions somehow and called Bridget to come and talk to them.

"Miss Browne…"

"Please call me Bridget, Thomas has told me so much about you."

"Bridget, you know, I'm sure, that Thomas is very dear to me. Be good to him for he will always be good to you." With that she turned and went back into the grubby cottage, closing the door behind her.

"I'm sorry, Bridget, it must be the shock of her thoroughly inappropriate marriage getting to her."

But they both knew she was right; doubly right as it so

happens. But being right is not always easy to bear and Amelia spent the rest of the day fighting a sense of outrage that made her want to strike out at her husband.

Thomas and Bridget did not know how to behave so both resorted to being overly polite with the other. Bridget was now Miss Browne and Thomas became Mr Davenport, if not in name at least in restraint of feeling. Both felt the heavy presence of Amelia and neither knew what to do.

Chapter 30

It was not an easy thing to do but Penelope insisted.

"It will be much easier when you get there," she said. "And Sally and I will be with you. By all accounts, she is a decent woman and will give you a fair hearing."

"I do not know, Penelope, I treated her so badly."

"So, rather than swallow humble pie, you would give up Great Little and go back to chancing your living in Bristol?" Rich words from someone who had never eaten a mouthful of humble pie in her life. But that is the way of those born to extreme arrogance, softened for Penelope only by her intense love for Sally and her deep friendship with Alice. Before these two, she had been friendless but now knew love in all its splendid glory. How love manages, somehow, to rub off the sharp edges is quite extraordinary.

Pushed and pulled into their only remaining vehicle, a light buggy in which Penelope took the reins and Sally perched on a tiny runner board at the back, Alice looked ahead with apprehension. She could readily have been sick at the side of the road as Penelope clattered down the lanes to Winterbourne Stickland. But she was just brave enough to swallow the urge and tell herself to buck up. The worst that could happen was being sent away, dismissed like a tradesman or a distant relative out of favour, and told not to come back again.

If that happened, Alice Roakes would do exactly as instructed. She would go away and never come back.

Then she thought of her baby son and all he meant, both to her and in memory of her beloved husband. She had to give his future, his security, one last attempt.

It was the type of day that late September brings usually once, sometimes twice each year. Half the sky was covered in clouds but they were light and moved swiftly across the enormous dome that housed Dorset. In the back of the buggy, Sally was forced to sit back to save herself from being jolted off as Penelope was driving the single horse hard. Sally was in prime position to watch the clouds but registered them with only a part of her mind; the rest was deep in figures. Yields met prices and wages merged with efficiencies. She made further savings as they scooted along the narrow lanes from Winterbourne Stickland to Okeford Fitzpaine, slowing only slightly as they pushed up Okeford Hill. She then extrapolated those savings to see what the position might be three months out.

But try as she might, the gloomy prognosis was that they would not see the winter through. The penalties and fines under the contract would wipe them out.

They had Paul's and Amy's discovery of a possible way forward but had been unable to find out anything of the investors lurking behind the public face of Grimes and Co. All they knew was that it could not be Grimes alone.

Presently, Sally closed her eyes to the whiter-than-snow clouds and thought about Penelope. What would she do when her chosen home went under the auctioneer's hammer? Would she go back to live with her parents? Would they broker another marriage to some ugly aristocrat, ugly in looks and even uglier in temper? Where would that leave her, indeed both of them? For life without her Pen was not life at all.

Penelope was not thinking a lot as she concentrated on driving the horse forward. It was her nature to concentrate on the here-and-now and to rely on instinct rather than analysis when faced with a decision. If challenged afterwards, she would think a moment and then say this had been one last-ditch effort. It had been unlikely to succeed but was worth a try. Who, other than Jesus, after all, would throw themselves at the mercy of their enemy when on their knees already? And look where it had taken Jesus; to a crude cross of wood set in the ground amongst common thieves. She did not go beyond that thought to the resurrection and life-ever-after bit for that was not how Penelope used her mind. And religion was something that happened to other people. Instead, she told Alice, as tenderly as she could, that it would be better than she expected, then whipped the horse and cried out for it to go still faster.

The interview with Eliza Davenport did go, in some respects, better than expected and, in others, distinctly worse. At least it started on a bright note.

For it was immediately obvious that Eliza was pregnant, several months so.

"Lady Roakes, I believe you had a child earlier this year." It hurt to refer to Mrs Beatrice as Lady Roakes but Eliza wanted to talk to someone who had carried a child and given birth at a later age. She was deeply worried, having become forty that spring.

"I did indeed, Mrs Davenport. Young Sir Beatrice is fine and healthy. He is five months old now. But I did have some difficulties when carrying him, particularly when my husband was murdered."

"Will you take a walk in the garden? There are some things I would ask you about." Eliza ignored the comment about murder, not from vindictiveness but because her mind was on the prospect of giving new life, not taking old.

Lady Roakes assented by standing up, grateful that Penelope stood too; she was not to be alone with Mrs Davenport or Arkwright as she had called her in the old days. Alice no longer pretended anything about the whole episode. Financial desperation worked as a broom, sweeping until the bare boards reflected the truth.

"What I did to you was horribly wrong and evil," she said as they walked across the lawn towards the summer house.

"It was."

"I… just… wanted to apologise again. I am truly sorry for what I did."

"I have a hard time believing that, Lady Roakes. It seems that someone has rewarded you handsomely for your wrongdoing by putting Great Little in your lap. Oh, I did not mean to… to suggest that you have had it easy with your husband's murder." Eliza felt her clumsy mistake, was suddenly all nerves with her old oppressor.

"I know you did not, Mrs Davenport, for you have proved yourself to be firm but kind and are, I am sure, above such remarks." She needed to move the conversation on. "Now, what are your questions on babies, madam? You have before you a veritable expert and I am entirely at your service." She screwed up her courage, stepped away from Eliza, turned and formed a curtsey prettily. It was formal and casual at the same time; it spoke of serious respect but did so in a humorous way. It was meant most sincerely.

And it elicited the faintest smile from Eliza Davenport, who had spent five long years doing the curtseying every day.

And that faint smile was seen by Penelope a discreet five yards to the left of the pair and met with a grin she swallowed quickly lest they glance her way.

The meeting between these two major landowners of North Dorset went less well in terms of a practical way forward. But even here, amongst disappointment, there emerged some hope for the future.

For these two strangers who knew each other so well found much in common in their present situations.

"I am brought to my knees, Mrs Davenport," Alice started.

You had me on my knees for five long years.

"I am sorry to hear it, Lady Roakes. How is this possible, might I ask?"

Well, Mrs Davenport is interested a little; more than I could ever expect by rights. Strictly, I have no rights. That leaves just hope to hang on to.

"My factor, Mr Tomkins, signed a contract…"

"Tomkins, did you say?"

"Yes, Mr Tomkins is our factor and a fine man he is too, only he overstepped his mark in regards to this contract."

"He was assistant factor at Sherborne Hall when I was in… well, a long time ago."

"I believe he was, Mrs Davenport."

What does this mean? Does Mrs Davenport favour Tomkins or not?

"Tomkins was very kind to me and to those dear to me at Sherborne Hall. I would not want to see him in hardship."

There I have my answer! But will it help?

"I too, madam, but I am sorely tested as to how to avoid it for

Great Little is bankrupt following this contract."

There, I have said it!

"Tell me, Lady Roakes, about the difficulties you have experienced subsequent to signing this contract. I too have had difficulties of late, mine might be quite different to yours or just the same. We should examine them together."

Without realising it, Eliza had walked them down to the Divelish. Recent heavy rain during the lengthening nights had caused a rush of water. Alice noted in looking behind her that Penelope no longer followed them; she must have slipped off somewhere, perhaps as they reached the big old beeches that started the woods like guardian angels, watching the lesser trees within. She decided to risk something, not knowing at the point of commitment that there were two parts to the risk she tumbled into.

"Mrs Davenport, might we sit on that large rock over there? The one that looks perfect for diving into the water. Then we could compare notes and draw out any common themes amongst the troubles we both have had."

Eliza agreed readily enough; thus, the first element of risk had worked out. If Eliza had refused superficially, without taking offence, much of the new and tentative relationship would have been washed overboard. Had Eliza refused stiffly, it would be total dismissal, the fear of which had curdled her stomach for the entire ride from Great Little to Bagber Manor.

Eliza accepted because she was troubled by her pregnancy, although delighted to be pregnant. She was also deeply concerned that her money had dried up. It had been an expensive year with expansion and improvement plans underway but then the most recent land purchases had proved far more expensive and Simon would not tell her who had sold the land, preferring excuse after excuse and then shuffling away with a promise to let her know next time. In addition, there had been too many accidents and minor disasters recently, combined with reports of unknown figures darting around in the shadows when all should have been quiet.

But before they sat down together on the rock that Thomas had found Elizabeth and Amelia lying on, Alice did an extraordinary thing. Something made her extend the first risk she had taken, giving it new life, new prospect of failure; Alice was raising the stakes but had nothing left to gamble with.

The large and smooth shelf-like rock was invaded by nettles and brambles on two sides and hung over the river below on the third and longest one. That left the shortest side as easy access with firm ground beneath. Eliza went first when Alice held back, perhaps an acknowledgement of moral status? When Eliza turned with a hand out for Alice to scramble up, she found her kneeling on the ground below the slab that Eliza stood on. The combination of step up to the rock and Alice choosing to kneel gave Eliza a huge height advantage.

"Lady Merriman, Mrs Davenport, I am deeply sorry for taking five years of your life and will endeavour wholeheartedly to give this stolen time back to you in the future. I will not rest until I have done something to repay you this terrible debt. If you could ever forgive me, I humbly beseech you to do so. I am all yours, madam, for the injuries I have done you." It was medieval in approach; virtually passing ownership of body and soul to another.

It was not the script she had rehearsed with Penelope. It was a considerable diversion, sufficient to make the playwright furious.

But it worked to an extent. Eliza stood completely still; memories of cruel treatment crowded into her mind. Was this the same woman she had suffered so badly under? Clearly it was, for she was apologising sincerely and profusely, throwing dignity aside as if running naked could somehow wash the sins away.

"Lady Roakes, off your knees please. With our common background, I have no desire to see you displaying aspects of servitude I deplore; naturally, you understand this. I cannot forgive you for the theft of five years. I am not ready to and do not know when and if I will ever be. But that does not mean we cannot put the past to one side, temporarily at least, and concentrate on working together as landed neighbours. Now sit with me and we will compare our problems for a while."

Alice had planned the first stage of her risk, but not the

second. She counted both parts afterwards as a success for it did not lead to total rejection. There is a limbo between Heaven and Hell and Lady Roakes had been assigned a place at the table there. Perhaps like her Little picture at home, she would spend all the days of history still to come sitting motionless at that table with a slight but wistful smile made of choice pieces of cut red and white glass for her lips and teeth respectfully. She would be content because the alternative was so much worse.

They had no paper and no pencil but made a list in their minds, briefly joining those minds together. They agreed to list the common griefs first and then the ones they suffered separately.

Chief amongst the common issues was an incredible increase in the price of land this year.

"I paid almost ten times the cost an acre compared to last year. It has left me very low in the kitty and without the resources to develop the land," Eliza started the conversation.

"I could not afford any land this year," Alice replied. "I had told Tomkins to buy odd fields up to one hundred acres in total but the cash I set aside for this was nowhere near enough. He had the sense not to spend the entire sum on just a few acres." Alice was at least grateful for this, whereas Simon Taylor had half-ruined Eliza with excessively expensive land.

"Another thing is how mysterious the whole land-purchasing has become. I cannot find out from Mr Taylor who it was who sold me the recent land at such a high price."

"Similar to my problem!" Alice exclaimed. "I cannot determine who owns a farm next to the Home Farm at Great Little, which changed hands a few months ago. It has caused no end of problems for they immediately dammed the river to make a lake and cut off water supplies both to the Home Farm and several of my tenanted properties. We have had to drive the cattle to land I have rented to the south of Great Little. Again, I cannot discover who is renting this to me but it is expensive and has to be paid for a year in advance."

Eliza had had no devastating fires at Bagber but she had noticed several careless mistakes and an apparent theft of a portion of the wheat harvest.

"Tomkins has sold the whole output of the estate to one buyer with huge problems arising." Alice moved on to the next point.

"I've not done that but I did have one noteworthy matter in this regard," Eliza said. "I sold most of my excess oats to a new buyer and the oats were all returned three days later with complaint that they were contaminated and mouldy to boot. I knew this to be false for I inspected each bin sold."

"What was the name of the buying firm?" Alice asked but knew the answer already.

"Grimes and Co. I recall because it is the same as an old gamekeeper at Bagber. He was dismissed before I returned here in '85 but lives on the estate at a very low rent because it is one of a pair of cottages I have not improved yet."

"That is the same name!" Alice cried out, anxious for Eliza to finish speaking so she could say it without interrupting her.

"Same as what?"

"The same firm that Tomkins signed with." Alice explained further about the imposing nature of the contract and the hopes that Paul and Amy Tabard had unearthed. Also, of their frustration because Alice and Penelope had been unable to find out who lay behind it in the hope that one of the principals may have broken the law at some stage. This would make the contract defunct and damages due. "It's a long shot and looking hopeless for lack of information as to who is behind the firm. Are you hearing me?" Alice stopped suddenly, aware that her voice had come out harsh and abrupt, like the old days. She had almost said 'Arkwright' in hanging a name at the end of that question. She grimaced to think what damage to their fragile relationship that would have caused.

But Eliza Davenport had not noticed; offence was not the reason she had stopped listening. Rather, it was her mind working on a problem that had eluded her; she was slotting subsidiary answers into a grid in her head. When sufficient answers were on that board, she would have the solution to her problems. And, likely, the solution to Lady Roakes' intense worries, too.

And she was sure that Simon Taylor would know exactly which answers to chalk upon the board she had fixed in her mind.

"Enough for now, Lady Roakes," she said, standing up as she spoke. The dismissal was plain to hear. Eliza had to be alone in order to think. No, not alone, just rid of her visitors and free to track down Elizabeth, who had ridden out that morning shortly after Simon had left.

The whole way back, they talked of the superficial. Once arrived at the house, no further refreshments were offered. Her visitors had to be gone as quickly as Eliza could manage. There was an irritating delay when Sally could not be found. Eventually, she was located in the housekeeper's sitting room, deep in conversation about ideas for further economies in a large household.

She curtsied to Mrs Davenport and mumbled her apologies. Eliza said it was fine. She just wanted them gone so that she could find Elizabeth.

And before the buggy was through the gates, Eliza had ordered her horse to be made ready. Elizabeth had not returned but Eliza knew exactly where her friend would be.

Chapter 31

Matthew had no idea what to do, where to try next.

Every route into the palace was blocked by sentries, who scoffed at the idea that he worked for the King.

"Just tell Herr Avercamps that Matthew Davenport is here to see him."

"I think you must have the wrong country, my fellow," the guards taunted him. "We don't have no 'Herrs' here, all are plain 'Mr', else you want to see a Lord and that's nigh impossible for commoners."

It was nonsense, of course, but their pikes barred the gates and told another story.

He had no house to go back to for they had given up their lease when they left London a few months earlier. Anyway, the problems back at Bagber meant that they could not afford such a luxury. He was staying in a seedy inn on the south bank of the river because it was half the price.

And at least twice the danger.

But he was taller than average and muscled too, plus a dagger in a scabbard that hung from his belt. Most thieves would think twice before launching an attack on a grown and armed man who was patently sober.

However, he still felt safer back in his nondescript room with the door locked and barred when darkness came. He knew this cut down the opportunities to get in front of Avercamps but reasoned better to be alive to try the next day than lying in some street gutter, wondering in his last moments on earth what had felled him from behind.

He tried each day to gain access to the palace, surprising himself with the ingenuity he deployed. Yet the guards always seemed to be one step ahead.

And then there was the ominous presence he had sensed on the third day in the capital; by the fifth day he was sure he was being followed. He noticed certain things, a quick closing of the air around a space when he turned around suddenly, as if a painter was employed to hurriedly scrub out his watcher every time Matthew looked back. He turned more frequently than usual, feigning indecision about where to go next, so swinging his head this way and that while he paused at street corners, using peripheral vision to the extreme. His ears also were alert for the hurried sounds of footsteps when nobody advertised their presence.

He had expected to stay a night or two in London, report to Avercamps one final time, then return to Bagber. He had brought with him just enough money for the journey and three nights in the city, allowing a small buffer in case he had to wait for Avercamps to free himself from some other project. There was no other money to spare. By the tenth day, he was down to his last few coins, even staying in the cheapest place he could find and barely eating at all.

And on the eleventh day, he left the seedy tavern for the last time, used a few of his remaining coins for a boat over the river to Whitehall, and settled down to await his luck.

He had told himself, if nothing turned up by lunchtime, he would start the long walk home. He had just enough money left for bread and small beer for the week he estimated it would take to walk the hundred-odd miles to Bagber. He would sleep in woods along the way and take his chances with the weather.

He tried two main tactics that morning. The first was to walk brazenly up to a gate as if he were the King himself. It failed miserably and he felt the lack of dignity when one cocky soldier caught his jacket on the hook of his pike and jerked him backwards.

"Good morning my old cock, at it again, are we?"

"I need to see Jacob Avercamps immediately."

"Not that old chestnut, my friend. Careful of the others!" Matthew had little control of his movements, being hooked firmly from behind. He almost collided with a scowling matron and her two young charges.

"Watch out, sir, my you are a clumsy one," the guard called while trying his best to destabilise Matthew completely.

He freed himself by twisting under the pike. Then he retired and thought about a new entrance and a new strategy.

It was almost as if the guards were promised a handsome bonus provided Matthew did not enter the palace.

Spot on, Matthew, with your observation.

Parchman was generous with his payments, efficient also. The bonus he had laid out was a tiny fraction of the profit he was making every day of the week. But it was a considerable sum, even when parcelled out amongst twenty guards. It was money well spent.

Matthew's second plan that morning was to wait for a change of the guards and try the same gate again. He knew the rota well after eleven days of trying. He knew the pair that came on at ten that morning was the least watchful. If he had any chance of getting through it had to be now.

He waited until almost twelve for his move. This was not indecision. He was waiting for a sizeable party. Just before noon, he saw a group of lawyers making their way to the entrance. Surely, he could manage to get in on the tail end of a bunch of attorneys clacking on about their cases as they walked?

He noticed the lawyers were strung out in twos and threes. It made a perfect setting for his move. But bad luck dogged him, as it had this entire trip.

There was one other component to this exercise. He had given threepence to a beggar upfront with another threepence promised afterwards. All he was required to do was make a commotion at the right time so that the distracted guards would not see Matthew slipping in with the lawyers.

The beggar had come to him with the idea. Hanging around the gates with a bowl by his crossed legs, he had noticed that Matthew was often there, trying to get in.

"For sixpence, I'll make a diversion so you can slip in, sir."

But even beggars can have employers and this one was no beggar anyway. He was in the pay of Parchman; more correctly, he was an employee of Sanderson and Sanderson. Usually, he moved crates of goods from one warehouse to the next and earned an honest eight shillings a week. These last ten days, he had made eight shillings a day and could not believe his luck.

Plus, today, as a special bonus, he also had threepence from Matthew.

Matthew, ejected once more from the palace gates, looked gloomily around. It was lunchtime. He should go back to Dorset. He could not try again that day for he was a laughing stock at the gate now.

But, for some reason, he was not ready to leave. Going back home to Eliza had enormous appeal but he could not return as a failure. He hung about until the middle of the afternoon, seeking inspiration from the palace walls, from the streets, the churches, the people themselves.

Finding nothing.

He thought of all his adventures in Ireland, from the last desperate escape across to Hotherington backwards, as if time was turned around and sprinting into familiar history, retreating from the unknown future.

It was a lucky move because if he had gone forwards from his arrival in Ireland, it might have been too late by the time he thought of Bridget Browne and the manuscript she had sent to the publishers. As it was, she featured towards the end of his five weeks in Ireland so, working backwards, he got to her with time to spare.

He had to think hard to remember the name of the publishers. It was something like Penderels or Pennington; it definitely began with a 'P' and had 'and son' to end with. Bridget had mentioned it a few times, saying she had left instructions for her father to get in touch in case they were caught by the giants. She had left bare details of the corruption Matthew had uncovered in the same instructions. It was worth a chance that the publishing firm had received this information and could, perhaps, assist Matthew in some way.

If only he could remember the name.

He was walking now, walking without paying attention to where he was going. The weather was blustery, like his feelings turned inside out. If only he could anchor on something and make headway somehow.

What was the name of the publishers?

More to the point, if the name of a publisher escapes you, where is the best place to ask?

There, right in front of him on the Strand was a bookseller.

He stood a moment, wondering at the joy of God's world, where answers evaded and then appeared right in front of your eyes. Was every event planned? Or was this life just a crazy haphazard series of unconnected happenings that was bound only by the love of the Lord?

He walked across the Strand and went into the bookstore. Had he waited another minute on the pavement, he would have bumped into Parchman, crossing the Strand to make his way back from his office in Whitehall by the back streets.

As it was, Parchman saw only the back of a head that seemed familiar. He shrugged and continued his line of thought about the opportunities at Bagber and Great Little. Soon, he would have them just where he needed them.

"Can I be of assistance, sir?" Matthew had been drawn to the first book he saw on entering the shop, a large edition with notes of Luke Davenport's *Man Against Man: Several Sermons Concerning the Way the Lord Would Have Us Live.*

"Most editions do not run to the full title."

"You know the sermons well, sir?"

"A lot of people do," replied Matthew. "But I believe I know them better than most."

"That's a big claim, sir, for the most popular religious writer of our generation."

Matthew did not reply, simply picked up the book and flicked it open, finding the sermon he wanted by judging the weight of the book and knowing how many pages to open.

Something made him hand the book to the shopkeeper and start reciting from memory the *Sermon Concerning Confronting Evil in All its Forms*. It took him back to the old church with his father thundering from the pulpit. Not that it was all thunder; Luke had known how to use his voice to best effect. Sometimes he would almost whisper, lulling the congregation with sweet reasoning before railing against evil, with his voice rising to the Heavens as the words poured out.

Matthew stopped after six minutes of word-perfect recitation.

"You will find a note annotation at the end of that paragraph.

I believe it is note 63. At the back you will find an interesting theory that there is a little of the devil in everyone, yet it is self-discipline that allows some to conquer the devil within. Just as society struggles for order, so each and every individual faces a fight to resist temptation and follow God's law. As a nation celebrates a great victory over the enemy so the individual should celebrate each day he or she follows God's law, not knowing what tomorrow will bring by way of new challenges."

"Sir, you are almost word perfect. How can that be?"

"I am Luke's son, Matthew. I helped him write some of the sermons," he said modestly. He had done much of the groundwork and also the detail behind the notes, which had not interested his father. He could recite most of the sermons like a child could trot out night-time prayers. "But, right now, I am pressed for time and need some information you might be able to help with."

The deal was done within minutes. Matthew signed both copies of *Man Against Man* the bookseller had, more than doubling their value. In return, the bookseller left the shop, leaving Matthew to flick through the books on offer for a pleasant hour. When he returned, he led Matthew out of the back door, across the yards of several neighbouring businesses, down a back alley in the fading light then twisting along other lanes. These were the very back streets that Parchman delighted in using for the very same reason that Matthew now found useful; they guaranteed anonymity for they made it impossible for a tracker to keep eyes on his quarry.

Presently, the bookseller led Matthew to the offices of Prendegast and Son, explaining to him that Mr Prendegast seldom came into the office due to ill health but that his assistant, a man named Michael Frampton, had expressed considerable interest in meeting him, having failed to do so during a recent visit to Dorset.

"That was because I was not at home," Matthew said, rather stating the obvious.

Chapter 32

"I am delighted to meet you, sir. I have been trying to track you down in Dorset."

"I am pleased too, Mr Frampton. I was unaware that you were looking for me as I have been in London these last eleven days."

"Just exactly how long I have been in Dorset, seeking you! I met with your charming wife and both your sisters but, other than that you had gone to London, they were unable to supply any information. Mrs Davenport said to try the George as you had stayed there before but they had no record of you there so my trail went completely cold."

Matthew looked embarrassed, studied the floorboards a moment.

"That was because I stayed at cheaper lodgings across the river to save money. I did not want my wife to worry so implied that I would quite likely stay at the George without actually saying so." He blushed again, seeing his dishonesty first-hand, as if viewing a Catholic at confession.

Mr Frampton made a show of looking through some papers on the table between them, shuffling and tidying but hoping to reduce Matthew's unease. He was no confessor and certainly no judge of the motives or reasons of others.

He resumed the conversation, stating why he had been looking for Matthew, giving the background of the letter he had received from Tobias Browne.

"I thought it quite strange for a publishing house to become involved in reporting fraudulent activity. I wanted to weigh up the situation and then discuss it with Mr Prendegast, the owner of our business. When I could not find you in Dorset, I returned to London and saw Mr Prendegast this morning. You must appreciate, Mr Davenport, that Mr Prendegast is not a well man. In fact, I do not believe he has long to live. As the weather deteriorates with the onset of autumn, he is struggling more and more with his chest. I did not want to add complications and stress so thought to determine the facts first. I only turned to him when I was unable to locate you."

"I am sorry, Mr Frampton."

"There is nothing to be sorry about. I do not own your movements, Mr Davenport. I merely told you this to aid in your understanding for Mr Prendegast became quite excited when I told him the barest details and begged me for more. It seems he had connections with your late father, God rest his soul."

"How so, Mr Frampton?"

"Will you come back to dine with my wife and me so I might explain in more genial surroundings?"

"Gladly, sir." As if cued by the invitation, Matthew's stomach rumbled loudly. He realised he had not eaten that day, nor the previous evening, for he was husbanding his reduced resources.

Mr Frampton lived a short walk from the office, in a road called Tulip Lane. He explained that a Dutchman who traded in tulips had built a lavish house there quite a few years earlier. He had run low on funds and sold a large part of his garden for development. Subsequently, Mr Frampton had acquired a modest three-storey home mid-way down the street.

Mrs Frampton was like Mr Frampton, open and warm. Despite the lack of warning, she welcomed Matthew and rushed to the kitchen to tell the cook to supplement their supper.

Matthew fell to the soup, fish and plum pie as if it had been a week without eating rather than a day and a half.

While he ate, Michael Frampton related the details of his journey and Mr Prendegast's interest in the matter.

"First and foremost, Mr Davenport, I was entertained by your wife, who was kind to me. However, if I might be frank?"

"Of course, sir."

"She was somewhat distracted by some problems with the estate. I got the impression they were serious and would beg you to go back quickly to assist her."

"I will depart the moment my business with the King is complete. I turned to you, Mr Frampton, because I hoped you might gain entry into the palace with a message for Jacob Avercamps."

"The adviser to the King?"

Matthew nodded in confirmation.

"I suspect you wish to see him about the matter of Sanderson and Sanderson."

"Yes, sir."

"You know that Mr Sanderson is dead, murdered a few months ago in his warehouse? He headed a reputable firm of traders, who specialised in supplying various items for the army and navy. I have been investigating these last two days since I got back from Dorset and then laid the whole matter before Mr Prendegast this morning." Michael Frampton explained his other purpose in going to Dorset, seeking information about Bridget Browne.

"She is safe in Dorset, sir." Matthew cut through him.

"I know and I had the pleasure of meeting her, too. I have written to Mr Browne, informing him that she is safe. But he asked me also to pass on some information about your findings with regard to Sanderson and Sanderson."

"Quite so, and that is why I need to see Avercamps yet have been frustrated in every attempt to get into Whitehall."

"I will go first thing in the morning and will find a way to get a message to him. I have been into the palace before as we bind certain court documents into books from time to time. I will take some tomorrow to give my real mission a pretence of normal business."

It was as they finished eating and settled back on their chairs that Mr Frampton told Matthew of the connection between Mr Prendegast and Luke Davenport, an association that stretched back to the latter days of the Civil War. Matthew listened intently, amazed to hear of his father's exploits as a young man.

"Better than tell you, Mr Davenport, if you bear with me, I will fetch your father's book and read a section to you, if you are so minded."

Matthew waited impatiently, until Mr Frampton arrived back with a slender book, much worn at the edges. His host coughed, cleared his throat and started to read.

Diary of a Young Man Who Knows Yet Nothing of the World

Matthew chuckled quietly when he heard the title. He had often been told by his father that he knew nothing of the world.

July 12th 1643. Today, I start my diary for a momentous thing happened this morning. I met the King and was overcome with admiration. He is not a tall man but is graceful and elegant in all regards. I bowed low when he entered the room. He came straight to me, said to his aide, "Is this the man you told me about?"

"It is, Sire. This is Davenport. He will do the deed that is required of him."

My ears pricked up at these words. I should explain, I am an adventurer, lending my sword to anyone who might appeal to the honest and romantic in me. I am eighteen and full of the enthusiasm of youth. I am much attracted to the King's cause for he seemed to me full of honour; a man treated ill by nearly all around him. I left home seven weeks ago at Whitsun, left my miserable home and drunken father. I stopped at my mother's grave and said a prayer for her. I prayed that she is happy where she is now, away from the drink and the violence it breeds.

I came to London like Dick Whittington before me; but not to seek my fortune, instead to seek honour in a world of grime, to find truth in a world of lies, or die in the search of it.

I threw myself in with the King's cause for it seemed the right thing to do; if necessary, I would spill blood for my monarch, for the order of things that has always been since time began. We moved with heavy fighting around the country. At first, we won each skirmish with ease as our opponents lacked cohesion and direction. But after just a few weeks, we noticed improved organisation, as if some great mind was behind them, controlling each and every movement towards their ultimate purpose.

It is a hard business, fighting your fellow countrymen, who seemed honest people gone astray.

And today, the first day of this diary, marked the culmination of my dreams for I was told I was to meet the King. I brushed the dirt off my clothes and borrowed a cloak from my officer, proudly informing my troop that I was to meet the King.

"Surely not? And you just a boy!" But it was me standing there in Oxford, now the capital of England since London turned against royalty. I do not know why for I had loved London during my brief stay there.

The King did not talk to me that day, nor any day after that. He looked at me for the briefest moment, then he moved away.

"He will do," he said. "Tell him what I require."

"At once, Your Majesty." The aide bowed and I bowed too. I wondered what I would say when my troop crowded around me wanting to know what the King had said to me.

The aide presently came back to me as I stood waiting.

"Come back tomorrow now scram," he said, raising his hand as if to strike away a fly.

"Yes, sir," I said and bowed again.

Mr Frampton laid down the book and looked up at Matthew.

"Much of this account is lost," he said, holding the book up for Matthew to take a look. "See, the next page has been torn out and the following section damaged by fire."

"There was a fire when I was a child," Matthew said. "I remember it well although I was only six or seven. Father lost much of his writing."

"It is a great pity for Mr Prendegast is keen to publish this diary, with your permission, of course."

"You have my permission, Mr Frampton."

"Please call me Michael."

"And I am Matthew. I can search his study at home and see what is there. Also, he had a dressing room off his bedroom. There were few clothes in there for it was piled high with books."

"Could you, Matthew? I know it would make old Mr Prendegast immensely happy to see his friend's first work published and I fear he has not long to live. Now, the next extract we have intact is November of '45 and Luke is in Ireland…"

"Where I was until recently!"

"Exactly and seemingly in much the same occupation as you were briefly employed in. He seems to have been working for the parliamentary forces by then. It would please Mr Prendegast so much to know what caused him to change sides."

"Does Mr Prendegast not remember? Does he suffer from memory problems?"

"No, his memory is strong but he did not meet your father until '48 when he too was in Ireland. Your father was a firm Parliamentarian by then and Mr Prendegast did not know he had worked for the Royalist cause until this snippet of the diaries came into his possession two years ago. "

"Then, Michael, I will endeavour to find what you lack although I do not know whether I will be successful. I shall do it as soon as I get back and in gratitude for your kind help in my cause." The more Matthew meant something, the more he sounded stiff, overly formal.

"You must stay the night here, Matthew. No, Mrs Frampton would not have it any other way. And nor would I. Now, I think bed calls for we both have busy days tomorrow."

He showed Matthew to a small guest room overlooking the street below. Matthew thanked him and said goodnight. Instinctively, he went to the window and pulled the heavy curtains aside to make a viewing point to the street below. He watched a long while but there was nobody waiting for him outside. With a satisfied sigh, he washed in the bowl and climbed into bed.

Perhaps he had finally got the upper hand after all.

But then, perhaps, there were a few more twists to come.

Chapter 33

Thomas went to see Grace, his sister. She was the nearest in age to him and the closest, too. Since her marriage three years earlier, he had seen less of her, although she had moved just a dozen miles to Sherborne Hall, the seat of the Earl of Sherborne.

Thomas went to see his sister out of unhappiness. He felt like kicking the stones along the ground, then striking out at the bending up-and-down hills, sweeping their topography to one side in order to confront the sun itself.

Or perhaps that was the son, as in the son of God. For Thomas was angry; as angry as he had ever been, even more angry than when he had heard of Grace's rape during the Monmouth Uprising. And even more angry than he had been at the cruel kidnapping and mistreatment of Lady Merriman, now Eliza Davenport and their dear sister-in-law.

For Amelia had been stolen from him, taken and given to a wholly unsuitable husband when Thomas had first claim on her. The injustice of it ate at him.

"Grace, I…"

"I know, Thomas." She had heard from Elizabeth. She took his head against her slender body and held it there, caressing it like a mother would do.

Her closest relative, her dear brother, was hurting.

"It's so unfair," he cried, the sound muffled against her elegant dress, the force behind the words lost against the ruffles and bows so that he sounded to her like a little plaintive boy.

Grace was a year younger than Thomas but she had grown up a little quicker. Perhaps it was when they were thirteen and fourteen respectively that she had overtaken him.

"I know, brother dear. We must pray for Mealy; pray that she knows happiness again soon."

But Thomas' grief was complicated by desire and by guilt. These three make a terrible concoction for they add temptation and self-loathing to the original misery.

"If only I had not gone away."

But then, I would not have met Bridget.

"I should strike off Grimes' miserable little head."

Then I would be a dead man, for the noose is not any weaker, any more likely to give way, simply because the motivation for the crime was love. And dead men have nothing to live for.

"What shall I do, sister?"

Wake me, sister, from this terrible dream; shake me, cut me, pinch me hard but wake me.

"You have a choice, brother. Either you wait for Mealy or you marry Bridget."

How cruel can I be that I would present it so coldly to my dear brother? But where is the kindness in wrapping the truth in false hope because it has a pretty sheen to it?

Grace pulled his head slightly away from her body, gave a look of quizzical concern, the type an older-younger sister gives her younger-older brother when she is not quite sure. But she loves whatever it is.

"But poor Mealy!" Guilt was playing games with him now; sending him one way then the other.

Sure enough, the absolute thought was not far away.

"If I marry Bridget, what will Mealy think of me?"

"What has she said for you to do?" Which showed the maturity, the detachment, Grace had over Thomas.

"To marry Bridget, but does she mean it?"

"You want to be told to marry Bridget, don't you?" Suddenly, Grace understood his purpose; he did not want the responsibility of the decision but also did not want to face up to leaving Amelia alone in the world. She gripped his hands. "I can't give you that instruction, Thomas dearest. I can only give you my advice, which is to follow your heart but to be honest with yourself in the process." She stopped, feeling the inadequacy of her words, then added, "For Mealy's sake and for Bridget's sake, you have to make that decision on your own. Nobody can help you and it would show disrespect to both girls should you shun the task."

It left Thomas no clearer for he was, indeed, seeking instruction. Or rather, absolution in advance from another. He pulled away angrily, then remembered who he was with and forced his anger back down, swallowing it whole.

But he left Sherborne Hall even more upset and lost than when he had arrived.

He was halfway home before he realised that he had not asked Grace the second question. It was too late to turn around; too late for his pride, that is. He slowed his horse then stopped, did what many young men have done over the countless generations; turned then turned back again, first towards the north, where Amelia was, then to his Sturminster Newton home where Bridget waited. He turned and turned until the horse snorted in complaint. Then he knew. Turning and clicking his horse into a loping canter, he continued to the bridge, suggesting he had opted for home and Bridget.

But at the bridge he did not swing left and cross it. Instead, he kept riding along the banks of the Stour. He would go to the new house of Big Jim that Thomas' firm had finished building that summer.

He would ask Big Jim, not the first question but the second that he had forgotten to put to Grace; what it was like to be a Catholic.

Because he wanted to know.

But it was not to be for Big Jim had gone to Wareham to meet with a large customer who wanted to haul stone from his quarry to the cathedral at Salisbury. Plain Jane met him at the door, looking even more ravishing in her early thirties than she had been four years ago when they had first met in Bristol.

Plain Jane had a child now, a sandy-headed boy of two who gave Thomas a grin and led him by the hand to play in a sandpit, half sodden from the recent rain that still hung in the air like a threat.

Plain Jane came out to the sandpit, a glass of beer in each hand.

"Thank you, Plainy."

"You're welcome, Thomas." She had warmed immediately to Thomas' nickname for her when first used three years ago. It had caught on. It was a crooked reference to her beauty, which she took to be a gift from God.

She asked Thomas what brought him to their new home in Fiddleford.

"Did you come for business or pleasure, Thomas? Or was it just to admire your handiwork?" She looked back at her house with joy. It was mostly brick but with bands of flint. It was long and low and had an enormous head of thatch, like an unruly boy who refused to sit down for his haircut. Inside, the kitchen was central for it was where they spent the most time as a family. Despite their growing wealth, Plain Jane did most of the household work herself, employing just two young maids who shared a room amongst the thatch and enjoyed light duties under their hard-working and easy-going mistress.

Thomas felt a wave of affection for this generous couple who took life head on.

"What's it like to be Catholic?" he blurted out, the words merging slightly in his excitement at posing the question. But Plain Jane got the meaning, just wondered why the question was asked.

"Why, it's a wonderful thing, young Thomas Davenport," she said, hiding some of the awkwardness they both felt behind her playfulness. She called for one of the maids to watch her son, then said, "If you would like to come to the kitchen, I can tell you a little more about it."

"So, Thomas, is it the beauty of the ceremony of Mass that appeals to you? Well, worse reasons have been given for conversion."

"Who said anything about conversion? I was just wondering what it was like to be... Nobody said anything about conversion." But his denial was a little too hotly put, like Peter, the Disciple, saying he knew nothing of that man they called the King of the Jews.

"Of course not, my mistake."

But the seed is planted, is it not, Thomas, my dear friend? And seeds have a habit of growing. Even in the unlikeliest of places.

"Now," she continued, "tell me more about Father O'Toole. What vestments did he wear and what did his sermon cover?" A little later, when they sat at the kitchen table with a glass of wine and listened to the wind building up outside, stripping the trees bare, she added, "You know, I was a convert, too." This time she got less of an adverse reaction. Had the wine mellowed his response or was Thomas thinking on the subject? Or had he moved on to something else entirely?

But then, how do you split life from religion and give time to each separately when they are two parts of the whole? Add love to that mix, Jane thought, and you have another Holy Trinity.

She would pray for her friend. She slipped into a short prayer that very moment as Thomas sat staring at the stove, the glass of wine untouched after the first two sips. She did not realise that she was adding her prayers to a long chain of prayers for Thomas. And those prayers collectively produced a ragtag of pushing and pulling that would lead Thomas in every direction until, finally, he chose for himself.

Father O'Toole had just risen from his knees. He had prayed for Thomas' soul, recognising something in the young man but unsure what it was. Matthew never knelt but bowed his head and prayed each day for all his family, but Thomas especially as he seemed so unsettled. Even more so since the matter of Amelia's marriage had hit Thomas head-on. Marriage between Thomas and Amelia was clearly not God's will. Not at present, at any rate.

Elizabeth, Grace, Eliza, Henry; all added their words to God on Thomas' behalf, all because they loved him dearly and saw his agony.

Mr Frampton worked his way through the streets he knew well, barely acknowledging the people he normally nodded to. He was keen to get back to Matthew as soon as possible. Parchman followed at a safe distance, changing his profile and apparent direction constantly in case this new fellow looked backwards. He did not seem to, suggesting he was either an expert or a novice. Parchman expected the latter, he could usually tell at a glance.

Parchman examined the fruit in a barrow while his quarry went into a bookshop. Were books his trade or his cover? Or perhaps it was just coincidence. He moved from fruit barrow to examining men's hats in a shop window, then on to a menu chalked up outside a narrow tavern that, he knew from old, went back and back into the mass of buildings behind.

How much longer should he wait? After twenty minutes, he went back to the hat shop, purchased a new hat, heavy coat and scarf.

"Do you want them wrapped up and delivered, sir?"

"No, I'll wear them now. I... um... have to protect my chest, it's prone to dampness." He felt like saying that he needed a good disguise for the wicked work he was about.

But then he would have to draw out his thin, pointed knife and slide it between the ribs of the shopkeeper when he should be keeping an eye out for the man in the bookshop.

"Of course, sir. Allow me to help with the coat."

"Can I help you, sir? Perhaps a book of sermons? You look the moralising type, if I may say so."

"Did you have a gentleman in here just now? I would say mid-thirties, jet-black hair and heavy eyebrows."

"Oh, there was a fellow that fits that description. He asked after a strange book I confess I've never heard of."

"Well?"

"It was a play called, let me see now, sir, it was, that's it, *The Trial and Execution of an Important Person.* I had to tell him that I did not have it."

"I wasn't asking about the book but the fellow. When did he leave?"

"Oh, almost immediately, sir. It must be three quarters of an hour since he was here." The bookseller looked at his pocket watch to confirm his conjecture on the time, an elaborate exercise that involved shuffling the books he held from hand to hand and back again.

"He really left almost immediately?"

"Yes, sir." The bookseller was not lying. He had left three quarters of an hour earlier but by the back door, which led directly onto Frampton's own back garden in Tulip Street. Frampton had suspected someone might follow him and had played this simplest of tricks to shake them off.

Parchman went back to his office in Whitehall, wondering whether there was any truth in such a strangely-titled play.

He did not like to own up to a clever move against him. The clever moves usually came from him.

"So, you avoided him?" Matthew asked. "I'm sorry to have put you in danger."

"Not a bit of it, Matthew. I have led far too peaceful a life. It adds a little spice to shake things up from time to time! But let me tell you what happened."

Michael Frampton had seen Herr Avercamps almost immediately on entering the palace.

"I went to the records room where I normally collect the documents and, by enormous luck, Avercamps was there. At first, I was not allowed in, was told to come back that afternoon when this important person was finished with the records. I passed a shilling to the guard and asked who it was. Imagine my delight when he said it was 'that Dutch man who is always around the King'!"

"Good Lord, so did you speak to him?"

"Yes, for twenty minutes. He was very interested in the message I passed on from you and has made an appointment for tonight."

"What time?"

"I should explain, Matthew, he does not want to see you, rather it is for me to go to the appointment."

"How so? It is me who needs to report to him?"

"He would like to see you but it is too dangerous for you to remain in London, especially carrying around the evidence you have concerning Sanderson and Sanderson. He wants me to take the papers to him. As it was, I was followed here after meeting with Avercamps, but I managed to shake them off."

"But the risk is the same for you, Michael. Why would you put your life in danger?"

"Precisely because I never have done so! More to the point, Matthew, you are needed most urgently back at home where your wife is struggling with the trials placed upon her. You must go home and as soon as possible."

Matthew agreed with this logic but had to say he had no money, meaning walking home was the only option.

"I'll give you an advance against your father's diaries," Michael said in reply. Matthew agreed with evident relief and they turned to preparations for his speedy departure from London.

It was a blessed day he had stumbled upon Mr Frampton.

Chapter 34

Paul Tabard had an idea.

"I can't sell silk all my life," he said to Amy.

"What will you do, then?" She bent over him where he sat with his boiled egg for breakfast, kissed him on the top of his head, right in the spreading bald patch. She wondered, if it was a son she was carrying, whether he too would go prematurely bald. There was an old wife's tale governing offspring and hair loss but she could not remember it.

"I am going to see Lady Roakes on Sunday." He explained his proposal and asked whether she would accompany him.

"Of course I will come, my love." She bent again, enjoying the feeling of her lips directly on his head.

They set off on Saturday afternoon after Paul's work had finished. It was the second Saturday in October and they fought into a wind that seemed set against them. The two hired horses that Mr Amiss had insisted on leant into that wind, shuddering at the penetrating cold. The sun was somewhere in the sky but they could not tell where.

"Just as well we know the way and are not trying to navigate by the sun!" Amy laughed, shouting to beat the wind.

"I should know the way by now!" he laughed back. "It must be my tenth time to Great Little."

Well, thought Amy, with such dedication exhibited, they should do what they can to assist him.

It was just a question of what they could do.

Despite the wind, the eleven miles to Great Little fell under foot and they were looking down from the rim to the estate below. It was the same deserted place of the last few visits; no builders, no servants scurrying to welcome the new arrivals. Tomkins came to the door and helped Amy slip from her side saddle.

"Careful, Mrs Tabard, we would not want to hurt the baby."

But the words were wooden and hollow; they were meant for there was nothing shallow about Tomkins but there was no fire, no substance, to them.

Here we have one defeated man, she thought as she touched the firm ground beneath her feet, wobbled a bit from tiredness and felt Paul on one side, Tomkins on the other, guiding her up the broad stone steps that announced Great Little to the world.

It was the perfect way to start their awkward request, for Lady Roakes was all about babies. Her own child, Sir Beatrice, was playing on the floor of the drawing room where she sat with the Dowager Duchess of Wiltshire. In the background, quickly straightening her skirts and apron, stood Sally. Amy got the impression she had been sitting with the others a moment before and had jumped up when the door opened and Tomkins announced their arrival.

"Welcome Tabards, how nice to see you." Lady Roakes rose from her chair and shook hands, then gave Amy a hug. "I can see your belly now, Amy! I trust the baby is growing well?" Amy noted the pretence at cheeriness; Lady Roakes was most certainly not feeling cheerful.

"The baby seems fine, Lady Roakes, I mean Alice." She had been told before to use first names and reacted promptly to Alice's raised eyebrows and mock-frown.

"You must stay the night," Lady Roakes said. "We are planning a light supper tonight that Sally will prepare, is that not so, Sally?"

"Yes, Lady Roakes. Would you like for me to bring some tea before I start the supper?"

"Tea, coffee or chocolate, I care not which," Lady Roakes replied.

Meaning bring whatever we have left in the larder and then find something, anything to eat tonight.

Sally curtsied and left the room with Tomkins. Together, they were now the full complement of staff at Great Little; a far cry from the Littles at Feast depiction on the stairs, where servants were tripping over each other to bring new delicacies to the high table.

Paul Tabard's proposal was simple.

"Back me and we shall be partners," he said in conclusion, before sitting back down on the low chair Amy had pointed him towards on arrival. It was so low, he felt he was on a par with young Sir Beatrice trying to shuffle across the rug, rather than the adults who occupied some different strata altogether. Amy had chosen it because it was directly opposite Lady Roakes. As her husband sank down, she saw her mistake but thought it would look silly to redirect him now.

"I would love to say yes," Lady Roakes spoke into the silence. That silence was filled with the expectation of youth and Alice's pitiful duty was to sweep out that hope and shovel in disappointment in its place. "But I just do not have the capital."

"It would not take much," Amy spoke up. "We've worked it out. We could start with just a hundred pounds."

"Amy, my dear, I don't have a hundred pennies, let alone a hundred pounds. I know it is bitterly disappointing but, even if I had the money, my duty is to my tenants first."

"I understand, Alice, believe me I do," Paul said.

But understanding is not necessarily accepting. It was a bitter blow. Paul saw his days spent, ad infinitum, in the silk warehouse or out amongst the houses selling to groups of ladies. Or gentlemen who wished to impress.

Alice had to leave the room and scooped up Sir Beatrice in her arms. She had had no choice in letting the staff go, including the two nurses who had cared for Sir Beatrice. Their work was now done by Alice, with Sally helping. Sally seemed to be everywhere those days: fields, kitchen, nursery and, of course, Mr Tomkins' office. Sometimes, Alice Roakes contemplated, it was only Sally that kept them all going, kept the place together, even if it was ultimately towards disaster.

Sally did it without wages. She did it for charity, for those she loved.

And now abideth faith, hope and charity, these three, but the greatest of these is charity.

Penelope helped where she could, particularly some practical matters of the estate where Alice was too emotionally tied to one cause or another. But her main input was the great strength she suffused into the others, especially Alice, knowing innately when to tease and when to encourage; jokes, endearments and caustic remarks slipped out at precisely the right time. Yet Penelope would have nothing to do with Sir Beatrice. She could not bear babies.

"I hold them in entirely the wrong way and they scream so when I look at the little beggars," she said in jest but meant the truth of it.

To Amy, Penelope seemed distant and condescending. She was very surprised when she was taken to one side and a meeting was suggested with her and her husband in the summer house in ten minutes' time.

Both Amy and Paul were there early, thinking they would be waiting for Penelope, only to find her sitting in a deck chair in the middle of the summer house. It was large and deep, going back into shadows beyond the sunlit area where Penelope sat. It seemed to Amy that the Dowager Duchess was holding court as they took up places on the bench seat that ran around the perimeter.

"Mr and Mrs Tabard, I have to say that I do not believe you." There was no suggestion of first name terms from Penelope. Paul and Amy sat still a moment as the words filtered through to them. Then Paul rose from the bench seat.

"Come, Amy, we are wasting our time here." He looked at Penelope's haughty expression and supposed she was mocking them, enjoying their disappointment in some sick way.

But another thought altogether crossed Amy's mind.

Why, she wondered, was Sally there, sitting in the shadows in the deepest part of the summer house? Her skin colour made disguise in deep shade easy. But Amy had sharp eyes and had sensed the presence of another.

"You may come out, Sally Black. It is best to know who is in on any conversation."

Sally hesitated until Penelope gave a tiny nod. Then she

moved but only to the periphery of the group; from deep shadow to lesser.

Penelope's nod was an instruction for Sally to join the meeting but also a command for Paul to sit back down again.

Which he did.

For there was something about the Dowager Duchess that made one hesitate to disobey.

"As I was saying before being interrupted, I do not believe you in your projections. I think you will need more capital. Do you agree, Sally?"

Two heads jerked up. Why was Sally being consulted? True, she was indispensable but that was as a servant. Why include her in a business meeting?

And then they found out why.

"Your Grace, I do agree." Her voice was strong and clear, inspiring confidence from the start. "I've given this great thought and…"

"But we only made the proposal just now," Paul interjected, then apologised when Penelope stared him down.

"We had considered it ourselves some time ago, albeit in a slightly different format," Penelope said in her commanding voice. There was no doubt which party was in control of the meeting.

"How so, Your Grace?" Amy asked, feeling they were in a land where nothing was familiar.

"Sally, please explain."

The essence of the counter-proposal set the Tabards reeling. It was dangerous, especially for Paul. But the rewards were there.

Penelope would borrow three hundred pounds from her mother, not her father, who would probably refuse it. This would be the injection of capital they required and would be easily sufficient. "Ownership will be one quarter to me," Penelope said. "One quarter to Lady Roakes, despite no injection of capital from that source, and one half for you, Mr and Mrs Tabard. You will have the right to buy us out after five years but not the obligation to do so." Penelope had taken on the partnership essentials having listened on the stairs to her father's many business deals being hashed out in his study at home.

"How is this possible?" Amy asked at the end.

"There is one requirement on Paul that makes all things possible," Sally replied. "Find out who is behind Grimes and Co and discover sufficient illegal activity for us to tear up the contract and take them to court for damages."

"That will put my husband at considerable risk." Amy involuntarily felt her stomach. Would she be left a widow to bring up their child alone? "These are clearly very dangerous people we will be dealing with."

"I will do it," Paul said. "We accept your terms."

Michael Frampton checked left and right before leaving his house. It was dark but in some ways that made it more dangerous, not less. He had a mile to cover. And he needed to do it quickly.

He ran, slamming his door shut, just as he noticed a shape forming across the street. Pounding his legs, he made it to the carriage waiting for him, sent by arrangement. It had two armed footmen and the driver had a shotgun propped against the seat.

He had made it. Stage one was complete. A mile in a carriage drawn by four strong horses and little regard for people jumping out of the way, takes little time. Stage two was upon them.

He edged the carriage door open as it started to swing around a large bend, with a door positioned in the middle of a long building facing the kerb. He waited, muscles tensed, holding the carriage door slightly ajar. He estimated ten more seconds. The driver was accelerating out of the bend, straightening the horses and showing no sign of slowing down.

Five seconds, four, three, two. He wanted to stay in the carriage and drive on, sink to the floor. But now was the time to swing the door open and act.

He jumped, probably a second too soon, hit the side of the steps, his shin scraping along brick. He registered the strike, would have paused to rub it but the ring of shot striking stone just above his ear kept him absorbed.

An arm reached out for him, stabilising him, pulling him up towards the private entrance. It was Avercamps.

"Have you got the papers, Mr Frampton?"

He felt in his jacket for the slight bulge.

"Yes, Herr Avercamps, I have the evidence."

Chapter 35

Paul and Amy Tabard did three things the very next day, having talked through their options that night. Straight after church on Sunday, they left for Dorchester. They rode hard through heavy rain to arrive at Mr Amiss' house in the early afternoon.

"We seek your blessing, sir," Paul said, after explaining the opportunity presented.

"You need it to proceed?"

"Yes, sir."

Mr Amiss thought quickly, running through the options and weighing up the risks.

"You have my blessing on one condition," he said. "That Amy stays here and that you, Paul, keep her and me informed at every stage of your investigation."

Amy protested briefly but saw the sense of Mr Amiss' insistence. At four months pregnant, she would be a liability and, as such, could endanger the safety of her beloved husband. For a moment, she tried to persuade Paul out of the decision they had talked over endlessly already. But this was half-hearted for she could see that Paul was determined to seize the opportunity. There were risks, certainly, but the rewards were substantial. She swallowed her fear and nodded her agreement.

Paul departed on the second task. Visiting his employer on a Sunday afternoon was irregular and the silk merchant was none too pleased to learn that he was losing his most able employee.

But what can you do when a young person shows, right in front of you, that they have found their destiny? You cannot sail a boat directly upwind. The merchant sought to tack this way and that but was bowled over with the force of that wind.

"You're making a mistake, young man, take it from someone who knows business inside out." But he went to his money box and counted out Paul's wages to the penny. "You'll be back within the fortnight, mark my words."

"Sir, I might be and am grateful that you are humouring me. But do not pay me the wages due."

"Eh?" Was this the time for a quick profit, the merchant wondered, or is it a trick of some sort?

"Sir, I wish to resign from your employment but do not wish it to be known as a fact. I would happily forgo my due wages in exchange for some weeks of secrecy as to this situation." It was a good approach and Paul suddenly decided to go one step further. "In fact, if you will allow me to take two pack horses loaded with silk to give me the appearance of a salesman in your employ, I will happily dispose of all the silk and take no commission on the sale."

It was too much for the merchant to resist. He produced a few questions as to the wheres and hows behind this strange request but quickly gave up in response to Paul's evasive answering. The appeal of saving three pounds in wages and making fifty pounds of silk sales with no commission to pay was too much to resist.

They shook hands like the partners they were not; the silk merchant now having a premonition that Paul Tabard would not be back within a fortnight, not back at any time.

For Paul had found his destiny.

That left Paul free for his third task and with the perfect disguise for the area he needed to be in. Remembering his commitment to Mr Amiss and Amy, but also thinking of practical matters such as clothes to wear and a stomach to fill, and lips to kiss, he returned first to their home.

"You will eat with me this evening," Mr Amiss commanded. "I would not have it any other way." His housekeeper prepared soup and cold beef with bread, peas and corn. He passed around a rich red wine, which they drank readily.

"Why don't you go in the morning?" Mr Amiss asked, looking at both of them. He could not be sure about being Amy's father. He often saw her mother in her but sometimes he thought he saw his own mother, long dead now. It came in flashes; the way Amy's mouth coped with disappointment or lit up in a broad smile when Paul, or even he, came into the room.

243

A lot of smiles he had seen over the years travelled not much further than the mouth, fading in brief lines of insincerity. But certain people, Amy and Paul amongst them, shone their smiles from deep within, lighting up every facet of their faces, their very beings.

That was why he had known early on that Paul was a good man for his daughter. There, he had said it. Amy, in all likelihood, was his offspring.

"Because I said I would do three things today and I've only done two of them." Paul's statement shook Mr Amiss back to the world of now.

A fresh horse was ordered from the stables on the corner and Paul mounted after a long kiss with Amy. He gathered the leading rein of the first packhorse in his left hand, making a chain of three horses, the latter two packed with silks to sell. It looked no different to a normal excursion for the best silk salesman in the firm.

"I'll be back before the end of the week," he promised. "And if I can, I'll get word to you before that."

He decided not to look back at his wife. He did not want her to see his tears. He felt like a soldier going to war.

Which he was, in a strange sort of way.

Knowing Blandford Forum well from previous selling trips, Paul decided to stay in the town centre because he was seeking gossip and a bustling town was a good place to start.

But an element of caution took him to the second and quieter hotel in town.

Early on Monday morning, after a breakfast he did not feel like eating, he got together his silk samples and started his familiar rounds.

Mrs Phillips at one of the several dressmakers bought thirty yards of a fine blue silk, described by Paul as 'cornflower blue, like the sky in June'. But she knew nothing of Grimes and Co, just that they had taken the old bookshop on Salisbury Street but not much seemed to go on there.

Mrs Bellew was much the same, purchasing forty yards of a deep crimson that Paul thought too strong a colour for dresses.

But each to their own; he could not be bound by his personal preferences.

"What's going on two doors down?" he asked as he wrote out the bill. "It's a new place, is it not?"

"Yes, Mr Tabard. A fellow called Grimes, I believe. It's quite a mystery as very few people go in and out and the rooms have been in a sorry state for some time."

"It is a mystery indeed, Mrs Bellew. I wonder if they have need of silk. I think I shall enquire."

"It's only a few gentlemen I see going in and out of there, sir. And they don't look like the types to buy silk for their ladies."

"Well, there is no harm in trying, I always say, Mrs Bellew. Thank you for the purchase. I shall certainly let you know if I succeed in making a sale to Grimes or his cohorts!"

"Please do," said Mrs Bellew, anxious for more gossip, even with it not yet ten o'clock in the morning.

Paul tried the door to Grimes and Co's offices. It was open.

"Hello," he called through the open door. "May I come in?" There was no answer, no sign of life.

He stepped down into a low-ceilinged front office with a large but bare cubby-hole desk, single chair and an almost empty bookcase in one corner. There were just a few papers on the bottom shelf. It took a moment for his eyes to adjust for the windows to the front were filthy, while the one to the side was boarded with what looked like the bottom of a crate, held with large nails hammered into the flaking plaster. There was one other door, presumably to a back office or store room. This door was closed.

Paul moved across the room, stopping each time a floorboard creaked. He made it to the bookcase, just the other side of the desk. Why the bookcase? Because the papers on the bottom shelf were the only visible source of information.

But just as he reached out to put down his silk samples and take up the papers, he heard a sound behind the rear door. He froze. Someone was approaching from the other side. He looked around desperately for somewhere to hide. He started back to the front door but stopped halfway across the room, realising he could not make it. He darted for the only other cover, crawling into the cubby-hole space below the desk, just as Grimes entered the office.

"Is that you, Mr Taylor?" he asked. "Ah, so it is. I thought I had heard the door opening a moment ago."

Paul, from underneath the desk, heard the commanding tones of Mr Taylor, whoever he was.

And then it came to him that if he had gone for the door, he would have run straight into Mr Taylor.

But, then again, perhaps he had escaped the frying pan by jumping into the fire. He would have had surprise and momentum on his side in a bolt to the door. He probably would have driven straight through Mr Taylor and be around the corner into Market Place before anybody took note of what he looked like.

But without any information at all.

He crouched in the cubby-hole, castigating his poor judgement. Above and around him, the two voices continued. Paul woke up suddenly to those voices. How foolish of him, for he had not been listening; a prime source of information was passing over his head while he was busy blaming himself for past decisions.

"Well, that should do nicely, Grimes. We need to step up the pressure now. How much damages have they actually paid?"

There was a laugh in response, actually more of a snigger. "Over three thousand pounds, Mr Taylor, and another two thousand is due at the end of the month."

"Excellent. Our backer will be pleased. He will be here on Thursday from London. We will meet at your house again, Grimes."

"Of course, sir, I'll have the wife cook something this time." So, Grimes was married. Paul could not imagine what type of witch would be attracted to a man like him. "Sir, when do you anticipate the auction of Great Little will take place?" That was definitely Grimes' voice. He had heard it before, during a visit to Great Little. Besides, the other man had referred to him by name now. But who was the other man? He had never heard of a Mr Taylor before.

"We will naturally follow the due process of the law in every respect prior to the auction."

"Naturally." The way that word was repeated, plucked from the preceding sentence, told Paul there would be nothing natural about the intended process.

"But I think we can safely count on ownership as our Christmas present." Grimes dutifully laughed at the joke the more senior man had made.

More senior, not just for the deference and the 'sirs' peppered into Grimes' speech, but for the authority and confidence Mr Taylor's voice carried.

And all Paul had was a voice.

And the name of Taylor.

"Sir, if you could come into the back office a moment, I'll outline my ideas for Bagber."

Paul heard the door scratch across the floor as it opened, followed by the sound of it clicking shut. He waited for the voices to fade, then scrambled out from under the desk and dashed to the front door.

It was only when he was back in his hotel room that he realised he had left his silk samples alongside the papers on the lower shelf of the bookcase in the office of Grimes and Co.

Parchman normally hated returning to Dorset, the county of his birth. It usually felt like he was sinking back into a past he much preferred to leave behind. There was nothing of the past about Parchman; he cared nothing for what had gone on before. His concentrations were the other tenses, present and future.

And Dorset to him was all about a past he had dragged himself out of.

But this time was different. He was looking forward to it. Generals need their confidence boosts every bit as much as the private soldier and what better way than to survey overwhelming strength on the battlefield? He decided to come down early and do a little extra surveillance prior to the meeting on Thursday. He would not announce his presence for that would defeat the purpose.

And he enjoyed being surreptitious; it was a form of entertainment for him to notice without being noticed.

Thus, he saw a young man dash from the offices of Grimes and Co, from his position in the gun shop opposite. He had been selecting from an array of very fine pistols and had just about decided on a striking pair decorated with little devils down the barrels. Then he saw the young man. It was someone he had never seen before. Parchman did not forget a face; another source of pride to him.

"Sir, would you like to acquire these for your collection?" the shop owner asked, breaking into Parchman's distraction. By inferring a collection, he gave Parchman the status of an experienced gun owner, also implying status and wealth, making a double dose of flattery. The other tactic he employed just as frequently involved not flattery but fear: only my guns can keep you, Mr Innocence, from the terrible harm waiting just outside my shop door.

But flattery was clearly the best option with this customer, who could never be mistaken as innocent.

"I'll take them but I'll have to come back later," Parchman replied, moving towards the door. The gun shop owner knew this tactic from old. Yet, this customer did not seem like a time-waster.

"I could have them delivered, sir. I just need a name and address."

"I said I would be back later." This was muttered quietly but with penetrating force. The shopkeeper looked at Parchman's face and wished he had not. He lowered his eyes and mumbled, "Of course, sir, just as you wish," before holding the door wide open.

"I'll see you later, sir," he called after Parchman, feeling a need to add something to save the sale but not really wanting to be heard.

"You will," Parchman called over his shoulder as he strode after the young figure he had seen. The shop owner closed the door as an act of security, thinking he might just shut up shop and take a few days off.

Parchman made the corner between Salisbury Street and Market Place just in time to see Paul disappear into the Crown Hotel.

"Interesting," he said to himself. "I'll need to pay a visit later." He pounded fist into palm as he spoke, as if limbering up for hard physical exertion.

"Sir?" A lady passing by thought he was addressing her.

"I was talking to myself, madam," he replied harshly, only the harshness disappeared like smoke into air as the short sentence progressed. He gave the lady a smile that was too full and tipped his hat. "My apologies for disturbing you, madam." This trip was going to be enjoyable, like a holiday. The lead up to the venom at the end was going to be every bit as entertaining as the conclusion itself.

He returned to the gun shop and was all charm as he paid a good price for the pair of pistols with the little grinning devils running down the barrels.

He knew that devils did not grin but that was beside the point.

He thus missed Paul's next manoeuvre who, exhibiting quick thinking, had darted into an hotel he was not staying at, in case he had been spotted by Grimes or Taylor. He did not know about Parchman spying on his own henchmen but his tactic served just as well with him.

He left the Crown by the back door some twenty minutes later and went up a side road, past several tall and imposing buildings to his own hotel, set back from the bustle of Market Place and in a quiet garden; near the centre of things but secluded.

He had another idea as to how to gain information about Grimes and Co and needed the hotel owner's assistance to make it work.

Chapter 36

The front parlour in the Davenport family home was barely ever used. Thomas, the only Davenport resident of the house, used the dining room and his father's old study, making it his own while barely changing anything. Even with Bridget and Tristan Browne staying, there seemed little point in opening up the largest room in the house.

But today was different.

"How many are coming?" Bridget asked over breakfast. Thomas counted them off on his fingers, in pairs to start with.

"Henry and Grace, Eliza and Matthew, Big Jim and Plain Jane, a couple called the Tabards who I do not know, Penelope and her maid. That makes ten." He wanted to add a couple being himself and Bridget, but that jarred because of Amelia. "And then there's yourself, Tristan and myself, so thirteen in total."

"Lizzie cannot come?" Bridget had slipped into using the shortened names of family members.

"She said she would try but her husband is keeping her at home all the time. I've seen her just once since we sneaked into Grime Cottage to visit Mealy."

"Tristan and I took off all the dust sheets in the front parlour last night."

"That was good of you, Bridget." It was back to first names but still overly polite, as if good manners were their protection against raw emotion. But being polite does not preclude looking and both Thomas and Bridget spent long minutes admiring the muscle movements and dappling of light on skin and hair whenever the other spoke.

Until Thomas looked away, thinking of Amelia.

The meeting was set for 11 o'clock. It started on time. There was one other attendee for Elizabeth made it a few minutes late, breathless from riding hard.

"Simon went out this morning," she gasped. "I waited thirty minutes and then had my horse saddled and came straight down here. Have I missed much?"

Elizabeth had not missed much. Thomas started the meeting again.

"Lizzie, this is Mr and Mrs Tabard." He turned to the Tabards. "And this is my sister, Mrs Taylor, married to Simon Taylor, who used to be a lawyer in town and now is land agent to Mrs Davenport at Bagber Manor."

"Hold on," said Big Jim, beating Paul Tabard, who suddenly wanted to ask something. "I think we'll get on an awful lot better if we use first names. Agreed?"

"Agreed," came the chorus back from nearly everyone.

"I am Paul and this is my wife, Amy," Paul volunteered. "I think we know all your first names so there is nothing to stop us moving ahead. Now, Thomas, did you say Mrs Taylor?"

"I did."

"And married to Mr Simon Taylor, who is a land agent at Bagber Manor?"

"Do you know my husband, sir?" Elizabeth enquired.

"No, well yes and no, sort of. Let me explain." Paul gave a detailed account of his adventures in Blandford Forum. "I did not see him but heard him with Grimes. I would know his voice anywhere."

"Commanding, condescending, imperious even?" Elizabeth asked.

"Yes, I would say all those things."

"Then you were hearing my husband, sir. But I am puzzled as to the connection with Grimes. I know he has Grimes living in a cottage on the estate but I thought that was charity and he despised the fellow; after all, he dismissed him a few years ago. Are you saying that they are in league together to bring down Great Little?" Elizabeth was very interested, suddenly hoping that discovering more about the emerging relationship between her husband and Grimes might explain why he had insisted that his daughter, Amelia, marry Grimes. Simon had just insisted that Grimes had been the first and only one to ask for his daughter's hand and, given her age at twenty-seven, he had accepted the offer.

"Better to have a husband of some sorts than to be an old maid."

It was too late to undo the marriage now, of course, but knowledge might ease Amelia's suffering a little.

"I don't know what I am saying, madam, as to his intentions. But I do know that they mentioned concentrating on Bagber as Great Little was close to bankruptcy."

"Good Lord!" And for once there was no one in the room who disapproved of the use of God's name in such manner.

"There is more to come!" Everyone turned their attention to Amy, who had stood up suddenly. She turned to her husband, her arms waving in excitement. "Paul, tell them of the next afternoon in your hotel."

"Yes, of course, I was coming to that, dearest." He cleared his throat while Amy sat down again, as close as she could to her husband, hands on her growing tummy. "If you recall, I left the offices of Grimes and Co in a rush, so much of a rush that I left my sample book behind on the bookshelf next to the papers I was reaching out to read. I was in a black mood that day, wondering how on earth I could gather the information I needed. I considered, in the gloomy way of a defeated man, that had I not been seeking precise information so ardently, it probably would have fallen into my lap, as is the way of the world. But seek it out and it eludes one. I was taking a cup of coffee in the Crown Hotel when it suddenly occurred to me that the answer lay right in my own hotel just up the street."

Paul went on to explain that the Forum Hotel was set in its own quaint garden and was set back from the heart of the town. "It's a popular place for the ladies of Blandford, who repair there for tea and to catch up with their friends. I thought, if anyone knows more information about Grimes and Co, it will be the ladies of Blandford. And what better excuse for a gathering of ladies than a travelling merchant stacked high with best quality silks and determined to sell them cheaply?"

"A little less of the salesman's talk, Paul!" Big Jim risked a joke. Then, when it worked, followed with another. "I expect those silks were discounted from the highest prices ever seen!"

"I do not deny it, Jim. It is a part of who I am. Now, I will continue without the self-promotion."

He had sought out the owner of the Forum and put a proposal to him that he be allowed to host a silk afternoon for the ladies of the town the very next day. It was all arranged. The hotel would bill Paul for the refreshments and receive five percent of all sales achieved but would pay for its own posters to be run off a local printing press immediately.

"It was very well attended. I had the additional benefit of selling my entire holding of stock!" He gave Big Jim a nod and continued. "Furthermore, the hotel owner wanted to repeat it four times a year and I was able to give him the address of the firm to write to. I sent a report to my former employer that evening, explaining what I had done and enclosing a draft for the full funds less the hotel's commission. It was a good plan and a resounding success." Paul was sounding like the businessman he was.

"Yes, dear, but tell them what you found out! About Great Little, I mean."

"Ah yes, I was forgetting myself. Several of the ladies attending knew quite a lot about Grimes and his activities, mainly because husbands were approached in their various trades. For instance, there is a successful grocer shop on Market Place. Grimes came in the other day and purchased a high quantity of rat poison."

"What's so strange about that? Maybe he has problems with rats."

"I've got it," Eliza shouted. "The oats we supplied to Grimes and Co were all contaminated by rat poison when they were returned to us. We had to burn the entire consignment. We lost a lot of money on that transaction."

"At Great Little we have had similar experience with rat poison." This was Sally speaking, the most knowledgeable in the room as to events on the Great Little Estate, because she had chosen to make herself so. "We had half our wheat returned for similar reasons and two of our wells had rat poison thrown in them. We've had to abandon them and dig new ones. Tell me, sir, did you hear from the gun shop?"

"The gun shop?" several people asked, wondering what was to come next.

"Yes, as a matter of fact, I did. But this was not a purchase. Two kegs of gunpowder were stolen several weeks ago."

"They say our barn caught fire after an explosion of gunpowder," Sally said.

There were other occurrences. A local builder reported, or rather his wife did, that Grimes had asked him to provide an estimate to build a dam on the river. He had declined the work when Grimes would not allow him to talk to Tomkins, the Great Little factor, about the effects the dam would have on their farms.

"But the builder knew someone else from outside the area was brought in to do it."

Another lady had dismissed a servant from her employment for being idle. She was concerned about his family, however, and went to visit a week later with a basket of food. She brought that basket home again for they had plenty of food and more than enough ale and gin. When pressed, the wife told her that her husband had been offered a job by Grimes and Co. "It's not difficult work," she had said proudly. "All he does is a few hours a day making mischief up Great Little way. And believe me, my John is good at making mischief!"

There was an awkward silence after the telling of these discoveries; nobody wanting to be first to broach what to do next, until Penelope sighed and stood up to address the room. She had been quiet up to now.

"For those of you who do not know me, I am Penelope, Dowager Duchess of Wiltshire. I am here today to represent Lady Roakes and the Great Little estate. Lady Roakes could not be with us today." Penelope did not offer a reason why; if you do not want to explain something, act as if no explanation is necessary. "However, I bring with me my assistant, Sally Black." Everyone turned to look at Sally, resplendent in the old red dress of Penelope's that gave her skin colour a dark red hue, deepening to black as the influence of the dress diminished. Thomas had only ever seen her dressed as a lady's maid and now noticed her fine features and elegant bone structure, if anything accentuated by her motionless pose, hands folded in her lap. Other than the question about the gunpowder, she too had said nothing during the meeting.

"Mrs Davenport," Penelope turned towards Eliza to a general groan.

"Mrs Davenport has a first name. It is what we agreed," Big Jim said.

"I have agreed to nothing." There was an element of overarching in her voice. She and Sally had not murmured their assent to first names. "Furthermore, I find over-familiarity a tedious matter. By all means, call yourselves Bert and Bob and Mary to your hearts' content but I will not indulge. Mrs Davenport, it seems clear that your estate at Bagber is next in the sights of our dear friends at Grimes and Co. The question we have to address is how we fight back against this attack."

Sally, watching from her seat next to Penelope, was overtaken with pride at the commanding nature of her mistress and lover. Yet, in private, she was so different, so ready to subjugate her own needs to those of her maid. She was overwhelmed with love for this proud, arrogant daughter of a shit-shoveller, wanted to hold her hand immediately but she knew all contact would have to wait until they were alone.

She stopped listening to their plans. This was Penelope's world of intrigue and excitement. She loved that Penelope loved it but her world, recently discovered, was helping Mr Tomkins in a hundred different ways. And she was good at it. She had more than halved the expenses of the estate inside a month. These strict economies meant a little more life for Great Little; a few more days could make all the difference to survival.

For where there was life there was hope.

They made three plans that morning, calling them A, B and C. But their names could just as easily be 'Go to the Authorities', 'Publicise their findings to force them to stop' and 'Fight back, meet steel with steel'.

They voted by private ballot. Big Jim tore a piece of paper

into fourteen rectangles and handed out pencils taken from the study next door. Each person then wrote their choice, 'A', 'B' or 'C', on their slip, folded it and handed it back to Big Jim.

Big Jim and Thomas then opened them and counted the vote before Big Jim declared the results.

"Plan A received no votes," he started to a ripple of approval. "Plan B scored as Plan A." Now the ripple became a flood.

For Plan C, to meet steel with steel, was everyone's choice.

Chapter 37

Thomas had charge of the lantern. He wrapped his coat around it to control the light it emitted. It proved just sufficient for them to see by in the moonless, overcast night that secured their secrecy.

The street was silent other than a dog yapping away at whatever worried it. But the sound blended into the night like colours folding into a book.

They were equipped for the task at hand; a crowbar and a set of lockpick tools that Big Jim had produced, giving rise to a few witty comments about why he would have such picks in his possession.

But there was no humour now as they made their way up Salisbury Street; instead, nerves mingled with determination.

This was stage one of the fight back and they did not want to report failure when they met the others for a debrief in the morning.

Thomas led with the muffled lantern. Paul Tabard came next; he knew the layout of the office. Then came Big Jim with the lockpicks. Last was Henry, with the crowbar. They each had their purpose as they worked their way up the street, rehearsing their roles silently as they went.

They hoped Henry's task with the crowbar would be unnecessary and their hopes were fulfilled. Big Jim picked the front door lock within a couple of minutes; minutes in which hearts beat like town hall clocks against the stillness of the night.

"There's the door to the back room," Paul whispered, his arm pointing, slightly blacker than the night. Thomas, Henry and Paul moved towards the internal door while Big Jim stood by the window as the lookout, hiding behind the shutters that had been left open; were probably jammed open. Soon it was pitch black again in the front office as the lantern went with Thomas into the rear of the building. They had decided it was too risky to show light in the front office, with its large window to the street, so the papers on the bookshelf would be unread for now.

But they hoped for far better findings in the back office.

In which it seemed they would be disappointed. The back office was actually a small storeroom, still five times the size of the office.

And it was completely empty.

"I don't understand," Paul whispered. "Grimes invited Taylor in here to see something."

"Perhaps they moved it afterwards," Henry whispered back. Even their whispers seemed like shouting in that still and black night.

"Or maybe we're not looking hard enough," Thomas added, his voice slightly louder.

"We can't risk full light," Paul said and nobody disagreed with him. They searched the room by one feeble lantern, feeling their way like blind men in the street.

They searched for an hour and found absolutely nothing. Except for one thing that Henry stumbled over in the middle of the otherwise bare floor.

"I've got something!" he cried under his breath but sending the words with such force, like waves crashing on a lonely shore.

"It's my sample book," Paul said. "And it's been cut to shreds with a knife."

"If they've found the samples, they know someone was here." That was Thomas, but he was thinking further ahead, like a chess player. "The question is, did they also know we would come back, so they left the shredded book to taunt us?"

"Let's get out of here!" Henry suddenly called. "It's a trap." As he spoke, the rear door leading out of the store room swung open. None of the three moved; each expected to hear the cock of handguns as figures moved into the room.

Only no one came. There were no deep dark shadows flexing across the grey-black of the night, as if stretching from poses of stillness, now launching out to take their quarry. Instinctively, Henry glanced back at the door they had entered by. It remained closed as they had left it. It was no encirclement, no

258

springing of a trap at all.

Paul took the muffled lantern from Thomas' hand and held it up, loosening the coat from the body of the lantern a little so that the rays broke free and increased the flow of light considerably. "We must have a little light, gentlemen," he said, wanting to confirm his suspicions.

Which was that the wind, picking up and blowing from the east, had swung the rear door open.

It took another ten minutes to be sure. They went together out of the door and into a small yard, bounded on three sides by wooden fencing that rose much higher than a man's height. There was an outhouse against the storeroom wall, but it contained nothing but a pump and an old pail. There was a tarpaulin covering a stack of something, right behind the outhouse. Henry loosened some of the ties and revealed a pile of building materials. It looked as if it had not been disturbed for years.

"There's only one other place to look," Paul said, holding the unmasked lantern up to illuminate a shed in the far-right corner. A large tree invaded from the yard next door, spilling years of natural debris onto the roof of the shed below. They walked carefully over to the shed, expecting something aggressive to come out of the door at any moment. But there was no movement, other than their own.

"Get Big Jim," whispered Thomas, pushing the door to the shed hard. "We need his lock-picking skills."

They abandoned the need to watch the door to Salisbury Street; nobody wanted to remain silent and still in the shadows at the front, when they knew so much was happening at the back of the building. Big Jim was fetched but nobody replaced him on watch.

It took a while longer to pick the lock to the shed but, eventually, it turned. Jim pushed the door, which opened inwards with a huge, grinding shriek as the hinge parts rubbed and jarred. They instantly stood stock-still, crouching into the shape of the shed for fear of being seen. There were several houses backing onto the yard and one, then another, showed lanterns and candles piercing the blackness.

Thomas reacted by shoving the others through the doorway and closing the door behind them. He expected the hinges to make a similar noise on their return run but it seemed they were in luck. Perhaps the door only groaned in the effort of opening and was happily quiet to close again.

They heard voices singing out.

"They're talking to each other from the windows," Paul whispered. It made sense to the others. Those woken by the screech of the hinges did not want to come downstairs into the hostile night, where they could not be sure what awaited them. Instead, they preferred to call out explanations from their respective windows.

The noise of the hinges was quickly ascribed to a cat, a dog, a fox and a drunk. They settled on the fox and slowly the windows closed again with the woken returned to bed.

Thomas moved first, sensing they had got away with it.

"Let's search quickly and get out of here." He flashed the lantern to produce a wave-like orange glow on the pale yellow of untreated wood that lined the shed.

The shed was brim-full of furniture and stacks of boxes, seemingly stacked haphazardly.

"Grimes has been busy," Paul commented.

And Grimes most certainly had been busy, carrying out the instructions placed on him. But those were not the instructions of Simon Taylor, rather they were those of his ultimate superior.

And Parchman chuckled in the street outside as he saw Big Jim being fetched to pick the shed lock and heard the door hinges scrape into the night. One careful instruction had been for Grimes to rig the hinges so that the plates moved against each other with a loud screech.

That way Parchman, hiding in an alcove opposite the office, could be sure that the four intruders had entered the shed. It was the warning he needed; everything he needed to move forward now, quickly and efficiently. They were entering the final stages in the demise of two great Dorset estates.

And Parchman, chuckling to himself as he walked off into the night, was going to enjoy every minute of it.

He kept to the deepest shadows, as was his way. He could see in the dark but remained invisible to others.

It was just one of the many skills he had collected in his varied life.

Inside the shed, in the yard off Salisbury Street, Thomas tried to organise the four of them to inspect each record stacked up there. They quickly realised that it was a hopeless task. There were dozens of old papers, written by various hands, dating back decades. They seemed to be accounts; both figures in endless detail and narratives, describing tedious journeys or fashions that shone like fireflies for a season. There were several diaries of people they had never heard of playing out their lives long ago.

It was a vast jumble of random papers, with nothing apparent linking them. They tried at first to put everything back after checking but soon that became impossible and the pool of discarded matter rose like a river flooding. To start with, they read the articles, desperately trying to find the relevance. They stopped when one or the other thought they had found a link, only to have it dashed on closer examination. After half an hour of false starts, they skim-read the documents. Then they discarded them on the basis of the titles alone.

Still, despite speeding up their work several times over, they had well over half the pile still to do when the sun gave suggestions of light but no warmth to the new day.

"We'll have to stop soon," Thomas stated what everyone was thinking. But they worked on a little longer, hoping to find the jackpot.

"It's like counting grains of sand on the sea shore." Henry said.

With one last effort, each one of the four plunged into the mass and drew out an item at random. Time was running out.

Despite the night being almost over, they each addressed their selection one at a time with the others watching, as if there needed to be an audience for this final act. Thomas went first. He had a large book containing three years' worth of fishing catches. It was written in a hand that matured over the three-year period, suggesting a child growing up as he recorded what he had caught.

Next it was Henry. He had a rent roll from his great grandfather's day.

"This by rights belongs to me," he said, flicking through the pages of neat columns written by a long-forgotten factor. "Hang on, someone has added something to the pages at the back of the ledger." He held up the pages for everyone to see.

"Yes," shouted Paul, if you can shout at whisper level. "This is exactly what we need. See, it has rent for these farms; innocent stuff but superimposed on the last two dozen pages are records written very recently if I'm anything to go by."

Just then a door banged; not a shutting sound at all but the swing of a door opening and bouncing against its stop.

"Grimes, are you there?" It was Simon Taylor, clearly not pleased to have ridden seven miles early on a cold day, just to find Grimes not yet in.

"Henry, where did you find that rent book?"

"In that box over there."

"Bring it with us. We've got to go this minute."

Henry and Big Jim scrabbled for the box. Thomas eased open the shed door, slipped through, closing the door behind him. He returned a minute later.

"They're both in the front room. Simon's giving Grimes a row about being late. They'll be distracted for a while."

"But we've got to walk straight past them," Paul said.

"No, I've found another way."

Their actual escape route was simple. They could climb the stack of building materials and from there jump to the roof of the shed. Once on the roof, they could climb along the overhanging branch and drop into the yard next door.

"See, it has a gate into the alley beyond," Thomas said.

The hardest part was moving the box so they stuffed the papers inside their coats and Thomas took the box back to the shed.

"Why's it taking him so long?" Big Jim whispered, exposed on the roof top. Henry was already down the other side and into the alley, while Paul was climbing along the branch. Jim had to wait to lend Thomas a steadying hand while he jumped from stack to roof.

Thomas reached the shed roof exactly when the door opened into the yard. For some reason, no one came out immediately. Perhaps Grimes turned around in the doorway to receive another blasting from Simon. It gave them just enough time to shimmy along the branch and drop down to the ground.

They were in the back alley, running hard and clutching the various papers and books inside their coats as they ran, before Simon realised that someone had been in the shed that night. He clambered up on the stack of building materials, saw the gate open in next door's yard.

"We've had visitors," he said to Grimes. "From now on you sleep here each night." He climbed down and went to see what had been taken. "It's a mess in here," he cried, "but the box is still there. If that was what they came for, they ran out of time." He kicked the box with his foot and it did not move; it was packed with papers hidden at the bottom of a stack of junk.

It was just as he had told Grimes to do. His anger faded a little; Grimes was an obedient dog. Then he grinned to himself; he would certainly miss his new wife sleeping in the office each night.

Back around the corner from Salisbury Street, safely in Market Place, Big Jim asked Thomas what had taken him so long back in the shed.

"I decided to give them a little sense of false security," he said, explaining that he had taken the empty box and stuffed it full of the discarded and irrelevant papers from the shed floor, then placed it carefully back where it had been before.

They walked to the Forum Hotel and, once safely in Paul's room with some breakfast inside them, they laid out their booty on the table and started to examine what they had.

Stage one of the fight back had been a success. Only, they did not know about Parchman and the knack he had for staying one step ahead.

Chapter 38

Amelia Grimes could not move from her chair. Her bones ached and her fingers were cracked with a thousand stinging cuts criss-crossing her fingers, palms and wrists.

It was her own fault for she had decided she could live with the dirt no longer. She had scrubbed, swept and mopped all day. Not only the interior but also the sloppily-maintained chicken house in the back yard and the front porch that leaned against the cottage as if it could stand no longer.

It was leaning like Amelia had leant before collapsing in her chair. Only she could claim exhaustion towards the end of a long day that had started before dawn, the moment Grimes had left.

The moment Grimes had left...

But he would be back soon, demanding to eat and drink. She would have to get something ready, some eggs and cold meat perhaps? The drink was easy; there was plenty of beer in the shed and a few bottles of brandy in the cupboard under the stairs.

She hoped he would get drunk enough to fall into bed and leave her alone for the night. When that happened, she slept in the other bedroom, slipping back into his bed at dawn.

She knew she had to get up and attend to his meal. She would sit a moment longer; just while the light from the sun sent its last rays across her face.

When she woke next it was pitch black. It was also cold, for the fire had gone out. She raised herself up out of the chair, straining her muscles against their weariness. She lit a stub of candle and took it across to the mantelpiece, where a clock stood. It gave the wrong time but still ticked on, trying desperately to catch up. She had learned to calculate the correct time by adding three-and-a-quarter hours to whatever it said.

But this could not be true any longer. She blinked, rubbed her eyes and got a spot of wax in one eye, picked it out slowly and steadily. Then she looked at the clock again. If nobody had changed the clock, adding the required time to catch up made it close to midnight.

And there was no Grimes home yet. For a moment, she blessed her luck. Perhaps, she thought, something had happened to him. Perhaps he was....

She shook herself, splashed water on her face to waken her further, checked the clock again. It said it was thirty-six minutes past eight. That made it nine minutes to midnight.

She would wait another hour and then go to bed.

In the spare bedroom.

She came to him in the early hours of the morning. She came in just a simple nightgown of her own with shawl and slippers donated by Elizabeth. She came while he was in a deep sleep; he had, after all, been awake the whole of the previous night.

She sat in a chair she carried over to his bed in the attic room that was his, realising that his bed was almost directly above the bed she was using in the room below. She sat and watched him while he slept. A sky without cloud and with a thousand tiny stars visible through the two small windows gave enough light for her to see his facial features and to see him twitch while murmuring in his sleep.

Some strange sensation tells us of the presence of another in the room. It does not always happen but, on balance, more often than not. Maybe waves pass from the sender, radiating emotion from deep within. Maybe they are picked up by a host of tiny receivers and sent by way of various channels within, up to the brain where they poke and prod, working their way in.

And maybe these waves take a while to penetrate and be absorbed. For he did nothing but continue his sleep for over an hour. Then, his eyelids flicked and closed again before opening fully.

"Bridget," he said.

"Thomas," she replied. And no more words were said. But he moved over in the bed and opened the blankets to invite her in.

Mrs Grimes woke alone in the spare bed. She did not know at first how long she had slept but it was clear from the bright ball of sun at about fifty degrees that it was mid-morning. She sat up suddenly and banged her head on the beam that sloped down over the tiny bedroom. Her hand flew up to rub it.

Was her husband back? She did not want to find out, felt tempted to snuggle back into the blankets and hide from the new day. But she knew her duty. Moreover, she knew that certain things could not be shrunk away from; they had to be faced. She pulled back the two thin blankets, wondering what it would be like to be there in winter, with no warm quilts and rugs. Swinging her legs reluctantly, she placed them on the floor, only to realise that she was completely dressed.

"I slept in my clothes?" she asked herself, shuddering at her slovenliness. "I'm getting like Grimes." She did not say 'my husband' for she could not bring herself to that statement, as if she could somehow avoid the reality of her situation by choosing words carefully.

She went like a mouse to the main bedroom. The door was closed. She stood for a moment, trying to hear snoring through the door. There was no sound she could discern so she turned the handle gingerly and heard and felt the click as the door released.

Inside, the room was empty. The bed was clean and made up; a small part of her exhaustive work the previous day. She felt hope rising again but fought it back down. It was unchristian to wish Grimes away for it inevitably meant wishing him harm. But her true feelings clashed with her religious conviction, sending great sparks into the air around her.

Or so it seemed in her mind for actually all was still and quiet, just a few dust mites dancing in the sunbeams that fell in from the large window at the top of the stairs. The weather was strange, like the morning after a storm.

She went into the bedroom, as if it was larger than it was and might reveal Grimes hiding somewhere in a nook or alcove or cupboard. She even opened a bedside cabinet door, perhaps expecting his head to stare back at her.

There was no sign of Grimes either upstairs or downstairs.

Amelia splashed more water on her face from the pail in the kitchen then went about a few essential chores. She fed the chickens and collected the eggs, boiled two of them, which she ate with some stale bread she wet with a little milk, the last of the milk. If Grimes returned now, he would, in all likelihood, demand a glass of milk as was his want before he ate breakfast. She tidied herself up, set her hair in the only mirror in the house, and put on her coat. She checked her purse. There was a florin and some pennies. It was enough.

She would go to the farm nearby and buy some milk, bread and a couple of spare ribs if they had any so that Grimes would have his breakfast whatever time he decided to return.

Bridget slipped down from Thomas' room, getting back into her own just before Tristan came in.

"Up already?" he said, knocking and opening the door as part of the same movement. "I wanted a word with you, cousin."

"I could not sleep so wandered around the house." It was not strictly a lie. She had wandered between the ground and first floor, trying to summon the courage to go up to the attic. "What words shall we share, cousin dear?"

"About what we are to do, Bridget, is all. We need a plan."

Bridget knew her plan but it depended, crucially, on Thomas and she did not know for sure which way he was leaning. She pushed but, also, she pulled for she hated to think of Amelia without Thomas.

But she wanted Thomas for herself.

"What plan, Tristan?" she asked, vaguely.

"I want to go back to Ireland," he replied, missing entirely her mood. "But first, I think it is important that you meet your publisher in London. I propose that we go there together and then go on to Londonderry." It struck him as a neat trip; first to London and then to Londonderry, like visiting two generations of the same family.

Bridget had to admit to the sense of this. She did want to meet with Mr Prendegast. But first she had to know where she stood with Thomas.

"Perhaps we can go in a week," she said, setting God a test in her mind. *Show me within seven days, Lord, what the direction of my life is to be.*

In fact, she was to know a lot sooner.

Thomas walked straight past Bagber Manor without even thinking to enter. He passed where his sister, his brother and his friend lived without a thought, for there was only one thing on his mind. He walked on, lost down a deep well of thought. It took a little over an hour from his home in the centre of Sturminster Newton to Bagber Manor, a little under an hour from there to Grime Cottage.

Hence, two hours of walking in which his mind went over one question time and time again.

"Mealy, did you really mean what you said when we were last together?" She would have to recall what she had said the last time for he could not bring himself to say it despite rehearsing it over and over again.

He changed a word here and a word there of his proposed question as he went along the banks of the Divelish, not noticing the leaves turning or the wind picking up to knock them from their perches. He slowed as he got near to Grime Cottage, feeling a weight in his stomach like a stone.

Yet he went on, knowing that he would have no peace until he had an answer.

When he arrived at Grime Cottage, he went straight up to the front door, noting with a builder's eye how much tidier and cleaner the outside of the cottage looked.

It was as if someone had started to care for the place.

He was about to knock on the door when the sound of female laughter rang out from the tiny bay window at the front of the house. He diverted, walking along a narrow flower border with a few roses, newly pruned.

Newly pruned, he noted. Someone was definitely now taking care of the place.

While his heart recognised the truth, his mind worked on a thousand variations; each one a speck more fanciful than the one before.

Thomas reached the window and looked in from the side of the bay. There were four people sitting in the parlour around a rectangular table. At the head was Grimes, the two sides had a local farmer and his wife; Thomas knew them because he had rebuilt a stone barn for them a few months ago. That left....

At the bottom of the table, facing away from the window, he saw Amelia.

And she was laughing while she acted the hostess, ladling out stew, beans and potatoes she had obviously cooked herself.

Thomas withdrew his head before Grimes looked up from his tankard. He had seen enough.

He had his answer now.

"But are you sure, Thomas?"

"I'm certain, Bridget."

"But Amelia?"

"Mealy is somewhat happily married, reconciled to it. I've seen it with my own eyes. Now, you have not answered me?"

"Ask me again, Thomas."

"Bridget Browne, will you please make me the happiest person in the world?"

"Now, just how might I accomplish that, Mr Davenport?"

"By marrying me, of course."

"I will, Thomas darling, I will. If you are absolutely sure, that is."

"I'm absolutely sure, Bridge," he lied, ever so slightly.

But telling a shade of a lie in love is far from the worst entry in the Great Book of Sin. He was sure but not absolutely so. And she, if she was honest, knew of his slight uncertainty but accepted his words at face value.

Both chose to ignore that little something that tore at the edges of their happiness. They would make it work.

Somehow.

Later that evening, before Grimes left for the bed he had rigged up in the offices of Grimes and Co, he beat his wife soundly.

She deserved it for had he not told her to be jolly with the company he had brought back with him and had she not looked rueful on several occasions?

269

Chapter 39

Adam Jollice considered himself a fair man and one who loved his job. His father had been a bailiff before him and Adam had learned his trade traipsing around with him from an early age.

"If I come down hard on someone," he would say to his wife, "it's only because there is no other way." And Mr Jollice was good to his word, only confiscating goods when he had exhausted every other possibility.

But this one was a puzzle. Normally, the creditor wanted repayment above all else and would be happy with any method that returned his capital. This gave Jollice considerable latitude to devise a solution with minimal damage to the debtor; the source of the satisfaction he gained from his profession. But Grimes and Taylor waved their court papers in his face, demanding that Great Little, in its whole and entirety, be delivered to them that very day.

It seemed they would not be satisfied unless Lady Roakes was brought to utter humiliation, being evicted from her home and sent onto the streets with nothing. There was no hint of compromise in their eyes, no solution for Adam to tease out of a difficult situation, leaving a little more happiness, a little more dignity than the day had promised at dawn.

It was just not the way he liked to do things but the law was the law and this creditor held the upper hand.

He knew the way to Great Little for he had been four times to visit when the Little family had been in residence. They had been notoriously short of money and behind with all sorts of payments. Each time he had visited before, he had managed to pull some solution from somewhere. As he rode down the long, gentle slope of the drive for the fifth time, he had little hope of producing such a miracle again.

Sally saw him first. She had risen from Penelope's bed. She had, unusually, not wanted to lie with her lover at all that morning. She had been working on a plan to sell the winter crops to a third party. It broke the contract with Grimes and Co but, she reasoned, desperate people must do desperate things. If she could get a cash advance for the winter crops and sell the remaining livestock at the market in Sturminster Newton where they had been driven the previous day, she might be able to get the cash together to meet the next instalment of the onerous contractual fine they had been unable so far to pay.

But Penelope had insisted on bed, pleading for just half an hour together or even twenty minutes.

And the sight of the Dowager Duchess on her knees was too much to resist.

She had risen first from the bed, making a joke that Penelope's time was up. She had gone to the window and seen Adam Jollice riding up to the front door.

"We have a visitor," she said, searching for her dress. "I don't know who it is. Where did you put my clothes, Pen?"

"On the chest over there. Will you meet this visitor, then?"

"Yes, Tomkins is away with the livestock at market. I'll need to be quick."

Penelope, in response, jumped out of bed, went to the neat pile of Sally's clothes and helped dress her maid. There was no time to do much with her unruly hair but Penelope did tie on a clean white apron.

"There you go, Sally, back to being a maid again. I wish…"

"What do you wish, Pen?" Sally stopped on her way to the door.

"Oh, it does not matter."

"Tell me, Pen."

"I just wish that our roles were reversed and I would be your maid." The words rushed out in a tumble so that it took a moment for Sally to take it in.

"You serve me very nicely, Pen, when we are alone, that is. It's enough for me." They kissed tenderly before Sally had to leave.

"I'll dress myself and follow you down. I'll wear the pink dress as I can just about do that up on my own."

"It's clean but not ironed," Sally replied.

"Then I shall just have to be the Duchess of Crumpleton!" They laughed, then Sally hurried from the room.

"I see," said Sally, standing in the drawing room where she had taken Mr Jollice. "Lady Roakes is too ill, distraught from the trials of recent months. I am not in Lady Roakes' direct employ. I am maid to her partner in business, the Dowager Duchess of Wiltshire."

"The shit-shoveller's daughter? I'm sorry, I should not have said that."

"Yes, the shit-shoveller's daughter," came Penelope's patrician voice from the doorway. "I am rather proud of my heritage, sir. And this time, I will overlook your rudeness, but this time only."

"Your Grace, this is Mr Jollice, bailiff for this part of the county." Sally curtsied to her mistress and went on to explain the reason for Adam's visit. Penelope sat down and concentrated her considerable gaze upon him. Sally saw with alarm that her lover had indeed dressed herself but had done so very clumsily. One boot had snapped its laces and was tied only a third of the way up so that it made a floppy, sucking noise when she walked across the room to take a seat. She did wear the pink dress and it was very crumpled. She also realised, on walking to stand behind where Penelope sat, that the dress had not been done up, only two of the thirty buttons from waist to neck were attached. She had clearly set out to do it but had been defeated by the fiddly task. Or more accurately, defeated by her own impatience.

But the Dowager Duchess was splendidly adorned in her best jewellery.

"How much is the court asking for, sir?" Penelope asked, substituting 'the court' for the real creditor as she was unwilling to acknowledge Grimes and Co's existence.

Jollice, to his credit, understood this reluctance instinctively; it was one component part of why he was good at his job.

"Your Grace, the court is asking for three thousand as the overdue instalment under the contract."

"And payment can be in kind?" Penelope asked.

Suddenly Sally knew what her lover was up to; why she was wearing all her best jewellery.

"No!" she gasped. "You cannot do it, Pen." Jollice's eyebrows raised when he heard Sally addressing the Dowager Duchess as 'Pen'.

"Be quiet, Sally, or I will dismiss you without a reference. I will not have staff members interfering in my business."

"But, Your Grace…"

"You may leave the room now, Sally. I need you to attend to matters in my bedroom. There is much mending to be done. Work there until I come to you. Now, go!"

Sally gave her lover a desperate look but Penelope turned away, back to Jollice, who confirmed that payment in kind was acceptable.

Penelope did not return to her bedroom after the bailiff left. She had no desire to explain herself to Sally. She wandered around the terrace, dropping down to the garden below before a driving rain and ice-cold wind drove her back inside. Her mind was running through what she had done, her body trembling with fear.

She was without possessions of any kind for the first time ever. It had taken every piece of jewellery to cover the three thousand pounds of debt owing. And that was just an instalment of the total debt due. All she had done was buy a few weeks, maybe a month at most.

And the price of that month was that, apart from the clothes she had, there was not one thing more that she owned.

Oh, but there was one. She owned the deeds to Sally Black who, herself, owned only her clothes and nothing more.

Suddenly, she was laughing. Great shrieks of laughter that brought Sally tumbling down the stairs and into her waiting arms.

"What have I done, Sal? The jewellery was everything I had left."

"You have me, Pen." That made Penelope draw away and look at Sally sharply. Did she know? Or did she mean something else entirely? She looked at the blackness that was Sally's face, looked deep into the mysteries of that face and said in the smallest voice she owned. "Have I been silly, Sally?"

"No, Pen, you've just been you."

Adam Jollice had a technique he employed when someone had paid in kind. He always asked for more than the value of the debt and then took the goods, in this case very fine jewellery, to one of a few traders who he held in high regard. He chose a jewellery dealer in Dorchester and rode there fast. He had to have three thousand pounds by midnight or he would have failed and ownership of Great Little would pass straight to Grimes and Co.

At least, he thought, his fees came out of the creditor's repayment. He would enjoy working out his bill as he returned from Dorchester.

"Will you advance me four on the usual basis?" he asked once the trader had examined the goods. The usual basis was the trader kept the goods for ninety days, allowing time for the owner to re-purchase them together with payment of his fees. After ninety days, they would be sold and the trader would keep the profit arising.

"I will, Adam," he replied, his eyes glued to the jewellery. They shook on it, only ever a handshake, then the trader continued, "I'll tell you because we are old friends, Adam, these pieces are worth considerably more than four thousand, I think I could sell this necklace alone for two."

"I only want four but if you could wait a maximum amount of time before selling, I am sure the Dowager Duchess of Wiltshire would show her appreciation once her fortunes revive," Adam replied. "Now, I am in a great hurry. Shall we drink a quick glass together? Then I must be on my way."

It was four o'clock in the afternoon. He had to collect and bag the money, hire a capable guard and get to Blandford that day.

It was possible, except he also had another call to undertake in Dorchester and then wanted to go back to Great Little after his meeting with Grimes and Taylor; this timetable was going to push the day to its limits.

"Do you challenge my authority, sir?" Adam Jollice was livid but knew from old exactly when to display his anger. "I repeat that the sum due including court costs was three thousand. I have here three thousand in cash…"

"Where did you get that?" Simon spluttered, unable to comprehend it.

"It's not your concern where it came from, only that I can hand it over to you in full and final settlement of the debt confirmed and enforced by the court. You should know that, Mr Taylor, being as you were once an attorney."

Grimes then spoke up, demanding to know why Jollice had counted it out two hundred pounds short.

"That's my fee, Mr Grimes, evidenced by this invoice," he said, sliding a single sheet of paper across the table. "Now, I'll be on my way if there's nothing else?"

It was fifty minutes short of midnight when Adam Jollice pulled his tired horse up to the front entrance of Great Little. This time he was met by Tomkins, who woke the ladies. Sally came down first, then Lady Roakes, severely despondent, roused by the night-time visitor yet not really roused at all.

"Is the Dowager Duchess here?" Adam asked.

"I'm coming, I'm coming." Her woken-from-deep sleep voice could not even pretend to mask the irritation. "What's all this about?"

Adam explained, producing eleven hundred pounds in cash, being the one thousand and half his fee. Only, he implied that there had been eleven hundred left from the original settlement.

"I took the liberty when in Dorchester of stopping to talk to Sir Philip Lacey," he said.

"Who is this Casey?"

"Lacey, Your Grace. Sir Philip happens to be, in my opinion, the best contract lawyer outside London. He is expensive but his fees should leave you sufficient to make the interest payments on your loan."

"Our loan?"

"Yes, Your Grace. The loan is in your name so that you may redeem the jewellery once you have the cash to do so. The

275

lender is well known to me and is unlikely to do anything in terms of disposal without letting you and I know."

"But how are we to get that huge sum to get the jewellery back?" Sally asked.

"That, Sally, is where Sir Philip comes in."

Adam was pleased with his long day's work. He would store it away to tell his son the moment he was old enough to appreciate the story.

That way, the boy would start learning the job from his father and, through the father, from the father's father.

Chapter 40

Penelope and Sally took the trap first thing in the morning. Penelope drove the horse hard, as she always did. They rattled along, bumping over the rutted roads, rain spattering their faces like sea spray.

"It's invigorating," Penelope cried in answer to Sally's plea to slow down. But she did slow down. She would not admit it but any want of Sally's became her mission to provide.

They had dressed carefully that morning, anxious to make the best impression, despite the lack of jewellery for Penelope to choose from.

"You know the strangest thing," Sally said, when Penelope had slowed the horse to a rapid trot.

"What, dearest?"

"I think you are even more beautiful without any adornments."

"You are my adornment now, Sal." As Penelope said these words, the fact that she legally owned her lover came back to mind. It seemed so wrong to own who you loved, as if you had to buy affection rather than find it in life.

Yet she was the owner and she could not, would not, give it up.

They reached Dorchester but Sally took their trap not to Sir Philip Lacey's house but straight to the home of Mr Amiss, where Amy and Paul Tabard lived.

"Can you stay with the horse, Sal? I just need to see Mr and Mrs Tabard a moment."

"No, I'm coming in with you, Pen. Your business is my business."

"And if I order you to stay outside?"

"Pen, my love, you are forgetting that we are alone."

"So?" But the defiance in Penelope's voice was traced through with uncertainty.

Sally did not answer directly. Instead, she jumped down from the trap and held her hand out to Penelope. "I'll take the three hundred to Mr Tabard. You stay with the horse."

"I had something extra in mind," Penelope muttered like a child as she handed over the money.

"I'll ask Mr and Mrs Tabard to come with us to see the attorney too, don't you worry, Pen. Just make sure the horse gets to drink from that trough over there and then tidy yourself up a bit while you wait for me."

Inside, Mr Amiss asked if the Dowager Duchess wanted to come in and take some refreshments.

"She sent me, sir, as she prefers to tend the horse. She is a little... shy, sir, is all."

It was hard to fit all four on the trap but they managed it. Amy sat on Paul's lap, precariously balanced on the tiny tilted-to-the-sky platform at the back. They would have happily sat on a bed of nails, however, for they had not expected the capital for their business to come in so soon. Amy had her arms looped over Paul's neck by necessity but she enjoyed that necessity very much indeed.

Sir Philip Lacey was stiff and formal, putting Penelope at ease instantly and putting her back in control.

After introducing the Tabards, she added that Sally was her maid "who helps a little with some estate business as she has an aptitude for numbers and such like. I thought it an idea to bring her along."

Sir Philip had two chairs for visitors in his office. He called in his assistant and asked for another to be brought in so that Paul might sit.

"Sally will bring it in," said Penelope. "Run along with Sir Pip's assistant, Sally dear, and bring a chair for Mr Tabard."

"Sir Pip?" Sir Philip asked, frown forming like weather on the horizon.

"Yes, it seems appropriate somehow," she replied. "To pop an inflated balloon is no bad thing from time to time."

Amy and Paul looked at each other, wondering if this would be the shortest ever client-attorney relationship.

But the dark clouds scattered, chased out of the sky by Sir Pip's great gusts of laughter.

Penelope, seemingly oblivious to all this, beckoned to Sally to bring the small briefcase she clutched, so that they could start the discussion.

And it was clear to Sir Pip after just a few minutes who made the decisions and why. He did not concern himself with the relationship between Sally and Penelope, just with the fact that Sally had an enormous ability to condense detail into salient points for action. Unlike Penelope, who Sir Pip liked immediately but could see was all front, operating entirely on instinct. He understood where the true power resided and how it was evolving.

Within fifteen minutes of starting, Sir Pip had called his assistant for another chair and Penelope did not suggest that Sally fetch it.

Penelope was useful to the meeting in two particular ways. She handed four hundred pounds to Sir Pip's assistant. But more importantly, she stopped proceedings after the first hour.

"Sir Pip, do you have someone that can carry a message speedily?"

"Yes, why? Do you want to summon Lady Roakes?"

"No, she is certainly not well enough. This has come very badly on her. I am her partner and can speak for her in all regards concerning Great Little. Rather than dragging Lady Roakes down here, I feel it imperative to broaden this matter to include Bagber Manor, which suffers from similar contagion, although not so advanced."

It was agreed to reconvene early the next morning. In the meantime, Eliza and Matthew Davenport would be summoned, plus Thomas as well.

"I'm sure you can all stay the night with us, Your Grace," Amy said when they had left the office several hours later.

"That would be acceptable, Mrs Tabard, my thanks to you." Penelope had feared otherwise and did not want to pay for staying at an inn, especially as someone of her status would have to take a whole floor.

"Would you mind sharing a bedroom with your maid?" Amy asked, working out the numbers and room allocations in her head.

"That would be tolerable this once," Penelope replied but was unable to hide the broadest of smiles.

"We made good progress today, sir," Paul reported to Mr Amiss during a debrief held in the small but elegant drawing room he had created on the first floor.

"I'm glad to hear it," Mr Amiss replied but looking at Amy. He was certain now that she was his daughter. "You will, I hope, consider setting up your firm's office in my house?"

"We couldn't, sir, the inconvenience to you..." But Paul stopped when he realised Mr Amiss was talking to Amy, not him. The rumours were true, then.

"Of course, we will... sir." And Amy knew it, too.

Chapter 41

Parchman liked shadows and dark corners. He liked to see more than to be seen. But there was a vanity in this for he delighted in his ability to move around unnoticed, to eavesdrop and then spring from nowhere. Particularly the springing, for he loved to see shock and fear spreading across faces.

But he knew today was not a day for springing out. Nobody on this grey November day would have a chance to register surprise or dismay at seeing him. He would be incognito from grey dawn to grey dusk, blending into that greyness as was his way.

For when the courts became involved, all the certainties were brushed away. True, Parchman relished uncertainty. But not this type. What he relished was the uncertainty of others caught in surprise.

Courts and magistrates meant a different uncertainty; they spelt out one thing to Parchman and he shuddered to think of everything he had planned unravelling.

Except the rope that held the noose about his neck.

But he was ready for this. He was ready for every eventuality he could imagine, provided he kept to the shadows, played it safe. He could rely on his cleverness, too. He ran through it all again in his head, one more time would do no harm:

1. *There is only the word of Taylor and of Grimes to link me to anything.*
2. *All the payments are untraceable and the money-carrier is lying in a ditch in the field next to Grimes' miserable house. He had served his purpose and was needed no more.*
3. *Provided I remain invisible, there is nothing to link me to the firm of Grimes and Co, however hard they look.*
4. *And the beauty of it all is that neither Taylor nor Grimes can name me without implicating themselves.*

It pleased him to list his cleverness once again.

Parchman had not been worried when Paul Tabard had first come on the scene, digging into Grimes and Co, poking his nose where it was not welcome. He had, nevertheless, asked quietly about the silk salesman and, as soon as he made the link, he felt alarm rising. It was too much to be a coincidence, this link to the early stages of the fraud Parchman had instigated. Tabard was the only part of the firm of Sanderson and Sanderson that remained, having fled when old man Sanderson was sent to the afterlife with a circle of bright red around his neck. Now, Tabard was begging to be dispatched in similar manner and Parchman would make it happen.

All in good time.

He had watched and waited in the shadows for too long now. Not that patience was not to be applauded but he sensed things coming to a head. He would be there for the climax.

He was in Dorchester, although nobody knew of his presence.

Nobody, that is, except the fat man who had recognised Parchman from his youth and claimed to be his uncle. Or was it great uncle? This uncle was lying down now in a quiet corner of the town, staring straight up with open eyes.

He was concerned about Paul Tabard. But Sir Philip Lacey sent shards of ice into him. He knew Lacey to be an intelligent man, astute and perceptive. And where he went, the magistrates were always close behind.

Which is why he was in Dorchester right now, outside the office of Sir Philip, trying to think of some pretext to enable him to get close enough to listen in to the meeting going on inside. There were several Davenports there, plus the Wiltshire brat. The connection of Roakes and Wiltshire with the Davenports and Merrimans told Parchman that they knew the target was both estates, first Great Little and then Bagber; they had worked out the link between them.

Congratulations, my 'friends', at least your joint-demise will be entertaining.

But it was all a game, for they had no evidence. Without papers proving the fraud, they could rant and cry until the sky fell down but they would be able to do nothing against him.

They might find something against Grimes and Taylor but he would always be safe.

In fact, it might be better if they did act against Grimes and Taylor. No one can talk with their neck stretched and their body dangling lifelessly on a rope.

For he had been far too clever for them, always several steps ahead. He grinned to himself in the shadows, remembering the cleverest thing of all. Last week, he had destroyed the entire contents of the metal box Grimes had hidden in the shed. It had contained all the records of their fraudulent activity. He had demanded Grimes bring it to him unopened, for fear something incriminating might escape. He had then set fire to a remote pigsty on the Bagber estate on Sunday morning when everyone was at church. He had fed every single item in the box to the flames, then thrown the empty box in for good measure.

Those delicious flames had chewed up the evidence, taking whole crimes in one swallow, never to be seen again.

"This is the line of attack I propose," Sir Pip was the only person standing in his crowded office. As well as those summoned by Penelope, Henry and Grace Sherborne had come and also the two Browne cousins. "Who is familiar with naval tactics?"

"My old tutor spent some time on naval battle stations and such like," Henry replied. "He had been a naval officer before he lost his leg fighting the Dutch."

"So, you may recall the forms of attack, My Lord?"

"I do, sir, at least in part. The traditional strategy consists of a line of ships that would bear down on the enemy's own line, cutting them in two. The cannon would fire and cause great destruction but much of the fighting was by boarding isolated ships, one at a time."

"Exactly, I could not put it better myself. Now think of us as the attacking line…"

The problem, Sir Philip, with your logic is that you have nothing to attack with. Parchman, posing as a beggar beneath the open window on the street outside, could hear every word. *You need firepower and you have none.*

Then he heard Penelope's voice above the others.

"Hush, sir, for all we know one of them might be posing as a beggar in the street outside, listening to our every word." Parchman sprang up, leaving his beggar's bowl with its few pennies, rushed for the nearest door he could see.

"Can I help you, sir?"

"Um, is this the alms house?"

"No, it is an attorney's office. For the alms house you need to go back along the street and…" But Parchman was not listening for he could just hear Penelope above him declaring that there was no beggar there that she could see, although there had been one once for he had left his bowl behind.

"With some money still in it if I am not mistaken," she called from the window.

Sir Pip's connections meant it was easy to get the ear of a magistrate and preparations were quickly made.

"Such a change, Pen, from just a few days ago," Sally said on their drive back to Great Little. The house had been selected as the base of operations, not least because it had fortifiable rooms in the cellar. They were going back to make ready.

"It looked like everything was lost then and now suddenly there is hope. The wheel turns very rapidly at times, Sal my dear." Even Penelope felt the pomposity of her words. Sally pinched her sharply and told her to come down from her high horse.

"I'm sorry, Mistress Black," Penelope said, after looking adoringly at her maid and lover.

They could talk freely, for they were alone on this trip. They were happy, full of hope and in love. They did not care that they had little protection against the persistent heavy rain and were already soaked through.

"If you will get the hot water from the kitchen, Sal, I will give you a bath and wash you all over when we get in."

"I would like that very much indeed."

"And then I shall dry you all over and dress you with great care." Penelope slowed the horse a fraction to better concentrate on Sally. "All this because…"

"Why, Pen, why all this?" Sally hoped Penelope's reserve would not get in the way. She knew what was coming and desperately wanted to hear it.

In response, Penelope brought the trap to a complete halt.

"All this I do because I worship and adore you." She clicked to the horse, snapped the whip above its head and concentrated for the last mile on driving as fast as she could while not risking the legs of their last horse.

But there was no time for baths when they pulled into Great Little a few minutes later. A band of militia under Colonel Hanson, the good friend of the Davenport family, was at the gate, trying to light fires in the rain.

And more were expected.

"Sir, do not stay out in the cold and wet. Come into the house, where at least it is dry," Penelope called across to him.

"I stay with my men, Your Grace."

"I meant the lot of you, sir. I would not have anyone out in this rain when there is at least a partial roof within. Put out those pathetic fires and follow us." Her commands required obedience and she received it.

"Sally," no abbreviations to her name now for they were in company, "jump down from the cart and find Tomkins. Take him this money and tell him to provision for forty soldiers and a dozen or more guests and to do so instantly. He may take the trap as we are done with it but he is to rub down and feed the horse first. Then come to the Great Hall for I shall need you to serve the soldiers and our guests when they arrive."

"Yes, Your Grace." Sally curtsied to the back of the trap and turned and ran for the kitchens, where she breathlessly tried to explain the situation to Tomkins, who clearly was not listening.

"What is it, miss?" someone asked. Sally turned to see a tall, thin man with brown eyes and a tired expression. He was wet, flushed and his hair stood on end.

"Who are you, sir?"

"Oh, he's a messenger from the palace," Tomkins answered. "We have a visitor arriving any minute."

"I rode as hard as I could," the messenger replied. "But my master was in a dreadful hurry, too. He has laid it all before the King."

"What, the King is coming here?" Tomkins clearly was having a hard time comprehending. Sally was quicker to understand.

"Who is coming, sir?"

"Mr Avercamps, sent by the King. He will be in within two hours. He is one of the King's closest advisers."

"Then we have no time to lose," Sally replied, feeling the urge to take control. "Mr Tomkins, go immediately to the village for supplies. Take the trap. I'll organise one of the soldiers to rub down the horse while you make a list of what we need, sufficient for a royal adviser and a band of hungry soldiers. Sir, what is your name?" She turned to the messenger, while also finding paper and pencil for Tomkins. "Sit, Mr Tomkins and concentrate on the list."

"Julius Byrne, Miss. How may I help you prepare?"

"Come with me, Mr Byrne, to see the mistress; both of them, in fact."

Most of the soldiers did not stay long. Adam Jollice arrived as the magistrate's delegate with Sir Pip. They brought with them two arrest warrants, for Grimes and Simon Taylor.

"We want to pick them up independently," said Sir Pip.

"Then, I'll send two separate troops," James Hanson said. "Which is the more dangerous?"

"Grimes, without a doubt," Penelope said. "He has the cruel look of another man I knew from some other difficulties in the past." She was thinking about Parchman and, through sheer instinct, had come up with the true source of power behind the illegalities. Yet, it was not quite enough volume of insight to make the direct association.

"Then, I'll go with that party and send my lieutenant to pick up Taylor. Will Mrs Taylor be at Bagber?"

"In all likelihood," Eliza replied. "She was there when I left yesterday. Simon forbids her to leave most of the time."

"So, we will be imprisoning two people and freeing one other."

"Far more by way of freedom than you imagine, sir," Penelope added, in her own acerbic way.

"Quite so, Your Grace, quite so."

The excitement increased noticeably when everyone learned that Jacob Avercamps was expected that evening. Sir Pip led that excitement.

"I know Avercamps well," he said. "We corresponded during the dark years." This was a reference to the reign of James II, now encamped in Ireland in a bid to regain his throne. "We met last year when he landed with the new King."

"What does it mean, his coming?" Penelope asked.

"I think it means there is a London element to this fraud we have uncovered. I mean some form of government involvement. I need to think on it a bit more." Sir Pip asked for a quiet sitting room and was shown Sir Beatrice's old study, the room he had died in. "Yes, just a glass of wine," he replied in response to the offer of refreshments. "And an hour on my own," he added pointedly when Penelope sat on the long sofa in the study.

"Well," she replied, rising again so quickly that she might have denied later that she ever sat at all, "I have things to do. Come, Alice, we have some preparations to attend to."

Colonel Hanson split his force into three. He took twenty men to Blandford, the shorter distance, to pick up Grimes. His lieutenant took ten to Bagber for Simon Taylor. The colonel left ten men behind to secure the cellar rooms.

"You say the cellar has two entrances?" Adam Jollice asked.

"Yes," replied Penelope. "As part of the rebuilding, we put in a new entrance from the kitchens. The original one goes from the pantry off the Great Hall. We had intended blocking that one off before we ran out of funds."

"Well, I am pleased you did run out of funds."

"How so, sir?"

"It means we can take each prisoner in without any risk of them seeing the other. Now, can someone show me the cellars? I want to select the two that are the darkest and dampest."

Simon made a lot of noise, shouting that he knew the law and would see them punished for their violation of it. He complained all the way back until the sergeant asked permission of the lieutenant and received a nod in reply.

"Go to it, Sergeant."

The sergeant pulled off his neck scarf and rode up to Taylor from behind. With a deft movement he put the scarf around his mouth, gagging him.

Simon Taylor continued his ranting but it was muffled and garbled, eaten up by the sergeant's none-too-clean scarf.

Ten men rode out for Simon Taylor. Eleven men returned, indicating their success. Eleven men and one woman, for Elizabeth insisted on coming with them.

Grimes was not so easy. It was one thing to locate him but quite another to secure the man.

They went to the offices of Grimes and Co but they waited in an inn at the other end of town, using Matthew Davenport as a scout, for they thought he was unknown to Grimes. They feared as the gloomy day came to its conclusion that they were too late and had missed him. Hanson considered going on, all the way to the northern fringe of Bagber Manor where Grime Cottage was situated, to see if he had already gone home. At six o'clock he did that but decided to split his force, sending his sergeant in command of a force of ten.

"See if he is at Grime Cottage and then come back here if he is not. If you find him, take him straight to Great Little and send one man back to me."

"Yes, sir," the sergeant saluted, called out nine other names and went to the inn stables for their horses.

The hours went by, one soldier in a dark and heavy cloak to cover his uniform, going up Salisbury Street at irregular intervals to meet with Matthew in a different doorway each time. Parchman saw him and knew what he was about. The soldier did not see Parchman, of course. Almost nobody saw Parchman, unless he chose to be seen.

Then, at nine o'clock, Grimes came walking up Salisbury

Street on his horse. He dismounted at the front and led the horse down the side alley to the back yard. Parchman saw Matthew walk away, strolling at first, then picking up speed as he turned the corner into Market Place.

The question that went through Parchman's mind was whether to warn Grimes. The thought entered and departed rapidly; rejected, application denied. If he warned Grimes, what would he achieve? Nothing in regards to his own safety and security. True, he would save a loyal henchman.

But henchmen were ten a penny.

And there was the risk that he would be caught by the soldiers. No, it was time to head for Great Little and the next episode of this entertainment that would, without doubt, end in the demise of both Great Little and Bagber Manor.

And he would not have to share the thrill and the satisfaction with anyone else; he was effectively a lone agent now.

Thus, Parchman hustled silently away and missed the fight that woke half of Salisbury Street and was the talk of the town for weeks after.

Ten soldiers against one man. It should have been easy but it was not.

By half past ten they had secured Grimes, tied and bundled onto the back of a horse. But Colonel Hanson had one of his ten dead and four wounded.

"I'll take him back," said Matthew, "if you can see to the wounded and inform the authorities about…" He did not say it, but one fine young man had died with a vicious swing of a wood axe to the head. Grimes had fought wildly with whatever came to hand and had received barely a scratch in return.

For Sir Pip had been adamant that they take the man alive.

Chapter 42

Simon talked within minutes. Grimes never spoke again. The two were held in different cellar-rooms, taken there by different entrances. Other than their guards, they saw no one.

Grimes retreated into himself; he refused to acknowledge the presence of anyone else. Simon Taylor, on the other hand, whimpered continually when the makeshift gag was taken from his mouth.

The interrogating team consisted of four people. Adam Jollice was in charge as the Magistrate's deputy. His opinion was the only one that would count. The Magistrate would decide whether to hold the pair for trial based on the report he received from Jollice, including conclusions as to which crimes had been committed.

Jollice could have taken the questioning all by himself. But he knew his limitations. He was too affable to invoke fear, too accommodating to generate uncertainty. So, he built a team around him. He chose Colonel Hanson, the leader of the local militia. His uniform added authority while his presence aided the interrogation. He asked Sir Pip, knowing that his reputation as a severe but honest lawyer would bring credibility, even if he did represent the opposing party in the civil case. And then, of course, Jacob Avercamps could not be excluded, had he even wanted to. Avercamps gave another dimension to the questioning. He did not often speak but his insight and knowledge terrified Simon Taylor when he did. It seemed to Simon that he was encircled and his case was hopeless. As a lawyer, he could see the jury weighing up the evidence.

And when that evidence came, in part, from a senior government official, there was little prospect of a 'not guilty' verdict.

Grimes said nothing, with very little expression to give away his thoughts. Simon, however, raised his terrified voice to a loud squeak and was about to protest against the expanded team interrogating him, when a voice inside him said to stop.

Don't be a martyr to some alien cause. Look after yourself. Only then can you fight back.

"That is acceptable," he said, trying to lower his voice and flatten it out, as if he did difficult interviews every other day of the week.

"Good," said Jollice, "we will commence then."

In reality, despite Jollice's position and Avercamps' seniority, Sir Pip led the charge and he did it in such a strange way that Colonel Hanson almost stopped the proceedings to ask for an explanation.

"Mr Taylor," he started, "we are deeply sorry to have inconvenienced you."

"What on earth…"

"But we must clear up some matters of serious concern to the courts regarding criminal activity. I am sure we can quickly resolve the outstanding issues and let you go on your way."

"I do not understand, sir." Simon's eyes grew so wide, Hanson could have jumped into them and swum around happily.

"The court has asked Mr Jollice, who I believe you know to be the bailiff, to investigate certain allegations about malpractice in the pursuit of a contract. Their concern, Mr Taylor, is that these amount to criminal activity. If we can dismiss these fears, we will be able to return you to your home in quick fashion." Sir Pip's deliberately verbose language left hanging in the air the question of what would happen if they could not dismiss the fears. But Simon was deaf to this point, just heard the promise of getting home safely.

And he started talking.

Parchman, disguised as a tradesman, brought in fresh produce for the kitchen and asked what on earth was going on below stairs.

"Just a couple of prisoners on a big fraud case," said Tomkins, rushing from one task to another, feeling ten years younger for his effort.

"Are the prisoners obliging the interrogators?"

"One is and the other is refusing to say a thing, so I've heard." Parchman knew who was keeping his silence and who was talking.

"I see you are very busy here," he said to Tomkins. "I would be happy to take refreshments to the guards in the cellar if it helps you."

"Yes, yes, thank you, my man. Take some loaves, cheese and beer from the pantry if you will." Tomkins was heading for the door as he spoke. It had not been this busy at Great Little for a long time.

Another weapon of Parchman's armoury was his ability to seem like one of the boys. He handed out the bread and cheese, produced an ample amount of beer and also a bottle of brandy he had pinched from the pantry upstairs.

"So, how's it going, friends?" he asked the soldiers. "We don't see much excitement in these parts and this promises to be a good show for certain!"

Within a few minutes he had confirmed his initial suspicion. Grimes was keeping strict silence, refusing even to confirm his name. Well, if the fool wanted to mime his head into the noose out of some misguided concept of loyalty, that was his lookout. It was exactly how he had thought Grimes would behave.

Taylor, on the other hand, was a different thing altogether. He had expected him to cave in under questioning but to put up a fight first. He had expected indignation and outrage for several hours. Apparently, Taylor has started talking immediately.

And he had mentioned the connection with Parchman quite a few times.

"Parchman, what sort of name is that?" said Parchman. "It sounds like something the Magna Carta got scrawled on all those years ago."

He left while they were still laughing, thinking to leave on a high note. Besides, he had the information and he had promised himself to leave the moment he learned his name was mentioned.

But he wanted to be around for the fun, especially when they found no evidence to link him to the crimes for which Grimes and Taylor would have to be punished.

They told Grimes he would swing for the crimes and all they wanted was confirmation that Parchman was behind the scenes, pulling the strings.

"You see, your friend Taylor has told everything, implicating you and Parchman in an intricate set of illegal activities that someone must pay the price for. If you would only talk you might be able to exonerate yourself, demonstrate your innocence. As it is, we have to assume your silence to be an admission of guilt."

Still no response.

"Clearly, Parchman has worked hard on you but your loyalty is misplaced. It is you who will swing, not him. We have written evidence. You thought, according to Taylor who has told all, that you had destroyed the contents of the metal box. Or rather, you took it to Parchman and he destroyed it. But, what you did not realise is that our enterprising agents investigating these crimes had already taken fistfuls of the incriminating documents and replaced them with some of the innocuous rubbish piled up in the shed at your offices." This news got a flicker of interest, perhaps Parchman had made a serious mistake and perhaps his faith in the man was misplaced? But no, Parchman had sworn he would never desert Grimes and there was no way to prove these charges. All he had to do was keep strict silence and their case would unravel. Taylor would talk but they could not convict on the basis of one man's word.

Grimes returned to a desultory inspection of the ground between Grimes and his questioners. Sir Pip lost his patience. "Oh well, have it your way. Guards? Take this pathetic being away. He is too blinded by loyalty and stupidity to see the way he is being used so there is little I can do to help him."

Outside, deep in the shadows, one soldier of the militia passed this news on to Parchman, receiving first a bag of coins and then a knife neatly inserted between the ribs. When they found the body the next morning, there was no bag of cash, just a body lying in a pool of its blood.

It was Parchman's ultimate move. But the strike was made more in anger than humour for when the soldier had passed on the news of the evidence pilfered from the metal box by Thomas, he knew he was undone. He should have acted when he saw them walking clumsily out of the alley that early morning. They obviously had wads of incriminating records stuffed up inside their coats.

He could have pounced then and knifed all four of them. It was well within his capabilities to have done so. But he had fooled himself that everything would work out well and had wanted to play this out, to see the final destruction of those that had humiliated him before.

And now were humiliating him again.

Epilogue

It snowed on their wedding day. Not a light spattering but a serious fall starting at ten the night before. By morning, there were eighteen inches on the ground and another eighteen inches hanging over them, as if the bottom of Heaven was falling out onto the earth below.

Bridget wore a red dress, the colour of the tulips that lay in the ground and refused to come up. It was late March, with Dorset in a grip of ice. Thomas wore green and when he carried her later that day, after the ceremony, the couple looked like a defiant tulip determined that spring was here.

When it was most decidedly not.

Everybody cheered but the snow muffled the cheers and swept them into silence. It seemed a muted world. They were both happy but not as happy as they could have been.

For eating away at them both, in slightly different ways, was Amelia. She had insisted that the wedding go ahead, even when Bridget took her courage in her cupped hands and offered Thomas back to her.

"He has always been yours, Mealy."

"I am a married woman, Bridge."

"But…" and the rest could not be said, not by Bridget at least. For Amelia's husband, Grimes, lay rotting in jail, awaiting trial. They had discovered the body of the money-carrier in the ditch below Grime Cottage in the big empty field that seemed to separate the Grimes household from the rest of the world.

Grimes had been accused of the murder of Russell Smith, a casual labourer without any family or friends; a loner who had met a very lonely end. It might have seemed unfair to Grimes for Smith had died not by his hands but at Parchman's doing. But, if it did appear unfair, Grimes made no complaint at all, not even any movement on his blank face when the charges were read out.

He had been accused by the magistrate but the higher court

had thrown it out in January; there was no evidence that he had killed Smith other than proximity to his home. He was still in prison, talking to no one, awaiting trial for fraud.

Parchman had disappeared completely, presumably with all the money the fraudulent contracts through Sanderson and Sanderson had generated.

For they searched the offices of Grimes and Co and found nothing at all. They searched in London too, both his office in Whitehall and at the firm of Sanderson and Sanderson. In the process, Robert Ferguson was arrested and questioned but his questioners came to the conclusion that he was innocent but incompetent. He was dismissed from his government post with three months' pay. When he collected his personal items from his government office, he picked up his money box from its hiding place under a floorboard but felt its lightness before he saw the broken lock.

"I'm sorry, Lady Roakes," Adam Jollice, the big-hearted bailiff had said, "but we have found no cash, not even a sixpence."

"Do we have the wheat that has not yet been contaminated?" Alice asked, much improved now from her illness.

"Yes, you have that."

"And the deeds to the farm in the centre of our land?" Penelope asked.

"Yes, that too. It is 316 acres of good farmland."

"The most expensive land we've ever bought," said Lady Roakes in half humour for she was fighting back now after giving up before, aware that it was only her friends and associates who had kept her from ruin.

And now everyone was at the wedding, even Amelia, buried in a dark brown bonnet, as if it was she under sentence rather than it looming over her husband. She had come for complicated reasons she could not begin to understand. Sometimes, she mused, things get so complicated that a simple wind is needed to blow the confusion away.

She thought of her father, also in jail awaiting trial. Talk was of indentured service in the colonies but seven years of unremitting hard labour might as well be a death sentence for someone of his age; Grimes, her husband, would likely survive it but not Simon Taylor. She thought of him when he had suffered his stroke four years earlier. How could there be such hatred within a man shown only compassion and care? Was anything missing from the attention the ladies of Bagber Manor had shown him? Love, perhaps? Can you love someone who only hates?

Amelia had gone to visit him several times, witnessing his pitying cries alternating with rage against the world.

She had once been to visit her husband. He had not looked at her, had not said anything. She had left, duty done.

Now, the love of her life was marrying another, a girl she barely knew but could see was solid and strong, a good match. She had insisted the marriage go ahead because... well, why had she insisted?

She sat on the hard bench in St Mary's, where Bridget, being an Anglican, had chosen to get married, and pondered that question.

Then God spoke to her and told her to love herself again. For only when you love yourself can you love others.

Matthew was uncomfortable in Anglican surroundings but endured that discomfort for the sake of the bride and groom. Increasingly his brother, Thomas, seemed disinterested in the true Presbyterian religion. He had stopped going to church in the Great Hall at Bagber Manor and went now instead to the Anglican church. Some might say it was infatuation with Bridget but Matthew thought otherwise, especially since Father O'Toole had arrived for the wedding. Why had Thomas written to invite him? What purpose could a Papist priest serve? He was a good man and had helped them escape but why bring him in now?

There was much to worry about with the way the world was going but at least one thing was certain. He was a father. Eliza had recently given birth to a little girl, a Lady Merriman of the future. He smiled as he thought about her. God was truly wonderful to give such gifts to him; first Eliza and then Baby Eliza.

He had consulted Eliza about the godparents.

"If you ask him, Matthew dear, you are tying yourself into that life. Do you want that?"

"A little part of me does, my love. Is that wrong?"

"No, dearest, it is natural to want conflicting things. But how shall we balance Jacob Avercamps with someone else?"

"Easy," Matthew replied, "we shall ask someone to be godmother who I never would have thought worthy."

"You mean Penelope Wiltshire?"

"How did you know, Eliza?"

"Because nobody on earth would stick up for someone like she would, should our little girl ever need that care. She's overreaching, crusty, imperious, arrogant and absolutely full of giving, despite herself."

Throughout the whole service, Thomas looked once at Amelia. Frustratingly, her head was slightly bowed as she talked to God and with her severe brown bonnet, he could see none of her face. He, too, had been to see Amelia and she had blessed his union with Bridget wholeheartedly, screwing up her courage and hoping Thomas would leave soon before her resolve broke down.

"You love her, don't you?"

"Yes, but…"

"But nothing, Thomas. You love her dearly and I am married to another so am not on the market. You have asked her and she has said yes, marry her and be happy." Would her advice be different had her husband still been charged with murder, for which there was only one punishment? Would she have slipped into Bridget's place at the altar at the last moment?

What benefit could there be to such endless self-questioning?

With the last vestiges of self-discipline, she had reminded him how beautiful Bridget was, something he could not deny, for it was a haunting, angular beauty that spoke of spirit rather than prettiness. "Also, she is so clever to be published so young."

It was true. She had gone with Thomas, Matthew and Eliza to London in December, only to find Mr Prendegast dead and

Mr Frampton in control of the firm.

"I am not surprised," Matthew said on hearing the news. "Mr Frampton said he was seriously ill when I came in September, unlikely to last the winter out."

"We are ready to publish," Mr Frampton had said, after congratulating them on their engagement. "We just need to discuss royalties and an advance. We also need to discuss what you will write next."

"Write next? You want me to write another book?"

"We would, Miss Browne. Your writing has a distinctive style that we feel will be popular. Let me tell you what we would really like." He outlined a book on the state of the nation from a female perspective. "We would like to see how you see the world around you today. We can discuss the main tenets in due course but there is yet another project we would very much like you to consider. We are starting a newssheet. It was never something that Mr Prendegast would entertain but it has long been a desire of mine. We, as a board, have committed to this and I would like to ask you to write a weekly column."

Bridget looked at Thomas. "Can I accept?" she whispered to her husband-to-be.

"Of course, you can, Bridge. I would not dream of holding you back."

It was towards the end of the meeting that another idea came to Mr Frampton. He had greatly enjoyed his evening with Matthew a few months earlier, when Matthew had come to him with a plea to get a message to Jacob Avercamps.

"Matthew," he said quietly, "will you do me the honour of matching Miss Browne's efforts with a column of your own? We are desirous that the newssheet we create should have quality views and opinions as its backbone."

"You want me to write?"

"Yes, Matthew, we most certainly do." The board had not discussed this for it had not been raised but Mr Frampton was sure it would go down well.

"I accept, sir!"

299

Mr Frampton smiled. In one afternoon, he had secured two quality columnists and signed Miss Browne to produce three more books over the next three years. The only thing left was Luke Davenport's diaries but he would hold that for now as he did not want to present too much change to the board so soon after Mr Prendegast had departed.

Many times, Mr Frampton had reflected over his life that one good deed deserved another and what goes around comes around. He thanked the Lord for his good fortune and then looked again at how he might spread that good fortune further.

Book One:

A New Lease On Freedom

1680s England is a disturbed place.

Thomas and Grace Davenport, from a Dorset Presbyterian family, seek their missing friend, Lady Merriman.

The Duke of Monmouth, illegitimate son to the old King, Charles II, lands with a small force in Dorset, seeking to depose his uncle, James II.

"For liberty and religion!" is his cry.

Thomas and Grace are more concerned with tracking down Lady Merriman. They meet the heir to the Earldom of Sherborne, who falls for Grace but a Catholic nobleman cannot marry a Puritan and it seems the match is doomed.

Monmouth is no leader; his following dissipates as he wanders around the West Country.

Thomas and Grace cannot escape the rebellion around them. They are embroiled in war.

Through battle, captivity and deceit, they finally come home in the aftermath of failed rebellion and all that means for Dorset and the whole country.

A must-read for those who love the history and drama of an emerging nation.

Book Two:

It Takes A Rogue

In 1688, England is on the brink of something terrible. And Dorset is in the thick of it. Will James II's dictatorial policies lead to invasion by William of Orange?

Thomas Davenport, a builder, has a diminishing workload due to national uncertainty.

Henry, the new Earl of Sherborne, has a deep secret to keep. Recently married to Grace Davenport, he walks a tightrope between loyalty and rebellion.

Matthew Davenport, exiled in Holland, jumps at the opportunity to return to Dorset as a scout for the planned invasion.

The Wiltshires are rich and aristocratic. She hungers after human warmth yet is ice-like with others. This is, until she meets Lady Roakes. Together, they learn that a rogue need not stay a rogue forever.

William gains momentum, people flocking to join him, some less salubrious than others.

Ambition, love and revenge make an intriguing tale that ranges across Dorset, causing anguish, adventure and suspense.

A must-read for those looking for an exciting story set amidst the forging of modern England.

The Story Continues

Parchman has slipped away. We do not know where, for elusiveness is Parchman's way. All we know of this man is that he will be back. Each defeat, every setback, drives a new resolve for a man motivated by revenge.

And hatred.

And loathing of what he can never have.

And, so, the story goes on. Like anybody in the here and now, we do not know what the future holds. Thomas and Bridget, Matthew and Eliza, Grace and Henry do not know what is waiting around the corner.

Perhaps the more astute have an inkling. Put yourself in Amelia's shoes for a moment. She faces great uncertainty yet has a philosophy that will take much strain. Perhaps she has an idea that the struggle is only just begun.

Only just begun for our players and only just begun for our country as it slips and slides towards the modern age.

Step back again and see things through the eyes of Penelope or Sally, who have only just started their journeys and much is still to come, or perhaps the older eyes of Mr Amiss.

There is much in Ireland still to resolve, constitutional matters to wade through. A country does not make itself; rather, it is made by countless small involvements from countless small people. There is a king in France who has a hatred of everything English, everything British. He will, no doubt, feature in tales to come.

Our characters will be back and more quickly than you might imagine. The next instalment of the Dorset Chronicles is circling around us and about to land.

So, hold fire, book four will soon be available. Everyone will be a little older but there is no guarantee they will be any wiser.